THE
STEAMY
KITCHEN
COOKBOOK

the STEAMY KITCHEN cookbook

101 Asian Recipes Simple Enough for Tonight's Dinner

Jaden Hair

TUTTLE Publishing

Tokyo | Rutland, Vermont | Singapore

Published by Tuttle Publishing, an imprint of Periplus Editions (HK) Ltd.

www.tuttlepublishing.com

Copyright © 2009 Steamy Kitchen, Inc.

ISBN 978-0-8048-4028-6 hc
ISBN 978-0-8048-4334-8 pb

With additional photo contributions from Diane Cu, Matt Wright, Matt Armendariz, Lara Ferroni and Carrie Hasson.

Distributed by

North America, Latin America & Europe
Tuttle Publishing
364 Innovation Drive
North Clarendon, VT 05759-9436 U.S.A.
Tel: 1 (802) 773-8930; Fax: 1 (802) 773-6993
info@tuttlepublishing.com
www.tuttlepublishing.com

Japan
Tuttle Publishing
Yaekari Building, 3rd Floor
5-4-12 Osaki; Shinagawa-ku; Tokyo 141-0032
Tel: (81) 3 5437-0171; Fax: (81) 3 5437-0755
sales@tuttle.co.jp
www.tuttle.co.jp

Asia Pacific
Berkeley Books Pte. Ltd.
61 Tai Seng Avenue #02-12
Singapore 534167
Tel: (65) 6280-1330; Fax: (65) 6280-6290
inquiries@periplus.com.sg
www.periplus.com

Hc   15 14 13 12   10 9 8 7 6 5 4 3
Pb   15 14 13 12   10 9 8 7 6 5 4 3 2 1
Printed in Singapore   1210CP

TUTTLE PUBLISHING® is a registered trademark of Tuttle Publishing, a division of Periplus Editions (HK) Ltd.

"To my Mom, who spent thousands of hours reciting family recipes over the phone . . . and to my Dad, who patiently translated when our Chinglish didn't suffice."

CLOCKWISE, FROM TOP LEFT: My dad; me and Mom on my wedding day; Three Pea Stir-fry; me and Nathan; Spicy Korean Tofu Stew; Andrew with my in-laws George and Sylvia; my Mom and baby me; Perfect Shrimp Fried Rice.

Contents

The story of

my Kitchen

I could start off by telling a story of how I learned cooking from my mother when I was a young girl . . .

But I didn't.

In fact, quite the opposite! My Mom is a fantastic cook . . . grocery shopping is her hobby and feeding people is her passion. When I was a little girl, I wasn't interested in cooking at all. I was constantly hungry and always wanted to eat! Plus, if I was anywhere near the kitchen when Mom was cooking, it never failed that I'd always end up with the crap jobs, like tediously pinching the itty bitty tails off the mountain of bean sprouts, shelling pounds and pounds of shrimp, peeling away the stringy thing off the snow peas, washing every bit of trapped dirt hidden in the bok choy. Of course, Mom would constantly rattle off kitchen wisdom, but hey, I was young and didn't care about cooking. I was too busy pouting with kitchen chores wondering when I could finally devour the fluffy pork bao whose steam was whispering my name . . .

So, I didn't become a kitchen rock star until I moved away from California (where my family lives) to a little town in Florida to start a family of my own with my husband, Scott. Suddenly, without easy access to good Asian markets, cheap Asian midnight eats and, of course, Mom's kitchen, I was forced to learn via telephone calls while digging for ingredients at the supermarket, tossing fragrant garlic and ginger in a wok and virtual taste tastes at the dinner table.

What a fine education it was. $448.63 in cell phone minutes later (which, by the way, is way cheaper than three years at a fancy culinary institute), I discovered that I was insanely good at cooking. I must have inherited Mom's natural talent of creating spectacularly simple meals for family and friends.

How it All Started

You might be wondering how I got from cell phone diploma to writing this book, and it's kind of a silly story. Right after we moved from San Francisco to this little town in Florida, Scott started a computer repair shop in the middle of a local strip mall, and right next door was a restaurant called "Bangkok Tokyo". I'd often walk next door to Bangkok Tokyo to grab a to-go order.

Well, one afternoon I was waiting for my order when I overheard a woman at the sushi bar just behind the hostess stand chatting loudly on her cell phone with her friend, " . . . come meet me for lunch! I'm eating sushi at the Chinese restaurant!"

WTF?!!

Bangkok Toyko? HELLO? Last I checked, neither Bangkok nor Tokyo was in China.

Oooooooh . . . I was upset. And yeah, I totally overreacted and took it personally, having just moved from San Francisco, one of the greatest culinary destinations and cultural smorgasbords. It didn't help that the week before I had watched a television celebrity chef feature an entire show on the foods of Thailand while wearing a Chinese cheongsam and cooking Japanese dumplings. Seriously, I'm so not kidding! (By the way, details have been changed to protect the guilty in case I happen to run into this particular celeb chef one day and then be forced to act all embarrassed, wondering if she has read my book! Ay-ya!)

Okay, back to the story. After the "eating sushi at a Chinese restaurant" incident, I cried and whined to Scott, wanting to move back to San Fran. And do you know what he said to me?

"Honey, don't you see that this is such a great opportunity for you?"

Welllll . . . truthfully, it went something like this: "Quit your bitchin'. If you don't like this situation, why don't you do something about it?"

And so I did.

I called a local cooking school called "The Chef's Table" and asked if I could teach some cooking classes, focusing on teaching Mom's family recipes, the virtues of fish sauce, how to stir-fry and, of course, the differences between Chinese and Japanese food.

That's how it all began. Oh, and the blog, SteamyKitchen.com? I started the blog because I needed a place to store all of Mom's kitchen wisdom and recipes. I was too lazy to write by hand, too unorganized to record audio notes and too scared to leave precious family recipes on my laptop hard drive. A blog was an ideal solution, and I named it Steamy Kitchen, as it perfectly described both my Mom and me, though in different ways. There's always something cooking in Mom's kitchen, a soup simmering away for hours or the flash-bang-cling-clang of her speedy wok master action. Basically, the kitchen was always steamy, with a variety of goodies cooking away. And then there's me. "Steamy" perfectly describes my fiery-hot nature and passionate personality.

What this Book is About?

This cookbook is a collection of Asian recipes that I prepare at home for my family and friends. These days, every one is limited on time, especially if you've got kids. If I don't get dinner on the table quickly, my rug rats will begin shimmy-ing up the pantry shelves to help themselves to sugary treats . . . so the recipes I've included in this book are fast. Most of the dishes are quick cooking or involve little hands-on time. There are a couple of exceptions—my Mom's Famous Crispy Egg Rolls (page 50) and the Pork and Mango Potstickers (page 46). I included them because these are super-awesome dishes and also because they are great for freezing and sav-ing for a lazy kitchen day or last minute party nibbles. Both recipes go from frozen to dinner table in about 15 minutes. Can't beat that!

Fast is not the only thing you'll find in this book. I love vibrant vegetables, aromatic herbs and ripe, juicy fruits. You'll find that each dish is incredibly colorful with fresh herbs, chilli peppers and veggies. Food comes so fresh these days—it's a shame to do too much to them other than a quick stir-fry in a pan!

But I think if there was one thing that defines this book, it's that the recipes are simple. Simple enough for tonight's family dinner. I've got lots of step-by-step photos to help break the steps down so you can visually see how to do something, like rolling Mom's Famous Crispy Egg Rolls (page 50) or deveining a shrimp with the shell-on (page 71).

Because I've been teaching hands-on cooking classes for a few years now, I'm really good at knowing what questions you'll want answers to and how to explain things clearly. At the end of class, people always proclaim, "I never knew it was that EASY!"

LEFT TO RIGHT: Actin' all crazy on the beach (from back row) Steve Anna, David Lebovitz, Elise Bauer, Adam Pearson, Romain, me, Matt Armendariz, Diane Cu; Ochazuke Rice with Crispy Salmon Skin, page 59; my boys Andrew and Nathan; my brother, Jay and I; Quick Vietnamese Chicken Pho, page 58; Andrew not wanting to go to school.

What is Asian Cooking?

I put a lot of thought into what "Asian cooking" really means, and it's more complex than just a section of a shelf at a bookstore. You see, I grew up in North Platte, Nebraska, in the '70s, during a time when I was the only Asian kid in my entire school. So, you can imagine some of the comments and attitudes that I had to endure as a child.

When we moved to Los Angeles, California, things changed. It was actually quite a bit of a culture shock for me, being surrounded by "my peeps" everywhere! No longer was I any different than the general population. When Scott and I moved to a small town in Florida to start a family... and as you read earlier, it kinda jarred me back to the days of childhood.

I think calling my style of cooking "Asian" will be short-lived because Asia is made up of so many different coun-tries! We don't use the term "European Cooking" as we can differentiate between French and Italian cuisines. And if I called what I specialize as "Asian" I would be just as guilty as the ignorant.

But at the same time, we've got to start somewhere. I hope this book inspires you to explore the ingredients in your local Asian market and play with them in your kitchen, and at the same time I hope to teach you some things about each spice, herb and vegetable, such as their origins and popular uses. And maybe one day, the foods of Laos will be just as popular as the specialties of Germany.

Having been born in Hong Kong, having grown up in secluded Nebraska, and having lived in crazy California and now in Florida, I think all Asian food is relative. It depends in part on geography (living nearby the bustling Los Angeles Chinatown versus having to drive four hours to the nearest Asian market in Nebraska), but also on learning how to take whatcha got and adapt it to your family meal. With several Asian online grocers in business (see the Resource Guide for a list) and many "ethnic" ingredients popping up at your regular grocery store, it's easier than ever to create fabulous meals with ingredients from all over Asia at home. This is why Martin Yan, Ming Tsai and Andrea Nguyen—my cooking idols—are such amazing chefs. They are able to keep the authenticity and essence of Chinese, Japanese, Vietnamese and Thai ingredients and help us integrate them into our American lifestyle without "dumbing down" Asian food. My style of cooking is really a combination of my Mom's home-style dishes and and of course influence from chefs and my fellow food bloggers.

With this book, I wanted to showcase all types of Asian ingredients, but specifically pantry items (like canned goods, bottled sauces and spices), frozen foods (fresh frozen noodles, dumpling wrappers) and preserved/dried ingredients (black mushrooms, Chinese sausage). And here's why. With our lifestyle, we don't necessarily eat Asian foods everyday, but I do like having the ingredients at my fingertips. I love going to my local Asian market once a month to stock up on ingredients that keep well in the pantry, refrigerator or freezer for weeks or even months at a time. I can combine any of these ingredients with a fresh vegetables, meat or seafood from my regular supermarket. That's exactly what I do these days and it's exactly how my Mom did it when we used to live in Nebraska and our nearest Asian market was a few hours away!

So, for example, pair canned black bean sauce with fresh clams—and 15 minutes later you've got a delectable dish.

Slather jarred sweet plum sauce over chicken and roast—for a savory yet sweet, moist chicken. Fresh noodles found in the freezer section paired with crunchy carrots and soft mushrooms make it to the table in less time that it takes to order a take-out dish.

This cookbook is a compilation of some very traditional Chinese recipes from my Mom, some not so traditional but modern take-out old favorites, and of course, some that my kidlets have chosen for you, like Chocolate Wontons (page 147)! Many of these recipes were inspired by some of my very favorite food bloggers that I am lucky to count as my friends. We are constantly swapping recipes, learning from each other and inspiring new creations. And you don't have to just depend on me to tell you that the recipes in this book work. The recipes were tested, and retested, by almost 200 of my dear blog-readers from all over the world, making this possibly one of the most well-tested cookbooks out there!

My wish is that you'll find this cookbook full of fantastic meals you'll share with your family and friends. It can't get any better than fast, fresh and simple enough for tonight's dinner!

Please continue the journey online with me at www.steamykitchen.com where I am constantly updating the site with new recipes, videos, clips from my television segments and links to other fabulous blogs. I'd love to hear your thoughts and experiences with the recipes, just comment on the site, email me at jaden@steamykitchen.com or find me on Twitter at www.twitter.com/steamykitchen.

xoxo,
Jaden

WHAT TO DRINK

After chopping, stir-frying, tossing and tasting in the kitchen, there's nothing I enjoy more than sitting down to a delicious meal with friends and family and a suitable beverage. We always keep a stash of chilled lager-style beers on hand. Their clean, simple taste immediately quenches thirst and is a fail-safe accompaniment to any Asian style dish. But sometimes, depending on the time of year or if we feel like something a little more upscale or festive, we pull out bottles of wine or sake. I've asked my friend Anu Karwa of Swirl Events to tell you about pairing wine with Asian dishes and Morgan Hartman of Vine Connections to tell you about sake. Aren't I lucky to have such experts as friends who can do that fancy wine and sake talk?

PAIRING WINE WITH ASIAN FOOD

The complexity of flavors—spicy, sweet, salty and sour—in Asian food makes pairing wine lots of fun. Here are some guidelines to pick the perfect wine to enhance, not overpower, your Asian meal.

Spicy dishes beg for a wine to balance the heat, not add to it. You want to stay away from anything too high in alcohol because it can intensify the heat. You also want to avoid highly tannic wines, which can add a bitter taste to highly flavorful, pungent dishes. For lighter Asian dishes, my "go-to" recommendation is Gewürztraminer from Germany. Its lychee and roselike aromas that hint at sweetness make it a natural fit. Another great pairing is a dry Riesling, such as a Kabinett-style, from Germany. Its slightly dry taste and racy acidity really works. Other options for spicy dishes with slightly more pronounced flavors or heavier texture, such as Spicy Korean Tofu Stew (page 112), include a Muscadet from the Loire Valley in France. For the more adventurous wine drinker, try the up-and-coming varietal of Torrontes from Argentina. A Pinot Gris from Oregon also makes a nice choice.

A dish accented with the fresh flavors of lemongrass, mint or cilantro (coriander), such as Vietnamese Summer Rolls (page 44), is complemented by a wine with a similar grassy, herbaceous profile like a Sauvignon Blanc, particularly from either New Zealand or Chile.

If you have a dish that is rich or fried, such as Firecracker Shrimp (page 48) or Asian Crab Cakes (page 83), cut through it with a highly acidic white wine also based on Sauvignon Blanc grapes such as the French Pouilly-Fume or Sancerre.

White wines aren't the only choices for Asian meals. Meaty dishes such as Indonesian Beef Satay with Peanut Dipping Sauce (page 93) or Hoisin and Honey Glazed Baby Back Ribs (page 88) that have intense flavors including chilli and garlic sauces or smokiness are best served with a light-bodied red wine. One of the least known but most worthy picks is a Chinon, a light bodied, savory and earthy red wine composed of Cabernet Franc grapes with distinct violet aromas from the Loire Valley of France. Another great option is a Pinot Noir from Willamette Valley, Oregon or New Zealand (looks for pinots from the Central Otago region). Hearty dishes such as Grilled Steak with Balsamic Teriyaki (page 90) are suited to medium-bodied spicy, flinty Shiraz. On the more adventurous side, try a Valpolicella from Italy or a slightly chilled Beaujolais Cru from France; both are perfect with pork dishes.

When in doubt, you can't go wrong pairing Asian dishes with Champagne. The effervescence steadily matches the many layers of flavor present in any Asian dish. Prosecco or a fresh and fruity Cava make excellent sparkling wine choices as well.

by **Anu Karwa**

ENJOYING SAKE WITH ASIAN FOOD

Sake, often labeled "The Drink of the Gods" by the Japanese, is making a new and improved debut in the wine and cocktail community. While many of us cringe with the memory of hot sake served in those funny carafes, premium, chilled sake has become the new rage. The word "sake" is used commonly outside of Japan, but it literally translates to mean all alcoholic beverages in Japanese. Sake as we know it, is created from rice, water, yeast, and koji (a mold used to convert starch to sugar for fermentation), and is brewed more similarly to a beer. However, Premium Sake should be served lightly chilled and consumed more like a fine wine. Lower grade sakes are often served hot to mask impurities and poor quality.

There are generally four types of sake, each requiring a slightly different brewing technique. Honjozo has a small bit of distilled alcohol added during the brewing process. Sakes without that added alcohol are labeled Junmai, literally meaning "pure" in Japanese, as they are made simply with water, rice, koji, and yeast. Ginjo and Daiginjo (the highest grade possible) are sakes that are distinguished by the degree of milling of the rice, a process that is necessary in order to get to the complex starches at the center of each grain for the best level of quality. Namazake, the final type of sake, is unpasteurized and difficult to find outside of Japan. These designations of sake combine to form the category of Premium Sake, a very special category that accounts for less than 15 percent of all of the sake produced today.

Premium sake, like a fine wine, is enjoyable on its own or paired with a wide variety of foods. Flavors of sake, depending on the style, range from light, fragrant, floral, and tropical, to rich, bold, and earthy. Some are on the sweeter side, others very dry. Nigori Sake, a popular style of sake that is unfiltered, and characterized by a degree of cloudiness, is on the heavier and sweeter side and perfect for spicy dishes such as Thai Coconut Chicken Curry (page 103).

Junmai Daiginjo sake, on the other hand, tends to be more delicate and floral, so lighter dishes like oysters with Asian Mignonette (page 38) or Baked Tofu Salad with Mustard Miso Dressing (page 64) are good choices. Some sakes, especially those coming from the more mountainous regions of Japan where root vegetables, pickles, and heavier meats dominate the cuisine, are brewed to be heavier, bolder, more earthy in flavor. Pair these with Grilled Lamb Chops with Asian Pesto (page 95) or Chinese Beef Broccoli (page 94).

For something a little different, try a lightly alcoholic sparkling sake (one popular brand is called "sake2me"), which is premium sake that's undergone a second bubble-inducing fermentation. It goes with a wide variety of Asian dishes, and can sometimes be infused with different flavors, such as Asian pear or green tea. Sparkling sakes can be enjoyed with any type of dish or as a fun cocktail.

Without a doubt, sake can be a great match for many different Asian cuisines, not just Japanese foods. Don't be afraid to experiment, as sake can be as diverse as fine wine, and certainly can complement a great meal, or just good company!

by **Morgan Hartman**

the tools

Okay, I admit I'm a gadget freak. My kitchen is so full of doodads that I've begun creeping over into my husband's garage area and also the kid's closet. Yes, I have a problem. But luckily for you, my editor only allotted a handful of pages to "Tools" so I can only highlight my tried, trusted and true. The Resource Guide (page 156) includes shops for buying specialized Asian tools.

Bamboo Spider These handy spiders (another word for strainer) have long bamboo handles and are perfect for lifting food from boiling water or hot oil. When deep-frying, I always use this bamboo spider to lift the food and the excess oil just drips away.

Bamboo Steamer I have a nice, big bamboo steamer that I set over my wok and use for steaming large batches of steamed buns, fish fillets and well, just about anything. They usually come with three or more trays (make sure that you rotate the trays during cooking so that the food in each tray cooks evenly). If you don't have a wok to set over, Helen Chen makes a steamer ring that you can use with any pot for just $6.00. It's genius. For small steaming jobs, I use any available empty pot with lid and a metal steamer insert that folds down like a flower.

Knives It took me twelve years of spending money on different knives before I finally found my soul mate and fell into a steady groove with the collection that I own now. In college, I got sucked into the magical world of infomercials and bought the super-duper Ginsu knives that can decapitate a soda can in one swift motion and the scissors that can cut a penny in half with just the power of your pinky. Well, those lasted for three months and then the only way to cut a chicken breast was to stab it repeatedly with all six knives in my hand, Edward Scissorhands style. As a working girl, to celebrate my becoming a useful member of society, I splurged on an expensive knife block that held like twenty-two different knives, each one designed to complete a specific kitchen task most efficiently. Need to carve a tomato into a butterfly? I had a blade shaped just for that task. But I hated those knives. They were too big for me and felt like I was shaking hands with an electric saw, not to mention twenty of the knives in the block went totally unused. I finally decided to save my money and just get one good knife that felt right in my hands. It was expensive, but it was the Ferrari in my kitchen and I loved using it so much that I went around the house every day looking for things to dice. It's been eight years and I still grab for that same 8-inch (20-cm) Shun chef's knife (www.kershawknives.com). And my latest love is a New West KnifeWorks Fusionwood Santoku (www.newwestknifeworks.com).This baby feels like a dream in my hands—it's sturdy, balanced and the wood handle is a piece of art. The only Chinese cleaver I like is Martin Yan's cleaver. It's about $40 and the knife has a small handle, very well balanced. It's got a traditional fat blade so you can use it to smash as well as to scoop and carry food. The blade edge is curved, so that you can rock back and forth to mince just like a regular chef's knife. Most of the other Chinese cleavers are straight edged, so you have to really use that up and down motion to Chop! Chop! Chop! And come 'on, who better to design knives than the King of Chinese American cooking? I remember watching Martin Yan on television, totally in awe that he could carve an entire chicken in eighteen seconds. Television trickery? Nope. I met Martin in person and yeah, eighteen seconds flat (www.yancancook.com).

Julienne Peeler I love this tool. I can julienne carrots, potatoes, zucchini or cucumber in seconds! The only brand I've liked is Oxo. Lay the carrot (for example) on a cutting board. Use a fork to skewer and anchor down the carrot on one end and then use the julienne tool to cut strips perfect for a super-quick stir-fry or noodle dish. Using this tool while the carrot is anchored down with a fork makes it safer and easier than trying to hold the carrot with your fingers.

Microplane Rasp Grater This is the perfect tool for ginger! Forget frantically mincing the very fibrous rhizome, just rub the ginger nub on the rasp grater and the fibers stay on top while the silky ginger pulp collects on the bottom.

Mortar & Pestle Pound! Bang! Knock! I love my mortar and pestle to smash, grind and smush (yes, that's a technical term) garlic, chillies, spices and herbs. Pounding the aromatics is a better way to release oils and flavors, even better than a food processor or a knife! Plus, it's fun to use.

Rice Cooker A rice cooker lets you have perfect rice each and every time with a push of a button. There's no pot watching, boiling over or over-cooking. Many rice cookers have built-in timers and a keep-warm function, so that you can fill the pot in the morning and come home from work with fresh, steaming-hot rice.

I don't think I could live without my rice cooker. I've used one my whole life! Since I consider my rice cooker even more important than a mixer, blender or even my coffee maker (gasp! I know!), it gets prime real estate on my counter. And the one I use is the mac-daddy version that's induction-heating-pressurized-rice-cooker (whew long name) in one, sleek, silver design by Zojirushi. I love it so much. It cooks rice, brown rice, wild rice, rice porridge (congee), sweet rice, sushi rice, delayed cooking and even keeps rice warm! If the thing vibrated, it'd be a fixture on my nightstand. But you don't need a fancy rice cooker at all. A great budget rice cooker is from Aroma Housewares, one of the most popular rice cooker companies in the U.S. They've got rice cookers starting from $29.00. The features that I would look for: retract-able power cord, rice warmer (so you can cook rice early in day and it keeps it cozy and warm for you), excess water catcher, quick cook option (speeds up your rice cooking by 20 percent).

Skimmer This handy metal skimmer has super-fine mesh that traps any scum, fats and oils lingering on the surface of your stocks and broths. WokShop.com sells them for less than $2!! This is a must buy. In fact, buy several and give them away to your friends.

Steaming Rack A metal steaming rack is helpful to prop the heatproof dish of food off the bottom surface of the wok. Water for steaming is poured into the wok, then the steaming rack in place inside, then your dish, then the wok lid. As you heat the wok, the water boils . . . which creates steam to cook the food. The higher the steaming rack, the more steaming water you can put in the wok. BUT—after laying your dish onto the rack, you might not have enough room to close the lid tightly! Look for steaming racks that are about 1½ inches (3.75 cm) or lower. You might have to refill the steaming water more often, but it's better than not being able to steam at all!

Tongs Shhh . . . here's my secret . . . I don't cook with chopsticks. In most Asian cookbooks, you'll see a pair of giant chopsticks that are meant for cook-ing (my Mom has and uses them) but I just find it easier to get a pair of really good tongs to grab, flip and fling the food. Now, there are good tongs and bad tongs. Bad tongs are the ones that are designed poorly and you end up pinch-ing that meaty part of your hand below your thumb. Ouch. The one I use is by Oxo. Best ever. For stir-frying noodles or long vegetables, I love using tongs, as it's easier to grab and toss ingredients. For stir-frying small items, a wok spatula is the way to go.

Wok is one of the most versatile cooking tools. You can deep-fry, boil, steam, pan-fry, stir-fry and it even doubles as a sled for small children. They are inexpensive and multi-purpose. I fry, steam, boil, braise and sauté in mine. There's always a wok on my stovetop, no matter what cuisine I'm cooking. Yes, I'm a total dork and even boil my spaghetti in my wok, just because it works so well. I have several in my kitchen, each for a different purpose or mood . . . but that's just my compulsive nature and it's not normal… so don't think you need more than one wok. In fact, you DON'T need a wok at all. A large frying pan with high sides (sauté pan) works just fine. If I can't convince you to invest in a $16 wok, that's okay. Just go on and be stubborn like that. **Shape:** If you have an electric stovetop, you'll need to get a flat-bottomed wok. If you have a gas stove, you can either use a flat-bottomed or round-bottomed wok with a wok ring. But first look at how powerful your flame is. Some wok rings sit up pretty high, and if you've got a weak flame that won't reach up and over the wok ring, you'll never get your wok hot enough. If you do have a weak flame, a flat-bottomed wok is the way to go. **Material:** Whether you have an electric or gas stovetop, I recommend getting a Chinese cast iron wok. I know many of you think heavy, thick and clunky when you think of cast iron, but not the Chinese version of cast iron! It's thin and incredibly light (mine weighs less than 3 lbs/1.5 kg)! It's a great heat conductor and the light cast iron will heat up evenly and retain its heat very well. Just like a beloved cast-iron pan, I love the feel of a well-seasoned cast-iron wok.

Carbon steel woks are also very popular. They heat up and cool down in a snap, are lightweight and very sturdy. There is also a flat-bottomed Chinese wok with a cast-iron interior and enamel exterior that are perfect for glass top or electric stoves.

Yes, you have to season the carbon steel or the Chinese cast-iron woks, but it's super easy. Instructions for seasoning should come with your wok, or follow the seasoning instructions on the Wok Shop's website (www.thewokshop.com).

The more you use your wok, the darker the patina will become and the more you'll fall in love with your wok.

If you want a pre-seasoned wok, give Eleanor Hoh, the Wok Star a shout. She'll preseason a lightweight Chinese cast-iron round-bottomed wok and ship it directly to your door with an entire stir-fry kit that includes a wok spatula, sauces and an instructional DVD. If you don't have a gas stove, she also has portable butane stovetops that are $65. I have one of these and lemme tell you— this sucker spews out more heat than my regular gas stovetop. Plus, they are great for camping or emergencies. Totally recommended (www.eleanorhoh.com). **How About Nonstick?** I know there are wok purists out there who shun non-stick woks. While I recommend a Chinese cast-iron or carbon steel wok, I still say use what you feel comfortable using. If you really, really love nonstick, then at least get the good stuff like Circulon, All-Clad or Calphalon. These are easy to take care and do not require seasoning. But they are expensive and you won't get the same results as a traditional wok! The non-stick surface prevents you from getting a good sear or browning of your meat or seafood, and the browning is what creates great flavor. Don't buy the cheap non-stick woks. Not worth it as they are . . . well . . . cheap, won't last long, are bad for the environment and not recommended for super-high heat. **Where To Buy:** The Wok Shop www.thewokshop.com owner Tane Chan has this smiling energy that is infectious! Buy from them online or give her a call to place your order. They've been online since 1999 and have every type of wok imaginable, including the carbon steel,

Chinese cast iron, cast-iron/enamel wok and instructions on how to season the wok. Love them, love them, love them. **Wok Care:** Immediately after cooking with your wok, wash the wok. Ideally, you should wash and clean the wok while it's still a bit hot so that it's easier to clean. Once seasoned, you wouldn't need to use soap, just hot water. Dry the wok thoroughly to prevent rusting. If the wok looks like it needs a little TLC, after drying, place the wok on your stove. Pour about a tablespoon of cooking oil on a wadded piece of paper towel. Heat the wok until very hot. Use tongs to rub the oily paper towel around and around the wok. Turn off heat and let cool.

So, whatcha waiting for? Go get a carbon steel or Chinese cast iron wok! Oh, make sure that you also get a wok lid with your wok! **Wok Spatula:** In Chinese, it's called "wok chuan" and basically it's a spatula shaped specifically for wok cooking, it's shaped like a bent shovel! Look for ones with a wooden handle on the end, so that it doesn't get too hot to grab. You'll use a wok spatula to move, flip, toss and scoop food around in your wok.

the ingredients

I live about 20 minutes away from a good Asian supermarket and some of you even further! The way I approach Asian ingredients is to choose those that store well, like canned pastes, jarred sauces, dried aromatics and frozen goods. This way, I can make one trip every few weeks and stock up on things like coconut milk, oyster sauce, dried shrimp and frozen noodles . . . and then visit my regular local supermarket for any fresh veggies, seafood or meats. Now, a spontaneous Thai curry dinner is really simple and literally ready in 15 minutes!

Here's a list of the most common ingredients that I've used throughout the recipes in the book. Take note that this is not an exhaustive list of Asian ingredients. For that I would need a volume of three more books to fill! But these are the ingredients that I use most in my home cooking: from curry pastes to fresh herbs and dried mushrooms.

My approach to Asian ingredients is that sometimes you've got to make do with whatcha' got. For example, fresh Thai basil is not always available in my local supermarket, and while I normally grow this in my garden, sometimes I'll just sub with sweet Italian basil. Same with chilli peppers—I often will use jalapeno chillies because that's what my market carries. (And also because the spice level of jalapenos suits me perfectly!) If you don't live near an Asian market, take a look at your grocer's "Ethnic" aisle, and you might be surprised to find many of the jarred, canned and dried ingredients there. I've also tried to provide you with as many substitutions for ingredients as possible in the recipes. The Resource Guide provides sources for ordering ingredients online. And for my gluten-free friends, I've included notes for your diet as well. (By the way, there are SO many Asian recipes that don't use gluten, so this is a perfect book for you if you are watching your gluten intake).

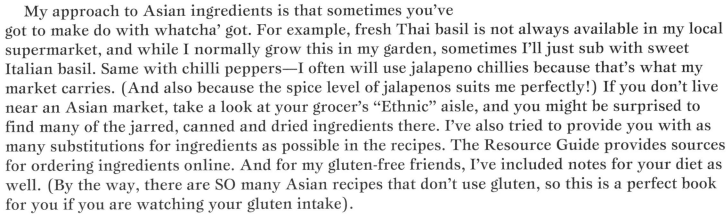

Bean Sprouts Bean sprouts, oh bean sprouts, how I love you now that I have my own kidlets to assign tail-pinching duties to! (Mom used to make me do this chore). Of course, you don't have to pinch the tails off, the tails are certainly edible, and most restaurants and cooks will cook the bean sprouts with tails-on. Bean sprouts are the sprout of the mung bean and are one of the quickest vegetables to cook! Just a minute in the wok or blanched and it's ready to eat. Personally, I love bean sprouts raw as a crunchy topping in my

Shrimp Pad Thai (page 137), Miso Ramen (page 66) or Thai-style Chicken Flatbread (page 37). Look for white stems that snap! Here's a tip to keep them fresh in the refrigerator. Wash the bean sprouts, discarding any that look a little soft or sad. Use a salad spinner to spin dry, or lay them out on a towel and gently pat to absorb the water. Store them in a plastic bag and also put a dry piece of paper towel in the bag. Close the bag. This is the best way to store bean sprouts . . . keep them as dry as possible! If you don't have bean sprouts,

you can just omit them from the recipe or sometimes what I do is take a long celery stalk, peel the stringy outer layer with a vegetable peeler and julienne into thin strips. The crisp-crunchy texture is very similar.

Bean Sauce or Paste Chinese bean sauce is made from fermented soybeans and different spices. There are a few different kinds of bean sauce, the brown bean sauce comes smooth or with whole beans (preferred) and is an essential component

LEFT TO RIGHT: Cilantro, green onions, lemongrass, Thai basil and kaffir lime leaves in the small bowl.

of northern Chinese cooking. It's pretty salty, so use just a bit at first and add more after tasting. Bean sauce has an incredible flavor—both salty and savory. Black bean sauce is made from fermented black beans and is used in Clams Sautéed in Garlic and Black Bean Sauce (page 77).

Bok Choy is Chinese cabbage and I love cooking with the beautiful spoon-shaped leaves (Simple Baby Bok Choy and Snow Peas, page 116). It's commonly used in Chinese cooking and the stalks are mild and crunchy while the leaves taste like cabbage. It's very healthy for you, full of vitamins A and C and a fab source of folic acid. My parents eat bok choy at least once a week! This is one of those vegetables that you can add to any stir-fry—you can cut them up into 1-inch (2.5-cm) sections, add the thicker stems into the frying pan first, followed by the leaves. My favorite part of the vegetable is the super-tender centers of each bok choy.

Breadcrumbs, Panko These are unseasoned Japanese breadcrumbs made from crustless bread and once you use panko,

there is absolutely no wanting to go back to regular, heavy, soggy breadcrumbs. Panko are more like "flakes" than crumbs and the end result is airy, super-crisp coating on whatever it is you're coating. You can use it to bread seafood, meats or vegetables and you can deep-fry, pan-fry (Asian Crab Cakes, page 83) or even bake for a healthier dish, like in Baked Crispy Chicken with Citrus Teriyaki Sauce (page 105). You can find panko at any Asian market and even at your regular grocer. Check the "Asian" section or the section that sells breadcrumbs. If you can't find panko, just use regular, unseasoned breadcrumbs.

Chili, Chile, and Chilli I've had fiery debates going on via Twitter and email on the correct spelling of chilli pepper (the fruit from the plant . . . I'm not talking about chilli con carne). In the past, I've always spelled the pepper "chili", my friends Elise and Matt spell it "chile" (as do many in America and in Spanish-speaking countries). But many of my Asian cookbooks use the spelling "chilli". Sigh . . . how confusing! Well, I asked my friend, Michael Ruhlman, for his opinion

and he cited late food historian, Alan Davidson's *Oxford Companion to Food* and Harold McGee, NY Times food writer and author of many chefs' food bible *On Food and Cooking*. Both believe that the double "ll" spelling is the way to go, pointing out that it is the original romanization of the Náhuatl language word for the fruit (*chīlli*). Whatever spelling you see in other books, on grocer's shelves or jar of hot sauce, just remember they all refer to the fiery hot members of the *Capsicum* genus.

Chilli Sauce I don't think I could ever be without chilli sauce. Wait. I think I say that about a lot of ingredients! Chilli sauce is a blend of chillies with other ingredients such as garlic, salt, vinegar and sugar. Chilli sauce is so popular in all countries of Asia, and it's very easy to make your own from fresh or dried chillies. Of all chilli sauces, there are two that are the most popular in the U.S., one is called Sriracha and the other is the Indonesian sambal oelek—a chilli-garlic combo. A staple at many Vietnamese restaurants (though originated from Thailand), Sriracha is like ketchup with a kick! I use it for everything, yes, even dipping in french fries (mix Sriracha with mayo). Its bottle is easy to spot—look for a green cap and a rooster logo—and you'll find it. Chilli garlic sauce, or sambal oelek, is thicker and great to add to a bit of soy sauce for a simple dipping sauce for dim sum. I also sometimes add a spoonful of chilli garlic sauce to stir-fries. Once opened, keep chilli sauce in the refrigerator. For a discussion of sambal, see page 24.

Chillies, dried You can find whole dried chillies at most Asian markets and you can soak them in hot water for a few hours to blend with some garlic or other seasonings to make a great chilli sauce, or you can throw them whole into your cooking. Of course, if you use them whole, you'll get the lovely flavor of chilli without all the heat. I personally like to cut each dried chilli in half, empty out and discard the seeds and add the halved chillies to my dish. This way, my kids aren't surprised with a zinger of a bite if a chilli seed (the source of most of the heat) is hidden in their food! The whole dried chilli is about $1^1/_2$ to 2 inches (3.75 to 5 cm) long and you can usually find them in your regular supermarket.

Chillies, fresh Of all ingredients, this is the most fun to play with. There are so many different chillies from all over the world and each has different levels of heat. In the U.S. you'll find finger-length chillies (medium spicy) to Thai bird's-eye chilli, which are tiny but will have you screamin' for your mama. Here's my tip. Use what you like and what you can find fresh in your markets. Generally (and I really do mean generally) the larger the chilli is, the less spice it packs. I try to find larger chillies because while I totally enjoy the flavor of fresh chillies, my spice tolerance really isn't that high. Jalapenos, while not Asian, are super-fresh and plentiful in my markets and I also grow them in my backyard. If you prefer even less heat, go for the big, fat banana peppers, which are incredibly mild but still have wonderful flavors.

Chilli Powder or Flakes Asian chilli powder is dried chillies ground into powder or flakes. It's very popular in fiery Korean dishes, like Spicy Korean Tofu Stew (page 112) and it's the heat that makes kimchi hot! Use sparingly at first, taste and then add more chilli powder if you need to into a dish. A little goes a long way, trust me. Oh, and one more thing. After you taste, wait 30 seconds before you add more chilli powder. Some chilli powder sneaks up on you, and its effect won't be apparent until a few seconds after you swallow! The powdered seasoning mixture, sometimes labeled as "chilli powder", is used to make chilli con carne should not be substituted for Asian chilli powder.

CLOCKWISE, FROM TOP: Curry paste, Chinese five spice powder, cinnamon sticks, shallots, ground and whole coriander, star anise and dried red chilli pepper.

Chinese Black Vinegar This is one of my secret ingredients in my pantry. Anytime that I think a Chinese stir-fry needs a little somethin'—a splash of Chinese black vinegar always does the trick. It's made with sweet rice that has been fermented, like fine aged vinegars. You can substitute with balsamic vinegar. You'll find that Chinese black vinegar is that indescribably secret ingredient in Chinese Beef Broccoli (page 94).

Chinese Rice Wine (or Sherry)
Shaoxing wine is the most popular Chinese rice wine, and it's made from rice and yeast. While you can drink good quality Chinese rice wine, it's not my cup of spirit. However, I can't imagine cooking Chinese dishes without it! I use Chinese rice wine in everything from marinating meats to a splash in my stir-fry to an entire cup in braises. You can substitute with dry sherry.

Chinese Sausage or "Lap Cheung" is found in the refrigerated section or in the dry goods section. Chinese sausage is sold in plastic shrink-wrapped packages in Asian markets. It is cured, so it lasts for a long time like Italian sausage. Keeps for about six months, sealed in its original packaging at room temp. Once you open, seal in plastic bag and refrigerate for up to another 6 months. Unopened, they keep in your pantry for 1 year, as they have already been cured. This is another of my secret ingredients, especially in Chinese Sausage Fried Rice (page 131). Everyone who's tried this sausage becomes addicted. I mean like loves it so much they'll sneak in your fridge and swipe the rest of the package home. It's salty-sweet and has little tiny pockets of fat that melt when cooked and flavor your entire dish. This is a must-try! There are few types of Chinese sausage, including duck liver. My favorite is just the regular 'ole pork. My kids think I'm the world's best mom when I throw a few links into my steaming rice—Chinese Sausage With Rice and Sweet Soy Sauce (page 129). There is no substitution—just buy the real thing!

Chives—Chinese. Chinese chives look like thick blades of grass—they are flat and dark green. They are stronger in flavor (and sweeter too) that the regular thin chives used in Western cooking, and you can add Chinese chives to any stir-fry, dumpling or egg roll filling. The flowering Chinese chives are stiffer, taller than Chinese chives, and are one of my favs to add to noodle dishes, like the Quick Noodle Stir-Fry (page 136). You can substitute with regular Western chives.

Cilantro. *See* **Herbs.**

Coconut milk is made by squeezing the grated pulp from a coconut, it's not the same as coconut water (which is the water found when you open a fresh coconut) You'll find coconut milk canned at any Asian market and mostly likely in the "Ethnic" section of your grocer (which, I hope one day will be obsolete and global ingredients will be found throughout the store). Coconut milk is unsweetened (not to be confused with sweet creme of coconut used for cocktails). There are many differences in each brand. The first pressing of the grated coconut results in very rich and creamy coconut milk (I loooove) and then the coconut pulp is soaked in warm water and pressed again. The subsequent is more watery, less flavorful. The best way to tell the quality of a coconut milk is to pick up a can and shake it. If it feels/sounds thick "schlonk-schlonk" (yeah, um, *schlonking* is a word) it's good. If it's watery "squish-squish" it's not as good. Personally, I go for schlonk. My fav brands are Mae Ploy and Chaokoh. There aren't really substitutions, unless you want to grab a coconut, grate and squeeze yourself. Don't even try to sub with milk and coconut extract—I'd rather have you skip the dish entirely than go that route.

CLOCKWISE, FROM TOP RIGHT: Dried rice noodles, egg roll wrappers, square wonton wrappers, round potsticker wrappers, jasmine rice tipped in the bowl, short-grained rice (popular in Japan and Korea) and dried rice paper wrappers for Summer Rolls.

Coriander, fresh. *See* **Herbs.**

Coriander, ground and whole Coriander is the seed from the coriander herb (better known as cilantro in the United States) and it can be found whole or ground. It's got a sweet, citrusy aroma and tastes nothing like the fresh cilantro/coriander! The spice is used in lots of Indian and Southeast Asian cooking and I love using it my Quick Vietnamese Chicken Pho (page 58). If you want to make your kitchen smell amazing, toast a tablespoon of the seeds in a dry frying pan!

Curry paste, Thai Thai curry paste is sold in little cans, pouches or tubs. I recommend the little 4-ounce (125-g) cans or pouches as they are easy to store and use. If you do buy the larger tubs, curry paste does keep well in the refrigerator for several months if you store it properly and keep it covered. There are many different types of curry paste: red, green, yellow and masaman. Each is made from a different combination of herbs and spices such as garlic, ginger, kaffir lime leaf, lemongrass, galangal, and of course chillies. If you're new to working with curry paste, it's best to add just a bit first into the dish, taste and then adjust. With coconut milk and curry paste in my pantry, I can make a fabulous seafood dish, like Mussels in Coconut Curry Broth (page 70), or the spicy-licious Thai Coconut Chicken Curry (page 103), both ready in just 15 minutes.

Dashi / Instant Dashi (Hon Dashi) is like the backbone of Japanese cuisine, flavoring everything from miso soup to braised chicken. It's a stock made of seaweed and dried bonito flakes. Instant dashi or Hon Dashi, is used in a lot of quick home cooking in Japan, and making it so convenient to whip up a bowl of miso soup in minutes! There are vegetarian versions of dashi made from dried shitake mushrooms—though I haven't found a vegetarian instant dashi. Also, instead of boiling frozen edamame pods in plain water, I add a couple spoons of instant dashi granules in the pot. You'll notice the difference in the taste tremendously!

Fish sauce is an essential ingredient in my pantry. It has a nice salty-sweet flavor to it, and you use it very sparingly, like Anchovy paste. A little goes a long way! There are several brands of fish sauce, the best one I've found so far is called "Three Crabs". Good fish sauce should be the color of brewed tea. Anything darker (like the color of soy sauce) is a lower quality brand. If you think that "fish sauce" sounds like a weird ingredient, guess what? A big chuck of the most popular Thai and Vietnamese dishes call for fish sauce! After opening, you can store fish sauce in your pantry or refrigerator.

Five Spice Powder Chinese five spice powder is a mixture of fennel, star anise, cinnamon, cloves and Sichuan peppercorns. But there are different spice blends and sometimes with more than five spices. It balances all 5 flavors of Chinese cooking: sweet, salty, bitter, sour and pungent. Just a pinch is all that's needed—it's a strong spice and can take over the entire dish if you use too much! It's great when mixed with sea salt to season chicken for the grill or just a few dashes can be added to any Chinese stir-fry. Five spice powder is a popular spice mix, you can probably find it at your regular grocery store.

Ginger is actually a root, the rhizome of a name of a plant I can't say 10 times fast, "Zingiber Officinale". It's one of the ingredients that I use in my everyday Asian cooking. When shopping for fresh ginger, look for ginger with smooth skin (wrinkled skin means the ginger is old and dried). For tips on how to prepare ginger see Jaden's Ginger Tips on page 33.

Green Onion (Scallion or Spring Onion) is part of my holy trinity of Chinese cooking, along with ginger and garlic. I use green onion in many of my dishes, either stir-fried with the garlic and ginger as an aromatic or sliced super-thinly on the diagonal as a raw garnish. To store green onions, remove the rubber band and place them in a small cup or glass jar that's filled with an inch (2.5 cm) of water. Insert the green onions, root side down and cover loosely with a thin, plastic grocery bag (I store fresh herbs this way too).

Herbs, fresh Fresh herbs are used as a major part of the ingredients, especially in Vietnamese dishes. I like to stir in fresh herbs at the very tail end of cooking, to keep its vibrancy and flavors. I also use fresh herbs as a garnish on top of a dish. Yes, the garnish makes a dish look prettier, with a pop of green, but my main reason is that I love snagging sprigs of the fresh herbs onto my plate to eat with the dish. Plus sprinkling the herbs on one side of the dish or on top makes everyone at the table happy. I can scoop a portion of the dish that doesn't have the garnish for my kids (they'll just pick out and waste the herb) and I make sure my big spoonful includes loads of herb, whether it's cilantro, mint or basil. To store fresh herbs, grab a glass or a ball mason canning jar. Add about an inch or two of water and stick the herbs in the glass like a bouquet. Cover loosely with a plastic bag (one of those thin plastic bags from the produce section of supermarket works just fine) and it should keep in the refrigerator twice as long as when normally kept suffocating in a plastic bag in your vegetable drawer! **Cilantro (Coriander):** Cilantro is what I call this fresh herb! When I was little, I didn't like the taste of fresh cilantro, picking every little itty piece out of the dish (mom loved it). Then one day, just out of nowhere, I craved the taste of cilantro and now can't get enough of it! (Okay, truth be told, I was preggers with Andrew and I think that had something to do with my tastes changing!) It's the most consumed fresh herb in the world and Asians use the leaves as well as the stems. **Mint:** This herb is so flexible—it can be used in savory dishes, desserts, cocktails and teas. It's refreshing and brightens any dish up. **Thai Basil** has a bit stronger taste than regular sweet basil that you find in supermarkets. But honestly, you can't really tell the difference in a dish! It's got purple stems and really beautiful purple flowers that look pretty as a garnish. Substitute sweet Italian basil if you can't find Thai basil.

Hoisin This Chinese sauce is made of soybeans and it's sweet, sticky and garlicky—which is why I describe it as "Chinese sweet BBQ sauce". It's used as a condiment for smearing on pancakes or buns for the popular Peking Duck and Moo Shu Pork dishes. I like hoisin sauce, but when I use it, it's with a light touch and in combination with other sauces.

Kaffir Lime Leaves are used in a lot of Southeast Asian dishes—the double leaves of the tree are incredibly fragrant and one whiff will instantly remind you of Thai dishes. You can use them like bay leaves, just tear the leaf (keeping it whole) in several places and drop in your soup or dish. If you can't get kaffir lime leaves fresh, check the freezer section or you can buy dried leaves. I also like to julienne fresh kaffir lime leaves into the thinnest slivers possible and add to a stir-fry. Substitute with a couple wide strips of lime peel. Grab a vegetable peeler and peel a strip of the thin outer green skin off the lime (avoid the white pithy part).

Kimchi I don't think I've ever been in a Korean family's home without the sight of kimchi in their refrigerator. Kimchi, or kimchee, is pickled or fermented vegetables and there are hundreds of different kinds. The one most popular is made of Napa cabbage, garlic, carrots and lots of chilli powder. It stores pretty well in your refrigerator and for me, the more it ages, the better it tastes! It's used as a spicy condiment, though I can make an entire meal out of white rice, kimchee and a few sheets of seasoned seaweed sheets (nori).

Lemongrass I grow lemongrass in the backyard because I use it so much! Lemongrass is well, a grass, that's native to Southeast Asia. You only use the bottom 4–6 inches (10 to 15 cm) of the thick stalk, as it's got a wonderful light lemony fragrance and taste. Look for lemongrass that is light green and fresh looking. Lemongrass is very fibrous and tough, so you'll either smash the stalk to release flavors and add to soups (remove and discard before serving) or mince it very finely. To use, cut the bottom 4 to 6 inches (10 to 15 cm) of the stalk (discard the rest) peel away the outermost layers of the stalk and discard. To infuse for soups, curries: slice stalk in half lengthwise. Use something heavy to bruise the stalk just a bit to release flavors. Rings: slice the stalk into super-thin rings. Mince: run your knife through the rings, back and forth to finely mince. Grated: my favorite way is to grate the lemongrass with a microplane grater. You'll get incredibly fine lemongrass without the fiber. I don't like lemongrass paste or powder (yuck). The frozen stuff is not bad, but I'd rather substitute with lemon peel. Grab a vegetable peeler and peel a strip of skin off the lemon.

Maggi Sauce Magical Maggi! This condiment is originally from Switzerland, but it is incredibly popular in Asia! It's like a more delicious version of soy sauce, though it contains no soy (but does have wheat gluten). A few dashes is really all you need to add that "umami" (that delicious, savory taste) to any dish. Next time you fry an egg, add a quick dash of Maggi! You can substitite with equal amount of soy sauce. It can be found in the condiment section of your grocery store.

Mint. *See* **Herbs.**

Mirin is Japanese sweet rice wine, very different from Chinese rice wine or sake and it certainly is NOT rice vinegar. I know, it can be confusing, as all three are so similar in name! Make sure you check the bottle and look for "sweet cooking rice wine". If you don't have mirin, substitute with four parts sake; 1 part corn syrup or sugar, dissolved. If you don't have mirin or sake, then try dry sherry or dry vermouth with the corn syrup or sugar . . . and if you don't have dry sherry or vermouth, then white wine. If you don't have white wine, well then it's time to go shopping.

Miso is an essential component of Japanese cuisine and it is made from fermented soybeans. There are so many different types and textures of miso, from delicate light and smooth to chocolate brown with bits of soybean chunks. It's found refrigerated in Asian markets and health food stores, but I bet you can also find it in your regular local supermarket as it's becoming more and more popular. Once you open it, keep it covered well and it will last up to six months in your refrigerator. The great thing about miso is that you can just take out a little scoop and make miso soup for one. White miso is called "shiro miso" and it's sweeter and less salty than the others. Of all miso, this is my favorite because the flavor is more delicate. The deeper the color, the saltier and generally stronger in flavor as it's aged longer. There's really no substitute for miso.

Mushrooms Canned, straw. This is a common ingredient in Chinese stir-fries and Thai soups. They don't have a lot of taste on their own (like many canned vegetables) but the texture is pretty unique, kind of slippery soft. I like cutting them in half lengthwise to make it easier to eat (and it's prettier too). **Fresh, shitake.** Shitake are Japanese black mushrooms, and you'll find plenty of shitake in your local supermarket, as it's widely cultivated now. The cap is light golden brown and the stem is woody. Store shitake in a brown paper bag in your refrigerator. **Dried, black.** Dried black mushrooms or shitake mushrooms are smokier and deeper in flavor than the fresh version. They are generally large and meaty and are used by vegetarians as a "meat substitute". These can be stored for a long time in your refrigerator or pantry. To use, soak them in water until soft. The thick mushrooms must be soaked for several hours. If you're in a hurry, microwave them in hot water. Start with 7 minutes and check. When I know I'll be using dried mushrooms in a dish, I'll actually soak them in water overnight. The soaking water is flavorful (discard the sediment at the bottom) and you can use this water when steaming vegetables, making rice or just adding to pot when making soup.

Noodles, dried Buckwheat (soba) noodles. This mushroom-colored thin noodle, which is popular in Japan, is made from buckwheat flour. It's usually served chilled with dashi-soy-mirin dipping sauce (yum) or in a hot broth. **Rice noodles or rice vermicelli.** This noodle is made from rice flour. It's one of the most popular noodles in Asia and come in many widths. The thin rice stick noodles are great for Vietnamese spring rolls and salads. The medium and wide widths are often found in stir-fried noodle dishes (Shrimp Pad Thai, page 137) and noodle soups (like the Quick Vietnamese Chicken Pho, page 58). Soak rice noodles in warm water and briefly boil. **Egg Noodles.** This pale yellow noodle is made of eggs and wheat. They are available fresh, frozen or dried. The dried egg noodles are dried in little bundles or coils. You'll have to soak them in warm water to loosen the coils before cooking. These egg noodles are used in Wonton Noodle Soup (page 60). See page 23 for information on fresh or frozen egg noodles. **Mung bean noodles.** These

LEFT TO RIGHT: Chinese rice wine, Sriracha hot chilli sauce, oyster sauce, sweet chilli sauce, soy sauce, coconut milk, sesame oil, Chinese black vinegar, fish sauce and hoisin sauce.

slippery noodles are made of mung beans and are gluten free! They are white when dried and clear when cooked. They are also known as glass noodles or cellophane noodles. They can also be deep-fried (my kids' fav!) and they magically puff up in just a few seconds time and great as a topping for salads or a stir-fry. **Potato starch noodles.** These Korean noodles are also sometimes called glass noodles and are used in the dish Korean Jap Chae Noodles (page 135). They are made from sweet potatoes and do not contain gluten. The noodles are called "dangmyeon" in Korean and are grayish in color when dried; they transform to clear color when cooked. **Somen.** This very thin, delicate Japanese noodle is made from wheat flour. They are usually served chilled with a dipping sauce and they are also served in broths.

Noodles, fresh Fresh Rice Noodles. These are my favorite noodles of all time, especially the wide rice noodles used in a Chinese stir fry. If I can find fresh rice noodles, I'll use them for Quick Vietnamese Chicken Pho (page 58). You can also find them in sheets that are rolled up; you can unroll them, fill them and then steam them. They don't keep that long—they'll dry out in the refrigerator, so use them

quickly or freeze. **Egg Noodles.** Fresh egg noodles are sold in plastic baggies or containers and are in the refrigerated section. They are also frozen in the package and store very well. The noodles are very quick cooking, and perfect for a hearty stir-fried noodle dish like Quick Noodle Stir-Fry (page 136) and the Garlic Butter Noodles (page 134).

Nori is Japanese for thin sheets of dried seaweed, usually sold in sealed packets of ten to fifty sheets. These are for sushi making, but their crispness doesn't last too long once you open the package. If you have a gas stovetop, turn on the flame, take one sheet of nori and wave it over the flame to toast and crisp up the seaweed for a shatteringly crisp texture. Nori also comes in other shapes—smaller squares and strips. I love to sprinkle seasoned nori on soup (Ochazuke Rice with Crispy Salmon Skin and Nori, page 59), plain rice, french fries or popcorn (page 53). Seasoned nori is usually seasoned with salt, and you'll see that right on the package.

Oil, Cooking For my everyday stir-fry or pan-fry cooking, I use canola oil as it's healthier than some of the other oils and it does have a high smoking point and a

neutral flavor. I also recommend vegetable oil or peanut oil, however, with so many kids with peanut allergies (what's up with THAT by the way?) I'm just afraid to use it in my cooking. Toasted sesame oil, which has dark amber color, has a very low smoking point but a pungent/distinct odor when using more than just a few drops or a dribble in a dish. Olive oil is fine to use for cooking, but the oil has a pretty strong flavor and you'll end up noticing the olive oil taste in your Asian food.

Oyster Sauce Yes, it's made from dried oysters. But no, you can't really taste the oysters! It's dark broth, thick and smooth; salty, smoky and slightly sweet at the same time. Oyster sauce is used to enhance the flavor of many stir-fries, noodle dishes and braises. There is a vegetarian version made from mushrooms, too. Once opened, keep it in the refrigerator, where it will last a long time. There's not really a good substitute for this sauce, however it's a very popular Chinese ingredient and you'll probably find it at your grocers.

Plum Sauce is sometimes called "duck sauce" because it's often served with roast duck in Chinese-American restaurants. It's a sweet, slightly tart dipping-sauce made of plums, apricots, vinegar and sugar. It's good as a dip and as a substitute for Sweet Chilli Sauce and even as a glaze for grilled chicken.

Rice There are so many different types of rice—jasmine, short grain, broken, sweet, brown, red and even black! The most popular rice is the long grain (I prefer jasmine rice and the short grain (used in sushi and popular in Japan and Korea). The long grain Asian rice (not basmati) is popular in China and Southeast Asia. The jasmine rice (popular in Thailand) has a beautiful aroma. Long grain rice is fluffier when cooked and the grains separate better. The short-grained rice is starchier, stickier and heartier. When mixed with a bit of seasoned rice vinegar, its texture is perfect for sushi, which requires the rice grains to stick to each other to form a ball. To cook rice, you must rinse the rice in several changes of cool water to get rid of excess starch and just to cleanse the grains. See page 129 on how to cook rice.

Rice Vinegar There are two types of rice vinegar (also called rice wine vinegar): seasoned (or sweetened) and regular (or unsweetened). Rice vinegar is less acidic and tart than regular white distilled vinegar. The seasoned rice vinegar is perfect for dressing sushi rice or for salad dressings as it includes sugar already in the mix. Substitute the regular rice vinegar with cider or white vinegar. To make sweetened rice vinegar, take $1/4$ cup (65 ml) unsweeteend rice vinegar, cider or white vinegar and add 1 tablespoon of sugar.

Salt Like the spelling of chilli (page 18) there is much confusion about salt! Not the spelling, but the fact that foodies and chefs are definitely passionate about their salts and there are different types of salts. The most common in households is table salt, but it's also my least favorite. The granules are very fine, the taste is bitter, the anti-caking agent just sounds gross, and the

added iodine is sooooo 1920s. I'm a natural sea salt and kosher salt gal. Most restaurant kitchens will use kosher salt in its everyday prep and expensive sea salt in finishing a dish, sprinkling it right after the dish is plated. I do the same. Kosher salt's larger granules are easier to use and feel (instead of spooning salt, I always use my fingers and hands to salt) and it's not as salty as table salt. And you can't beat sea salt's natural taste and flakey texture. I don't know what kind of salt you use at home, (and since the measurements of these different salts are so different), instead of putting exact measurements, like "$1/2$ teaspoon of salt", I've used "generous pinch of salt" throughout the recipes. I'm a big advocate of "season to taste" as your "salty" may be my "bland". Start with a generous 3-finger pinch of salt (probably twice for kosher and sea salt). You can always add more.

Sake is Japanese fermented rice wine and the best sake is drunk chilled. The so-so sake is served warm to mask its inferior quality. Sake has a higher alcohol content than beer or wine, and like wine, there are many different types and price points. Daiginjo is the top quality stuff (I'd use this for drinking and not cooking). For cooking, you can always substitute with dry sherry or dry vermouth.

Sambal The word *sambal* refers to a Southeast Asian (Indonesia, Malaysia, Singaporean) relish or condiment made with ingredients like chillies, salt, garlic, vinegar, sugar and others. Sambal is usually served at the table, so you can spoon some on your own plate as you need. I have a sweet chilli version (page 26) that is great tossed with cooked noodles, used as a dipping sauce or topped on plain chicken.

Sausage, Chinese, *see* **Chinese Sausage**

Scallions or Spring Onions, *see* **Green Onion.**

Sesame Oil, Toasted or Dark Sesame oil is the oil from toasted sesame seeds. The dark sesame oil has a very strong flavor and fragrance, so only a few drops to a teaspoon is all that's needed in a dish. Otherwise, your entire dish will end up tasting like the sesame oil! It's used as part of a marinade for meat and seafood for Chinese stir-fries, but mostly added towards the end of a dish as the sesame oil smokes at high heat. Buy sesame oil in glass bottles and store away from heat and light, it turns rancid pretty easily. If you don't have sesame oil, add regular cooking oil to toasted and crushed sesame seeds.

Sesame Seeds These itty bitty seeds are used whole in cooking for its nutty, sweet aroma with a rich, buttery, nutty taste. They come in shades of pale ivory, brown and black. The ivory colored sesame seeds are probably untoasted or unroasted. You can use them as is, but for maximum flavor, toast them in a dry frying pan on medium-low heat for 2 to 3 minutes or until golden brown and fragrant. The brown and black sesame seeds are pre-roasted (check the label) and are beautiful and provide a nice contrast in your dish.

Shallots are small, anywhere from $1^{1}/_{2}$ to 3 inches (3.75 to 7.5 cm) across. They are sweeter and milder in taste than onions and are a very popular ingredient in Asian cooking. You can add them to your stir-fry along with the garlic and ginger, or you can deep-fry them for a crispy topping on a dish. Store shallots in a cool, dry, well-ventilated place, just as you would store your onions or garlic. Substitute shallots with finely minced onion.

Sichuan peppercorn Contrary to its name, the Sichuan peppercorn (sometimes spelled "Szechuan") is not a peppercorn, but rather a berry from a bush. Put a couple of pods between your teeth and chew—you'll get a numbing, tingly sensation all inside your mouth and lips.

Contrary to what people think, Sichuan peppercorn is not really spicy in your face hot. It has a citrusy, warming and woodsy aroma and flavor. Try making a flavored salt with Sichuan peppercorn (page 24).

Soy Sauce/Dark Soy Sauce This essential seasoning is made from fermented soybeans mixed with some type of roasted grain (wheat, barley, or rice are common). It tends to have a chocolate brown color, and a pungent, rather than overly salty, flavor. Dark soy sauce is used in Chinese cooking and is a bit richer, thicker, and more mellow than the lighter varieties. I use both the more full-bodied dark soy sauce in many Chinese meat stews and braises and the lighter variety, which I refer to simply as "soy sauce" in the recipes as my everyday soy sauce.

Sriracha Sauce. *See* **Chilli Sauce.**

Sweet Chilli Sauce is my "ketchup"— it's sweet, vinegary and just barely a hint of spice. I use it as a dip anything for Mom's Famous Crispy Egg Rolls (page 50) and Firecracker Shrimp (page 48) as well as in stir-fries (Thai Chicken in Sweet Chilli Sauce, page 104). Two great brands are Mae Ploy and Lingham (thicker, spicier and less sweet than Mae Ploy). When my assistant, Farina, eats at a restaurant that doesn't have sweet chilli sauce, she makes her own concoction from a combo of ketchup, hot sauce (Tabasco), sugar and salt. If you have Plum Sauce, you can use that as a substitute.

Tamarind comes in blocks of pulp (with or without seeds) or prepared in jarred form as a paste (sometimes called "concentrate"). To make tamarind paste out of the blocks, in a medium sized bowl, combine a golf-ball sized piece of tamarind and ½ cup (125 ml) of hot water. With a fork, smash and "knead" the tamarind to extract as much pulp as possible. You can also use your fingers to knead as well. The consis-

tency should be like thin ketchup. Drain and discard the tamarind solids, reserving the water. If you're using the concentrate form, measure straight out of the jar.

Tea leaves, whether white, green, black or oolong all come from the same bush, Camillia Sinensis. The differences arise in the processing. Green and white teas are not fermented and the oolong and black tea are semi fermented and fermented. Chinese drink tea like water and of course, loose leaf tea is best (supermarket tea bags = stale tea dust!). In addition to drinking tea, I've got a recipe where I'm using tea to smoke and flavor salmon (page 80).

Thai Basil. *See* **Herbs.**

Tofu/Bean Curd (though tofu sounds sexier) is made out of soybeans—soft and firm. The soft, or silken is lovely eaten as is with a ginger-miso salad dressing. It's also used cubed in miso soup. The medium and firm tofu are perfect for baking (Baked Tofu Salad with Mustard Miso Dressing, page 64) stir frying and pan frying, as they hold up better in the cooking process (see chapter on Vegetables, Tofu & Eggs, page 108). Tofu has very little taste on its own, so it takes on whatever flavors you have in the dish. It's incredibly healthy for you and inexpensive to buy. They don't last too long in the refrigerator, though, so use within a few days of purchase. Tofu often comes in a plastic tub covered with a thin plastic film. Slit the film and drain all the water out. To store, you can put the tofu in a bowl or container, fill with cool water, cover and refrigerate. Check the expiration date and if the package puffs out with locked in air and the package looks like it's about to pop, discard (tofu is doin' something funky inside). Soft or silken tofu also comes in a paper carton that does not need to be refrigerated. It's much silkier, smoother and more delicate than the tub version. It's difficult to use for stir-fries (but great for Tofu and Clams in a Light

Miso Broth, page 117), but handy to keep in the pantry.

Wrappers From egg rolls to summer rolls and potstickers to firecracker shrimp, Asians love to wrap their food! **Wonton Wrappers:** Find wonton wrappers in the freezer section of an Asian market. They are very thin and square. To defrost, place package unopened on the counter for 45 minutes, or overnight in the refrigerator. Do not attempt to submerge the wrapper package in warm water or microwave to defrost. It doesn't work well that way. Once the package is opened, always keep the wrappers covered with a barely damp paper towel to prevent the edges from drying. If they do happen to dry, you should just trim off the dried edges. **Potsticker Wrappers:** Same info as above, but they are round instead of square. They are also called gyoza wrappers. **Egg Roll Wrappers:** Same info as above, but they come in large squares, 9 inches by 9 inches (23 x 23 cm). Look specifically for spring roll wrappers or egg roll wrappers. Where I live, my local non-Asian market has fresh egg roll wrappers for sale in the produce section. I generally will tell you not to buy these fresh "pasta sheets" that are marketed as egg roll wrappers. They are way too thick and just taste too starchy. You want very thin egg roll wrappers that crisp up beautifully. **Rice Paper.** Dried rice paper comes in different sizes and thickness and is used for summer rolls and is available in Asian markets. My favorite brand for summer rolls is "Three Ladies"; it's a bit thicker and better quality than the others. Look at the ingredients on the package. Don't get the ones that include "tapioca" as an ingredient. They are micro-thin and very difficult to handle. See Vietnamese Summer Rolls (page 44) for more information on how to use and handle.

the basics

I hope that these recipes for chilli sauces, dips and stocks will be some of your favorites, whether you use them to cook dishes in this book or adapt them in your own recipes. The chilli sauces store well and are great to put out on the dinner table every night to add a little fire to your meal, and the dipping sauces (like the Cashew Nut Dipping Sauce, page 30) are great for satays, chicken wings, summer rolls or even carrot and celery sticks! The stocks are the basis of many soups (stocks made from scratch always make a difference!) I also use stocks to flavor my stir-fries and when steaming vegetables—they just add an amazing dimension of flavor! Make a big batch of stock and freeze them in freezer bags, plastic containers, silicon cupcake trays or ice cube trays so that you have homemade stock whenever you need some. Have fun with these recipes!

Sweet Chilli Sambal

My friend and talented chef, Jeremy Hammond-Chambers, taught me how to make a sweet chilli sambal and I've been hooked ever since. Sambal is a condiment usually made with chillies—lots of chillies. I'm not a big blow-off-your-tongue spice gal, so I like using very mild chillies. This recipe is definitely a favorite of everyone who tried it. In fact, I make a massive batch of Sweet Chilli Sambal, can several jars and give them away as presents.

MAKES 4 CUPS (1 LITER)
1/2 cup (125 ml) hot water
1 walnut-sized piece of tamarind pulp or 1 heaping tablespoon tamarind paste (also called "concentrate")
1 lb (500 g) sweet chillies, roughly chopped
2 onions, each chopped into 8 pieces
8 cloves garlic
1 1/2 cups (350 ml) cooking oil
1/4 cup (40 g) palm or light brown sugar
2 1/2 tablespoons fish sauce

1 If you're using tamarind pulp, combine the hot water and tamarind pulp in a bowl. Smash the tamarind pulp with a fork to dissolve as much as of it as you can. Let sit for 10 minutes. Discard the pulp, keeping the tamarind water.
2 Process the onions, chillies and garlic in a food processor with the oil until a rough pastelike texture is reached. Place the paste in a non-reactive pan over very low heat and cook for approximately 1 hour stirring the mixture regularly to make sure it does not stick or burn. Add the tamarind water or concentrate, palm sugar and fish sauce and cook further until the mixture becomes sticky, thick, salty and sweet, about 1 hour. At this point the oil should have fully separated from the paste and will be sitting on the top. Cool and store in refrigerator.

> TIP: The general rule is the larger and fatter the chilli, the milder it will be. At the market, look for chillies that are labeled "sweet" or "stuffing" chillies. If you enjoy the flavor but no spice, then feel free to use red bell pepper as a substitute.

Asian Flavored Salts

Creating a flavored salt is the simplest way to add a dash of Asian flavors to anything you serve. They make fab gifts too—just bottle each flavor in a jar and give as a set. Try to use good salt—sea salt is best, followed by kosher, but I would steer clear of regular table salt. Use flavored salt in any way that you want—in place of regular salt or as a finishing salt to sprinkle on just before serving. It's great on steamed vegetables.

Sichuan Peppercorn Salt

1 tablespoon Sichuan peppercorn
3 tablespoons sea salt or kosher salt

In a dry, heavy-bottomed frying pan, toast the Sichuan peppercorn over medium-low heat until fragrant, about 3 minutes. Let cool and grind to a coarse powder in a spice grinder or mortar and pestle. Combine with sea salt. In addition to a lovely dipping salt, your house will smell wonderfully aromatic all day.

Citrus-Ginger Salt

1 teaspoon grated fresh ginger
1$^1/_2$ teaspoons grated orange and/ or lemon rind
2 tablespoons sea salt or kosher salt

Preheat the oven to 200°F (95°C). Place a sheet of parchment paper on a baking sheet and spread out the grated ginger and citrus on the paper. Bake for 30 minutes, or until completely dry. Combine with the salt.

Vietnamese Pho Salt

2 teaspoons whole coriander seeds
3 whole cloves or $^1/_4$ teaspoon ground cloves
1 small star anise
$^1/_4$ cinnamon stick or 1 dash of ground cinnamon
3 tablespoons sea salt or kosher salt

In a dry frying pan over medium-low heat, toast the spices until fragrant, about 3 minutes. In a spice grinder or mortar and pestle, grind the toasted spices to a coarse powder. Combine with the salt.

Ginger Scallion

Vietnamese Dip

The quality of your fish sauce has everything to do with this sauce, known as *nuoc cham* in Vietnamese. Look for tea-colored fish sauce. This dipping sauce is perfect for Vietnamese Summer Rolls (page 44).

MAKES ABOUT 1 CUP (250 ML)
3½ tablespoons sugar
¾ cup (175 ml) warm water
3 tablespoons lime juice
2 cloves garlic, finely minced
4 tablespoons fish sauce
½ teaspoon chilli-garlic sauce or ½ teaspoon minced fresh chilli pepper (or more, depending on your taste)

In a bowl, add the sugar and warm water, and stir until the sugar is dissolved. Stir in the remaining ingredients. Taste and add more fish sauce or chillies if desired.

Ginger Scallion

Here's proof that you don't need to add ingredients to a wok to fry. If you pour hot cooking oil over herbs or aromatics, the heat of the oil will "pow" or flash-fry the ingredients, releasing its aromas, and natural oils while keeping them bright and fresh. This is my magic condiment, transforming a plain, poached chicken into an explosion of vibrant flavors. I also use it for any steamed or fried fish … and sometimes I even just mix it in plain rice! It's important that you use a medium heatproof dish to pour the hot oil in. The oil will sizzle a bit, so you want some room in the bowl. Plastic and thin glass are not good options as they will melt or shatter! You can make the sauce in a small pot if you don't have a heavy heatproof dish. I suggest that you chop up all the ingredients for this sauce and have them ready for "powing" just before serving.

MAKES ⅓ CUP (80 ML)
2 green onions, minced
½ teaspoon finely minced garlic
1 tablespoon freshly grated ginger (see Jaden's Ginger Tips, page 33)

½ teaspoon minced red chillies
¼ teaspoon rice vinegar
Generous pinch of salt
⅓ cup (80 ml) high-heat cooking oil

In a heatproof dish, combine the green onions, garlic, ginger, chillies, rice vinegar and salt. Mix and set aside. In a wok, heat up the oil. When the oil is hot and just starting to smoke, carefully pour the hot oil into the heatproof dish on top of the ingredients. It will sizzle—please be careful!

Apricot Sweet Chilli Sauce

My kids love this for dipping Mom's Famous Crispy Eggrolls (page 50), Firecracker Shrimp (page 48), Vietnamese Summer Rolls (page 44).

MAKES ABOUT 1 CUP (250 ML)
½ cup (125 ml) apricot marmalade
½ cup (125 ml) sweet chilli sauce

In a bowl, mix the ingredients together. If sauce is too thick, thin with 1 tablespoon of water.

Thai Dipping Sauce

Sweet, spicy, sour and salty! The four flavors of Thai cuisine describe this delicious sauce perfectly. Use this sauce for Crispy Fish Cakes (page 36). You can leave out the chillies if you like.

MAKES ABOUT ½ CUP (125 ML)
2 teaspoons sugar
¼ cup (65 ml) warm water
½ to 1 teaspoon minced chillies
1 clove garlic, finely minced
1 teaspoon rice vinegar
1 tablespoon freshly squeezed lime juice
2 tablespoons fish sauce
2 teaspoons chopped cilantro (coriander) leaves

In a bowl, add the sugar and warm water, and stir until the sugar is dissolved. Stir in the remaining ingredients. Taste and add more fish sauce or chillies if desired.

Chilli Garlic Sauce

I grow several varieties of chillies in my back yard—always the ones that are a bit milder than the mouth-on-fire stuff at the Asian markets. Rather than use the store-bought chilli sauce, sometimes I just make it from scratch, because it only takes about 5 minutes.

Plus, it's fresher tasting and you can jar the rest and keep in the refrigerator for a couple of weeks. When I'm feelin' frisky, I'll make a massive batch of it in the wok and store them in sterilized jars to give to friends. It makes a hot gift.

Try making this chilli sauce with the larger, milder chillies—you'll really get the full, fruity flavor of chilli, not just the searing heat. (See page 18 for information on chillies).

MAKES 1/2 CUP (125 ML)
1/2 cup (125 ml) cooking oil
4 fresh chilli peppers of your choice, chopped
8 cloves garlic, finely minced
One 2-in (5-cm) piece fresh ginger, peeled and finely minced
2 green onions (scallions), finely minced
1 generous pinch of salt
1/4 teaspoon sugar

1 In a wok or small pot, add the oil, chillies, garlic and ginger.
2 Turn the heat to medium-low. The oil will begin to heat up and gently sizzle the ingredients. As soon as you start smelling the fragrant aromatics, turn the heat to low. Cook on low for 1 minute. Add the green onion, salt and sugar. Stir and remove from the heat and let cool.
3 Store unused Chilli Garlic Sauce in a clean jar and refrigerator for up to 2 weeks.

Chilli Garlic Sauce

Chinese Dipping Sauce

This is a very versatile dipping sauce. It's great for Pork and Mango Potstickers (page 48), boiled Wontons (page 60) on their own, or just having at the table as a sauce. You can use homemade Chilli Garlic Sauce (recipe on this page) or use store-bought chilli sauce.

MAKES 1/4 CUP (65 ML)
1/4 cup (65 ml) soy sauce
1 tablespoon rice vinegar
1 teaspoon sugar
1/2 teaspoon very finely minced garlic
Chilli Garlic Sauce (recipe on this page), as much as you want
Few sprigs fresh cilantro (coriander), chopped

In a small bowl, whisk all the ingredients together until combined.

Fried Garlic Oil

Steamed vegetables can get really boring, so I started making garlic oil to keep handy. I use it to drizzle on steamed vegetables just before serving, whether it's broccoli, cauliflower or carrots. It's also great on simple grilled or steamed fish too, adding a rich, nutty garlic flavor! Make sure that you strain out all the garlic bits, as garlic does not store in oil at room temperature. Take the strained garlic cloves, slice and toss them in that evening's noodles or vegetable dish. The toasted garlic is lovely and mild.

MAKES 1 CUP (250 ML)
1 cup (250 ml) cooking oil
10 cloves garlic, peeled and smashed

In a cold wok or saucepan, add the garlic and oil. Turn the heat to medium-low and cook until the garlic is golden brown, about 5 minutes. Remove from the heat and let the garlic cook a little further in the hot oil. Strain out all the garlic and reserve for another use. Let the oil cool completely and pour into a clean, glass jar. Cover tightly. Keeps for 4 to 6 weeks.

Sweet Soy Sauce

My children simply cannot live without this sauce. This is Mom's recipe, and she uses it for the Chinese Sausage With Rice and Sweet Soy Sauce (page 129). I make a nice batch of it and store in a jar in the refrigerator for up to 3 weeks. You'll find tons of uses for this sauce—over steamed rice, over steamed vegetables, broiled or steamed fish.

MAKES 3 CUPS (700 ML)
3 tablespoons high-heat cooking oil
3 cloves garlic, minced
1 shallot, minced
1 cup (250 ml) soy sauce
$1/2$ cup (125 ml) dark soy sauce
$1/4$ cup (65 ml) rice wine (or dry sherry)
$1/2$ cup (100 g) sugar
$1/2$ cup (125 ml) water
$1/2$ teaspoon sesame oil

Heat the cooking oil in a wok or saucepan over medium heat. When oil is hot but not smoking, add the garlic and shallots. Fry for 30 seconds, until fragrant and slightly browned. Carefully remove the shallots and garlic, leaving the flavored oil. Add remaining ingredients and simmer until thickened, about 5 to 10 minutes. Store in a clean, tightly covered jar in refrigerator.

Cashew Nut Dipping Sauce

Vietnamese Summer Rolls (page 44) are sometimes served with a peanut-based sauce, but I loved my friend, Jeni's (www.oishiieats.blogspot.com) version that uses cashew nut butter. If your regular supermarket doesn't carry it, check a health food store.

MAKES ABOUT 1 CUP (250 ML)
1 tablespoon cooking oil
3 cloves garlic, finely minced
2 tablespoons hoisin sauce
1 tablespoon sugar
1 tablespoon chilli garlic sauce
3 tablespoons cashew nut butter
$2/3$ cup (160 ml) water, divided

In a small saucepan over medium-low heat, add the oil and, when just starting to get hot, add the garlic and cook until lightly browned, about 30 seconds. Add the hoisin sauce, sugar, chilli garlic sauce, cashew nut butter and half of the water, stir well and simmer for 30 seconds. Whisk in the rest of the water if you want a thinner consistency. Keeps in the refrigerator for up to 1 week. If sauce is too thick after storing, whisk in a bit of water to thin it out.

Peanut Dipping Sauce

This is great for grilled satays (page 93), Vietnamese Summer Rolls (page 44), or just as a dipping sauce for sliced cucumbers, carrots or celery as a snack. Smooth or chunky? I like the chunky.

MAKES 1 CUP (250 ML)
2 teaspoons cooking oil
2 cloves garlic, crushed in garlic press
1 teaspoon grated fresh ginger (see Jaden's Ginger Tips, page 33)
3 tablespoons sweet chilli sauce
2 tablespoons hoisin sauce
$2/3$ cup (160 ml) water
3 tablespoons peanut butter (smooth or chunky)

Heat the oil in small saucepan over medium-low heat. When the oil is just starting to get hot, add the garlic and ginger and fry for 30 seconds until fragrant. Add the sweet chilli sauce, hoisin sauce, water and peanut butter and stir until smooth. Simmer until thickened. Let cool. Keeps in the refrigerator for up to 1 week. If the sauce is too thick after storing, whisk in a bit of water to thin it out.

Broccoli Stem Pickle

My mom never wastes any part of the broccoli. Instead of discarding the thick stem, she peels the tough outer layer and makes a quick pickle to serve at the table.

2 to 3 stems of broccoli
2 teaspoons rice vinegar
$1/4$ teaspoon finely minced garlic
1 chilli, thinly sliced
Pinch of ground coriander
Pinch of salt
Pinch of sugar
Drizzle of sesame oil

Use a vegetable peeler and peel the tough outer layer of the stem to expose the lighter colored, tender stem. Cut the stem into 2 to 3-inch (5 to 7.5-cm) sections and then thinly slice lengthwise. In a bowl, toss the stem sections with the remaining ingredients and serve as a condiment at the table.

Broccoli Stem Pickle

Carrot Daikon Pickle

I could eat this Vietnamese condiment by the mounds! It's easy to make, it only takes 30 minutes to pickle and stores for a few weeks in the fridge. Have these on the table for any Vietnamese dish.

1 cup (150 g) carrot matchsticks
1 cup (150 g) white daikon radish matchsticks
Generous pinch of salt
1 tablespoon sugar
1/4 cup (65 ml) rice vinegar or white vinegar

Toss the carrots and daikon with the salt, sugar and vinegar. Let sit at room temperature for at least 30 minutes. If not using immediately, you can add an additional 1/4 cup (65 ml) vinegar to cover the vegetables, stir and store in a glass jar or plastic container for up to 1 month.

Asian Pesto

Pesto doesn't always have to be just boring basil. Jazz it up with a trio of herbs popular in Asian cooking—cilantro, mint and basil. Freeze what you don't use in small plastic resealable bags and defrost anytime you need a quick, flavorful topping to chicken, fish, lamb or noodles.

MAKES 1 CUP (250 ML)
3 cloves garlic
1 chilli, coarsely chopped
1/4 cup (40 g) unsalted, roasted peanuts
1/4 cup (8 g) fresh cilantro (coriander) leaves
1/2 cup (16 g) fresh Thai basil or sweet Italian basil leaves
1/2 cup (16 g) fresh mint leaves
3 tablespoons freshly squeezed lime juice
1 teaspoon sugar
2 teaspoons salt
1 cup (250 ml) cooking oil, divided

In a food processor or blender, combine the garlic, chilli and peanuts. Pulse until finely chopped. Add the fresh cilantro, basil, mint, lime juice, sugar, salt and 3 tablespoons of the oil. Process until the mixture becomes a coarse paste. Remove and stir in the remaining oil.

Mom's Chicken Stock

My preference when buying chicken is to purchase the whole chicken, instead of just buying parts (unless I'm going for Baked Garlic Chilli Wings, page 43) and hack it up myself. It's cheaper and I get to have the bones for chicken stock that I place in a large bag and freeze. When buying chicken wings, I'll also save the flapper or tip and throw them in the freezer bag as well. For Chinese chicken stock, all you need is a full bag of bones (about 2 chickens worth) and a few aromatics. If you'd like to make chicken stock out of a whole chicken, by all means do!

Mom's tip with making stock is to boil the bones hard for a few minutes to dislodge any bloody bits and yuck stuff that's lurking in the bones. The boiling action scrubs the bones and also produce the most clear and clean tasting stock you'll ever have.

MAKES 4 QUARTS (3.75 LITERS)
4 lbs (2 kg) chicken bones, hacked into 2 to 3-in (5 to 8-cm) sections, exposing the insides of the bones as much as possible
One 4-in (10-cm) piece of fresh ginger, cut into coins (see Jaden's Ginger Tips, page 33)
8 cloves garlic, smashed
8 green onions (scallions), cut into thirds (roots discarded)
One small handful (about 1/2 oz /15 g) fresh cilantro (coriander) stems or leaves

1 Bring a large stockpot filled with water to a boil. Once it reaches a boil, add the chicken bones. Keep the heat on high and boil the bones for 3 minutes. Pour out the water (you'll notice a lot of scum and yuck!) and rinse the bones. Add the rest of the ingredients as well as enough water to cover the bones by 2 inches (5 cm). If you are using a whole chicken (not just bones) then fill with enough water to cover by 4 inches (10 cm).
2 Bring to a boil and immediately turn the heat to low and simmer for 1 1/2 to 3 hours, skimming the surface periodically.

The surface of the stock should be barely bubbling. Alternatively, you can put all the ingredients into a slow cooker or pressure cooker (follow instructions provided with your appliance for making stock)
3 Strain the stock and discard the solids.

Vegetable Stock

Vegetable stock can taste pretty thin with just boiling, and a tip that I learned from Chinese chef and author Kylie Kwong from Australia is to sauté the vegetables first before adding water and simmering the stock. If you have dried Chinese black mushrooms, they are fabulous in the stock and add a hearty flavor profile to the stock. You can throw in the dried mushrooms as is, or you can hydrate them in water overnight and then throw the mushrooms in the pot along with the mushroom soaking water (though be careful not to pour in the sediment at bottom of mushroom soaking liquid).

MAKES 4 QUARTS (3.75 LITERS)
1 tablespoon cooking oil
3 carrots, peeled and sliced on diagonal
3 celery stalks, sliced on diagonal
1/2 onion, cut into large chunks
3 dried Chinese black mushrooms, washed well
One 4-in (10-cm) piece of fresh ginger, cut into coins (see Jaden's Ginger Tips, page 33)
8 cloves garlic, smashed
8 green onions (scallions) stalks, cut into thirds (roots discarded)
One small handful (about 1/2 oz /15 g) fresh cilantro (coriander) stems or leaves
4 quarts (3.75 liters) water

In a large stockpot over medium-high heat, add the oil. When the oil is hot, add all the ingredients except water and sauté for 3 minutes. Add the water. Bring to a boil and immediately turn the heat to low. Simmer for 30 minutes to 1 hour, skimming the surface periodically. Strain and discard solids.

Seafood Stock

The tricky part of making seafood stock is to make sure that it doesn't taste too fishy. You can use fish bones, fish meat, shrimp shells, crab shells and even lobster shells for the stock. Fry the bones/shells in a bit of cooking oil first to mellow out it's strong fishy taste and to give the stock a much deeper, round flavor.

MAKES 4 QUARTS (3.75 LITERS)
1 tablespoon cooking oil
Enough seafood bones and shells to fill a 4-quart (3.75-liter) freezer bag
One 4-in (10-cm) piece of fresh ginger, cut into coins (see Jaden's Ginger Tips, page 33)
8 cloves garlic, smashed
8 green onions (scallions), cut into thirds (roots discarded)
One small handful (about $^1/_2$ oz /15 g) fresh cilantro (coriander) stems or leaves
4 quarts (3.75 liters) of water

In large stockpot over medium heat, add the cooking oil. When the oil is hot, add the bones and shells and sauté for 2 to 3 minutes, until the shells turn pink and the bones are white. Add the remaining ingredients. Bring to a boil and immediately turn the heat to low. Simmer for 30 minutes to 1 hour, skimming the surface periodically. Strain and discard the solids.

Meat Stock

As with Mom's Chicken Stock (page 31), you'll want to do a hard boil of the bones first, discard the water and scum, rinse the bones and then proceed to make the stock. I know it's an extra step, but you'll be rewarded with a rich tasting and clearest stock ever. I always like to have pork meat in my meat stock, and will just buy whatever's on sale at the market. If you don't have meat bones, that's fine, just use pork meat, like Boston Butt.

MAKES 4 QUARTS (3.75 LITERS)
4 lbs (2 kg) combination of boneless pork meat, pork bones or beef bones
One 4-in (10-cm) piece of fresh ginger, cut into coins (see Jaden's Ginger Tips, page 33)
8 cloves garlic, smashed
8 green onions (scallions), cut into thirds (roots discarded)
One small handful (about $^1/_2$ oz/15 g) fresh cilantro (coriander) stems or leaves

1 Bring a large stockpot filled with water to a boil. Once it reaches a boil, add the meat and the bones. Keep the heat on high and boil the meat and bones for 3 minutes. Pour out the water (you'll notice a lot of scum and yuck!) and rinse the bones. Add the rest of the ingredients as well as enough water to cover the meat and bones by 4 inches (10 cm).

TIP: To transform these stocks into a soup or broth, season with salt or fish sauce. I prefer fish sauce, and just a few dashes will do.

2 Bring to a boil and immediately turn the heat to low and simmer for $1^1/_2$ to 3 hours, skimming the surface periodically. The surface of the stock should be barely bubbling. Alternatively, you can put all ingredients into a slow cooker or pressure cooker (follow instructions provided with your appliance for making stock).
3 Strain the stock and discard the solids.

CUTTING BELL PEPPERS
1 Bell peppers can be difficult to cut with all its bumps, ridges and curves. Here's a great way to get even thin slices perfect for stir-fries or Vietnamese Summer Rolls (page 44).

2 Slice off the top and the bumpy bottom of the bell pepper
3 Lay the bell pepper flat on its side and cut into the pepper. Move the knife along the inside of the pepper as shown, "unrolling" the bell pepper.

4 When you get to the end, remove and discard the middle seedy section.
5 Slice thinly into strips. Don't forget the bumpy bottom and the top! You can slice those up or just save them for soups or stock.

JADEN'S GINGER TIPS

During cooking classes, my students always say that they love the taste of fresh ginger, but complain that it's a pain in the butt to peel and chop! Half of the students shamefully admit that they buy the pureed stuff that comes in a jar or tube.

Eeewwww!

Call me a ginger snob, but that jarred pureed stuff is just plain nasty and chemically tasting. There is definitely something suspicious about a food item that sticks to the roof of your mouth. Especially when it's not chocolate, peanut butter or caramel.

So, I'm going to share with you some of my secrets for cooking with fresh, delicious ginger . . .

HOW TO STORE GINGER

* Refrigerate: I use ginger so much that I buy a big massive root once every couple of weeks. The best way to store ginger is to place it in small paper bag in your vegetable crisper drawer.

* Freeze: When I have one of those moments at the store and forget that I already have two pounds of ginger in the refrig . . . and end up with ginger overload, I use the handy microplane grater to grate the entire root. Lay a sheet of plastic wrap on your counter and spoon the ginger on top in a nice even line. Roll up tightly, twist the ends like a long, skinny piece of candy and freeze. When you need, just unwrap, snap off a chunk and it defrosts quickly. Or just re-grate on your microplane grater while frozen. It's a clever idea I learned from food blogger Lunch In a Box!

HOW TO CUT AND USE GINGER

How I want to use the ginger determines how I cut the root.

* Flavor stocks or cooking oil: Sometimes, I don't want a strong ginger flavor in a dish, but I want my oil to be fragranced and flavored by the ginger. When using ginger to flavor oil, wash well, but don't bother peeling. When using it to flavor stock, peel the ginger with a vegetable peeler or scrape the skin with a teaspoon. Then cut the ginger into $1/4$-in (6-mm) or thinner slice coins. If your ginger is pretty evenly shaped, then the slices will look like coins! Take the side of your chef's

knife, lay it on a ginger coin and "whack" it to loosen its fibers and release its essence. You can also use the butt of your knife to gently tap the middle of the coin. Basically, you are looking to bruise the ginger without breaking it. You can now add the coins to your stock.

If you're using the coins to flavor cooking oil, heat up your oil in a wok or pan on high heat. When the oil is hot but not smoking, add the ginger coins (usually about 3 coins) and let the ginger fry for 30 seconds. If I want a little stronger flavor, I turn my heat to medium and let the ginger infuse the oil for a little longer. Don't let the ginger burn! Combine the ginger with smashed garlic and you have a start to a classic Chinese stir-fry. At this point you can remove and discard the ginger.

* In a stir-fry, a sauce or dressing: There's nothing more annoying than getting a fibrous piece of ginger stuck in your teeth. No matter how long you spend at your cutting board mincing this stubborn root, it's never going to be as fine as the method I use. I use a microplane grater to grate fresh ginger. It works wonderfully—the fiber stays on the root and doesn't end up in your dish! You'll end up with fine, silky ginger without any fibers. It's easy and it only takes 15 seconds to grate enough for a dish. You can use this directly in your cooking or squeeze the pulp with your fingers to release and use the ginger juices.

I also have a Japanese ceramic ginger grater but it's a unitasker that takes up space in my drawer. Hate peeling gin-

ger? It's an awkward affair with all those bumps, crevices and curves. Yes, you could use a spoon, but pssst . . . here's a secret . . . I don't always peel it. If you use a microplane grater, most of the peel stays out of the way. Because the ginger is so fine, you'll have to take extra care not to burn it. When using it in a stir-fry, start with a wok at medium-high heat. When oil is hot but not smoking, add the grated ginger and stir-fry for 15 seconds. Turn heat to high and immediately add your stir-fry ingredients. Sometimes, I don't add my ginger and garlic until the middle of the stir-fry process, to ensure that the delicate aromatics do not burn.

* As a condiment: Sometimes I love sprinkling fresh ginger threads on top of my dumplings, steamed chicken, noodle soup or vegetables. I want the fresh, crisp, tingly sensation—but if the ginger piece is too thick, it's just too strong and fibrous. If you are REALLY good with a knife and have the patience of a sloth-watcher, slice the ginger as thin as you can. But I'm not patient, nor really that deft with sharp, pointy objects. I cut off all the little knobs protruding from the main body of the ginger. I just want a nice 3-inch (7.5-cm) smooth piece (save the nubs for soup). Peel the skin with a vegetable peeler. Now continue using the vegetable peeler and peel paper-thin slices of the ginger root. After you've got a pile of slices, line them up and use your chef's knife to cut further into ginger "threads". You'll end up with fairy angel thin slices that you can use fresh, uncooked.

1 Use a spoon to scrape off the thin, brown skin. You can also use a small paring knife.

2 Grate the ginger with a microplane or rasp grater. You'll get beautiful ginger without any fibers!

Appetizers & Little Bites

If I had my choice, my meals everyday would just consist of **little bites** and dessert. The lovely people in Spain and Hong Kong have it right, with their tapas bars and dim sum carts!

Friends who come over for dinner always know to come hungry, as I always have a little somethin' for them to nibble on while I finish preparing our meal. These recipes are soooo delicious that I always have to remind everyone not to eat too much, otherwise they'll ruin their appetite for the rest of the evening!

FAR LEFT TOP TO BOTTOM: Pretty green tops of carrots; making breakfast with the boys; me and my girlfriend Kelly.

Crispy Fish Cakes

These fish cakes are extra special when wrapped in rice paper wrappers and tied with a long piece of chive, inspired by chef Ken Hom. Pan-frying the little bundle makes the wrapper crispy. The rice paper wrappers are the same wrappers used to make Vietnamese Summer Rolls (page 44). The chive tie is optional, but it just looks so cute tied like a package! If you have trouble finding long, thin Chinese chives (which are thicker, stronger and flatter than western chives), use a long piece of green onion (just the green part of the green onion). As always, choose a fish that you enjoy eating. The type of fish is pretty flexible here, since the fish will be pureed along with the herbs and seasonings. Tilapia fillets are inexpensive and work great in this fish cake!

The type and amount of fresh chilli pepper that you use is up to you. If you enjoy spicy heat, choose a small, skinny fresh chilli. If heat is not your thing, but you still enjoy the flavor of fresh pepper, go for the bigger, fatter chilli peppers or even minced red bell pepper.

MAKES 8 FISH CAKES
1 tablespoon cornstarch or flour
$1/4$ cup (65 ml) water
Eight 9-in (23-cm) round dried rice paper wrappers
8 Chinese chives, softened in hot water (optional)
2 to 3 tablespoons high-heat cooking oil
1 recipe Thai Dipping Sauce (page 28), for serving

FOR THE FISH CAKES
$3/4$ lb (350 g) fish, cut into 1-in (2.5-cm) chunks
2 tablespoons finely minced fresh cilantro (coriander)
$1/4$ cup (25 g) panko bread crumbs (substitute with regular bread crumbs)
2 teaspoons freshly squeezed lime juice
2 teaspoons fish sauce (substitute with 1 tablespoon soy sauce)
2 cloves garlic, finely minced
1 teaspoon grated fresh ginger (see Jaden's Ginger Tips, page 33)
$1/2$ teaspoon minced fresh chilli pepper
$1/2$ teaspoon salt
1 teaspoon ground coriander
$1/4$ teaspoon sugar

1 In the bowl of a food processor, add the Fish Cakes ingredients. Pulse until the mixture becomes a coarse paste. Divide the paste into 8 equal portions.
2 Combine the cornstarch (or flour) and water in a small bowl and mix well to make a slurry.
3 Fill a large, shallow dish with warm water. Dip one rice paper into the water for 6 seconds and let the water drip off. Transfer onto a clean, dry surface. The wrapper will still be a little stiff; don't worry, as it will soften up.
4 Using your hands, form one fish paste portion into a flat, square patty, about 3 x 3 inches (7.5 x 7.5 cm), and place in the middle of the dampened rice paper. Fold the top of the rice paper down over the patty, and fold the bottom of the rice paper up and over the patty. Dip a pastry brush (or use your finger) into the slurry and paint the remaining left and right sides of the rice paper. This will help secure the wrapper on the fish cake. Fold over the right and then the left side, making sure there are no air bubbles. Tie the fish cake with a chive, if using, and place on a clean, dry plate lined with plastic wrap. Cover with another sheet of plastic wrap to prevent drying. Use a towel to wipe your work surface before laying down another rice paper wrapper. Repeat with the remaining fish cakes.
5 In a large, nonstick frying pan over medium-high heat, add the oil. When the oil is hot, add 4 of the fish cakes, making sure that they do not touch each other, otherwise they'll stick together. Fry for 3 minutes on each side. Fry the remaining batch. Serve with the Thai Dipping Sauce.

Thai-style Chicken Flatbread

I make my own pizza dough from time to time, but when I want to make an impressive appetizer last minute, I buy a ball of premade pizza dough or, even easier, a package of naan or flatbread from the supermarket. This chicken flatbread is inspired by one of my husband's favorite restaurants, California Pizza Kitchen. When we were still dating in San Francisco, we'd just hop on the subway and walk to the CPK near Union Square. Those were fun times as many sweet nothings were whispered in my ear over a shared pizza. These days, with two loud, yappin' giggly boys at the dinner table, there's no more whispering! (Okay, replaced by footsies!)

SERVES 4 AS APPETIZER OR SNACK
1/2 lb (250 g) boneless, skinless chicken, cut into bite-size pieces
2 teaspoons soy sauce
1 teaspoon honey
1/2 teaspoon cornstarch
2 tablespoons olive oil
2 medium flatbreads or naan
1/2 cup (125 ml) Peanut Dipping Sauce (page 30)
8 oz (250 g) fresh shredded mozzarella
1 1/4 cups (125 g) fresh bean sprouts
Few sprigs fresh cilantro (coriander)
1/2 cup (80 g) roasted peanuts

1 Preheat the oven to 375°F (190°C).
2 Combine the chicken with the soy sauce, honey and cornstarch and let marinate at room temperature for 10 minutes.
3 Heat a nonstick frying pan over high heat. When hot, add the chicken pieces and sauté for 2 to 3 minutes, until cooked through.
4 Brush the olive oil all over the edges of the flatbreads or naan. Spread the Peanut Dipping Sauce on each flatbread. Top with the mozzarella and cooked chicken. Bake for 5 to 8 minutes, until the cheese is melted and the edges are golden brown. Remove from the oven, top with the bean sprouts, fresh cilantro and roasted peanuts.

More Options
■ Instead of the Peanut Dipping Sauce, you can use the Cashew Nut Dipping Sauce (page 30).

Raw Bar with Asian Mignonette

I'm what you call a "food adventurist". If it's stinky, weird or wiggling, I'll want to eat it. If you've watched Anthony Bourdain or Andrew Zimmern on location in Asia, I'm sure you know what that means. For many others, raw oysters and clams are considered pretty adventurous eats for the home kitchen. Normally, I only eat raw oysters and clams at raw bars, leaving the difficult work of prying open the rock-hard shells to trained professionals who are more patient and deft than I. But recently, at the freshest seafood counter in town, my inner daredevil kicked in and my need to conquer the shell. Plus, it didn't help that my four-year-old son Nathan was in the shopping cart and asked, "Mommy, how come we can't buy oysters?" Yeah, and what was I going to say, "cuz Mommy can't open them?" I'm Nathan's superhero! How could Super-Mom be defeated by a 3-inch (7.5-cm) tight-lipped marine mollusk?

Nathan picked out each oyster and chose not the cute, itty, bitty Littleneck clams, but the mammoth 4-inch (10-cm) Cherrystone clams. Words cannot describe the debacle that I went through to open a dozen of each. That pointy, thick knife with the big wooden handle called an oyster knife? Useless on the clams. I headed to the garage to find my husband's tools. A hammer, chisel and the vice grip in the garage didn't even crack the things. Power drill, level and the wire cutter, nada. Even the Jedi force was no match for these guys. I finally admitted defeat and recruited my husband (after I tiptoed back from the garage and laid his tools back EXACTLY where they were). Of course, sensible Husband knew that the smartest thing to do was search "how to shuck oysters and clams" online . . . 10 minutes later, he had all twenty-three open. Did you notice that there is one lone clam that is unopened in the photo? The stubborn sucker wouldn't budge. Once they were all opened, I just stared at 'em and they stared right back, thirsty for some kind of light, Asian-flavored sauce. I'm not a fan of the traditional jarred horseradish and cocktail sauce, mainly because those strong flavors mask the delicate taste of the seafood. So I called Jim, the owner of the Lucky Pelican in Sarasota, Florida, and begged him for the recipe for his killer Asian Mignonette. Many thanks to him. If you don't have seasoned, or sweetened, rice vinegar, use the unseasoned rice vinegar and add a pinch of sugar.

SERVES 4 AS APPETIZER
1 dozen fresh oysters in shell
1 dozen fresh clams in shell

ASIAN MIGNONETTE
1 teaspoon water
2 tablespoons sweetened (seasoned) rice vinegar
1/4 teaspoon red or green peppercorns
1 teaspoon finely minced ginger
1 teaspoon finely minced shallots
1/4 teaspoon whole coriander seeds (optional)

In a small bowl, whisk together the Asian Mignonette ingredients. Shuck the oysters and clams. Serve the Asian Mignonette, oysters and clams on a bed of crushed ice.

HOW TO SHUCK OYSTERS AND CLAMS

Do you really think that I'm going to attempt to teach you how to open those things? Well, instead of pretending like I'm a mollusk-shucking expert, I asked Executive Chef Rich Vallante from Legal Seafoods (www.legalseafoods.com) for some tips. If you happen to make an "oopsy" and mangle the meat a bit, no worries, just flip the oyster or clam over for presentation. Chef Vallante has an online video showing both methods on Legal Seafoods' website at www.legalseafoods.com. Here we go. First off, there's a difference between an oyster knife and a clam knife, and of course, different techniques!

SHUCKING OYSTERS

The oyster knife should have a solid blade, pointed end and a good, solid handle. You'll also need a kitchen towel, as that oyster blade tip is pretty sharp!
1 Place the oyster on a stable surface, flat side up/curved "cup" side down. This is how the oysters grow, and the cup will hold the juices in the shell. The top of the oyster is also shaped like an elongated "D". The curve of the "D" is the front of the oyster.
2 Look for the natural hinge on the back of the oyster. This is a muscle and this is the spot where you'll start working. With a towel to protect your hand, hold the oyster steady with one hand. With your other hand, shimmy the oyster knife into the hinge as if you were opening a paint can. Pop the top off like a paint can. But don't push the knife too far in, or you'll damage the meat.
3 There's a muscle in the top front of the oyster, so run your knife at a 45-degree angle along the top of the shell, avoiding the meat. Once you sever that muscle, the top of the oyster shell should come off.
4 Run your knife along the bottom of the oyster to cut the muscle that is on the bottom. Be careful and try to keep all the juice in the shell!

SHUCKING CLAMS

The clam knife is flexible, thinner than an oyster knife and has a rounded tip.
1 If you look at the clam's mouth, you'll find on one side that there's a small section where it's just slightly more open. It may be hard to spot, but usually it's on the side.
2 Cradle the clam in one palm, and use your other hand to position the SIDE of the clam knife right on that spot. Slide the side of the knife into the clam, just until you can feel that you're in, but no further. You don't want to damage the clam or cut it in half!
3 Keep pushing your blade in, angling towards the top. You'll be scraping the top of the shell, severing the 2 muscles on top. This is why a flexible knife is needed!
4 Pry open the shell and run your knife along the bottom of the clam—there are two more muscles below.

SHELLFISH TIPS FROM JOHN THE SEAFOOD GUY
The seafood guru at my local market tells me that the best way to determine whether an oyster or clam is fresh, alive and well is to knock them. Specifically, knock two against each other or one against the counter. If they sound hollow, throw them away. Also, oysters and clams should be closed super-tight (um, YEAH, I know). When you get home, grab two different-sized bowls, one that fits inside the other. Place the oysters and clams in the smaller bowl. Fill the larger bowl with ice and put the smaller bowl inside, on top of the ice, and refrigerate. According to John, if stored properly (cold and dry), they'll last for a few days like that. But I always go by the rule of eating them the same day or next day.

Great Grandmother's Crispy Potatoes with Sweet Soy Pork

I recently found out that my great-grandmother was Indonesian. I've never met her, and my Mom only has a handful of memories of her, one of them being a dish similar to this recipe. Of course, I've tweaked the recipe . . . how could I not? It's just in my nature to mess with things and make it my own, even when it is already perfection. Traditionally, this dish is saucier and the crispy potato chips are stirred right into the meat sauce, but I've lightened it up and cut back the sauce to keep the potatoes crispy. You can use store-bought potato chips (thick kettle chips work great) or make your own potato chips like my Great Grandmother did, I'm sure. But, I guess the downside of perpetual tweaking is that traditional family recipes will evolve so much that it's hardly recognizable at all. Who knows what kind of tinkering' my own kids will do to this recipe when they grow up? Oh Buddha help me if my kids will interpret this recipe as a lump of cold canned chilli dumped on greasy potato chips. If you don't like the crunch and bite of fresh green onions, just fry them along with the garlic and shallots. Sometimes I also like to add some fresh chillies to spice it up.

NOTE: Kecap manis is the seasoning used in this dish, which is an Indonesian thick, sweet soy sauce. The sweet-salty sauce is sweetened with palm sugar and flavored with star anise and garlic. You can find it at most Asian markets next to the regular soy sauce under the popular ABC brand. If you don't have access to kecap manis, substitute with dark soy sauce and sugar. Another great substitute is the Sweet Soy Sauce (page 30).

SERVES 4 AS APPETIZER OR SNACK

1 lb (500 g) ground pork
2 teaspoons soy sauce
1 teaspoon Chinese rice wine
2 teaspoons cornstarch
Freshly ground black pepper
1 tablespoon high heat cooking oil
3 shallots, minced
2 tablespoons kecap manis (substitute with 1 tablespoon Chinese dark soy sauce plus 2 teaspoons brown sugar)
2 teaspoons white vinegar or rice vinegar
1/4 cup (65 ml) water
6 oz (175 g) crispy, plain flavored potato chips (I prefer thick kettle cooked)
1/4 cup (15 g) chopped green onion (scallion)

1 In a bowl, mix together the ground pork with the soy sauce, wine, cornstarch and black pepper. Marinate for 10 minutes at room temperature.
2 Heat a wok or frying pan over high heat. When the wok is hot, add the oil and swirl to coat. Add the shallots and fry until fragrant about 30 seconds. Add the ground pork and cook until no longer pink, about 3 to 5 minutes.
3 Add the kecap manis, vinegar and water and cook for 1 to 2 minutes to let the entire thing bubble away and thicken. Taste and season with additional kecap manis or soy sauce if you are using unsalted potato chips.
4 Place the potato chips on a large plate and dish the ground pork mixture all over the chips. Top with chopped green onions.

Shrimp Chips with Spiced Beef and Crispy Shallots

When I was little, Mom used to fry up a big batch of these shrimp chips to snack on, usually when company came over or for special holidays. They are as light as air and the crunch that you can get is so loud! My brother and I would hide under the massive oak dining table and hoard a stash of shrimp chips and eat them. But of course we chomped so loud that it wasn't long before mom found us and scolded us for eating too much fried stuff.

Recently, we were having friends Shawn and Wendy over for dinner, and since Shawn is a big meat-lovin' guy, I topped the shrimp chips up with savory beef spiced with warming cinnamon and coriander. Shawn will tell you they were fantastic. As I recall, he ate almost the entire batch by himself. The crispy fried shallots add a nice flavor and crunch but the chips are still great without them if you don't have any. You can either buy them in a plastic tub or glass jar at an Asian market or make your own.

If you don't want to top the shrimp chips, they're also great served alone and dipped into Peanut Dipping Sauce or Cashew Nut Dipping Sauce (page 30) just like my Mom serves them!

SERVES 6 TO 8 AS AN APPETIZER OR SNACK
4 oz (125 g) uncooked Shrimp Chips or "Prawn Crackers"
High-heat cooking oil for frying
2 cloves garlic, finely minced
2 green onions (scallions), minced
1 lb (500 g) ground beef
$\frac{1}{2}$ teaspoon ground cinnamon
$\frac{1}{2}$ teaspoon ground coriander
$\frac{1}{4}$ teaspoon Asian chilli powder or ground red pepper (cayenne) (optional)
1 tablespoon soy sauce
2 teaspoons fresh lime juice
$\frac{1}{4}$ teaspoon sugar
$\frac{1}{2}$ cup (85 g) diced red bell pepper
$\frac{1}{4}$ cup (25 g) store-bought or homemade crispy fried shallots (optional) (see Note)
Sriracha chilli sauce, for the table (optional)

1 In a wok or pot, add 1 to 2 inches (2.5 to 5 cm) of oil and turn the heat to high. When the oil reaches 375°F (190°C), add 4 to 5 shrimp chips at a time. They should puff up and fry up in just a few seconds. If the chips do not puff up immediately, your oil is not hot enough. If they begin to burn after a few seconds, your oil may be too hot. Remove once the chip has puffed up and drain on a baking rack. Be careful as you add the chips in— the oil is hot! Try sliding them in at the side of the wok or lowering them in with a big spoon or spider.

2 Set a wok or large frying pan over medium-high heat. When a bead of water sizzles and evaporates upon contact, add 1 tablespoon of the oil and swirl to coat. Add the garlic and green onions and fry until fragrant, about 15 to 30 seconds.

3 Add the ground beef, cinnamon, coriander and chilli powder, and fry until cooked through, about 2 to 3 minutes. Add the soy sauce, lime juice and sugar, stir well and continue to cook for an additional minute.

4 Spoon about 1 tablespoon of the cinnamon beef onto each shrimp chip "cup", top with the red bell pepper and, if desired, the crispy-fried shallots and Sriracha chilli sauce.

> **NOTE:** To make crispy fried shallots, slice 5-8 whole shallots very thinly. Deep-fry the shallots in hot oil (375°F/190°C) until golden brown. Remove immediately to avoid burning (they burn easily!) Store leftovers in an airtight container.

Lettuce Cup Appetizers

This dish is an experience in textures and sensations…the cool, crisp lettuce cups cradles the warm filling. As you take a bite, you'll first taste the bright, sweet, juicy mandarin orange, then the savory chicken and then the crunch of water chestnuts and the mild bite of red onion.

The best part of this recipe is that the ingredients are so flexible. You can keep it light and use ground chicken or turkey, or try it with ground pork or ground beef—it's totally up to you. My kids love this when I substitute diced green apples for the red onion. Try to dice the vegetables into roughly the same size so that they cook evenly and are easier to eat.

To make this dish a full meal, include 1 cup (160 g) of cooked jasmine rice per person. My kids like to spoon the cooked rice along with the filling into their lettuce cups.

SERVES 4 TO 6 AS APPETIZER OR SNACK
$3/4$ lb (350 g) ground chicken, turkey, beef or pork
2 teaspoons soy sauce
1 teaspoon Chinese rice wine (or dry sherry)
1 teaspoon cornstarch
2 teaspoons high-heat cooking oil
1 to 2 cloves garlic, finely minced
1 teaspoon grated fresh ginger, (see Jaden's Ginger Tips, page 33)
$1/3$ cup (150 g) chopped red onion
4 to 6 fresh shitake mushrooms, diced
4 peeled water chestnuts (fresh or canned), diced
2 teaspoons rice vinegar
$1^1/_2$ tablespoons oyster sauce
16 cup-shaped lettuce leaves (Boston Bibb, Butter head, Iceberg or any lettuce with cup shaped leaves)
One 11-oz (312-g) can mandarin orange sections, drained

1 In a bowl, marinate the ground poultry or meat with the soy sauce, wine and cornstarch for 10 minutes at room temperature.
2 Heat a wok or large frying pan over high heat and when hot, add the oil. Swirl to coat and add the garlic, ginger and red onion. Fry for 15 to 30 seconds until fragrant. Add the ground meat. Cook until lightly browned, about 2 minutes. Stir in the fresh shitake mushrooms, water chestnuts, rice vinegar and oyster sauce. Simmer for an additional 1 to 2 minutes until the meat is cooked through.
3 You can assemble the lettuce cups by spooning a heaping tablespoonful of filling into each lettuce cup and topping with the mandarin orange slices or you can serve the ingredients separately for your dinner guests to assemble themselves.

More options
Remember how I said this recipe is flexible? Raid your fridge. Finely diced green bell pepper, celery, frozen peas/carrots work great in the stir-fry. Even top the lettuce cups with chilled, shredded carrots!
■ For a fun crunch, take a skein of mung bean noodles (also called cellophane noodles or vermicelli—see page 22) and break it apart with your hands. Heat about $1^1/_2$ inches (3.75 cm) of high-heat cooking oil in a small pot or wok. When the oil reaches 350°F (175°C), slide a few noodles in and watch them puff up. It should take less than 5 seconds. Drain on a rack. The light, airy, crunchy bits of noodles make a wonderful topping for these lettuce cups.
■ For a bit of salty sweetness, you can also dip the back of a teaspoon into a jar of hoisin sauce. Smear the hoisin sauce onto the lettuce cup before adding the filling.

Baked Garlic Chilli Wings

You could not find more opposite personalities than mine and my husband's, especially when it comes to food. He'll long for a deep-fried hotdog with crisp french fries and I'll crave something silly like braised tofu. The difficult part about being polar opposites is the choice of restaurant—casual sports bar or the Vietnamese hole-in-the-wall restaurant?

But when the situation involves chicken wings, we're smooth sailing. He's a drumette guy, I'm flat and flapper gal and we never have to fight at the table.

These wings are baked after a quick marinate. To intensify the flavor, I like to stir-fry a combination of garlic, lemongrass and chillies then toss the baked wings in to coat. If you don't have time to marinate the chicken, bake the wings naked. In your wok or frying pan, stir-fry the garlic, minced chilli and lemongrass until fragrant and add the marinade ingredients (minus the garlic). Let cook for 30 seconds to thicken and toss in the baked chicken wings.

SERVES 4 TO 6 AS AN APPETIZER OR SNACK

2 lbs (1 kg) chicken wings
1 tablespoon high-heat cooking oil
1 fresh chilli pepper of your choice, minced
2 cloves garlic, finely minced
1 stalk lemongrass, bottom 6-in (15-cm) thinly sliced, or
    2 shallots, thinly sliced

FOR THE MARINADE

2 cloves garlic, finely minced
$\frac{1}{2}$ teaspoon five spice powder
2 tablespoons brown sugar
2 tablespoons hoisin sauce
2 tablespoons soy sauce

1 In a large sealable plastic bag, mix together the Marinade ingredients. Add the chicken wings to the bag and seal, squeezing out all of the air. Massage the wings so that the Marinade coats them evenly. Let the wings sit in the Marinade for 15 minutes to overnight.

2 Preheat the oven to 375°F (190°C).

3 Arrange the wings in one layer on a sheet pan. Bake the wings for 20 minutes or until cooked through. Set a wok or large sauté pan over high heat. When a drop of water sizzles and evaporates upon contact, add the oil and swirl to coat. Add the chilli pepper, garlic and lemongrass. Fry until fragrant, about 30 seconds. Take care not to burn the aromatics! Add the baked chicken wings and toss until well coated with the seasonings.

More Options

My favorite shortcut for this recipe is to combine a package of Chinese roast duck seasoning powder (it comes in a small envelope) with 1 tablespoon of water and use that to marinate the wings. I like the NOH brand of seasoning.

■ Keep your kitchen clean and grill outdoors instead of bake. Grill the wings over direct, high heat, 5 minutes on each side. Then move to indirect heat, cover and grill for 10 minutes to finish cooking. Bring your large sauté pan outside too, and when the wings are done, clean a section of the grates and place your pan directly on the grates, turn your flame to high and sauté the aromatics. Toss with the cooked wings.

■ You can make the flavors Chinese by replacing the chilli and lemongrass with $\frac{1}{4}$ cup (15 g) chopped green onions and 1 teaspoon grated fresh ginger.

Vietnamese Summer Rolls

I used to be really uptight about making super perfect summer rolls. If it didn't look just so, I'd tear the wrapper, carefully save the filling and start all over again. Then, I had children and priorities changed. If I don't get food out to the table fast enough, the tots strut over to the pantry, shimmy their way up to the fourth shelf and help themselves to a smorgasbord of junk food. So, I learned to roll faster and didn't give a toad's tongue about neat rolls. The big eureka moment smacked me in the head when visiting friends Diane and Todd in California. Diane taught me after dipping the rice paper in water to fold it in half like a semi-circle before piling on the filling. This makes the wrapper more sturdy and easier to roll. The vegetables and meat spill out over the edge, making the summer rolls even more appealing and beautiful. Vietnamese Summer Rolls are wonderful as a complete meal on its own and is especially fun if you lay all the ingredients out on your dinner table so that each person can roll their own. Have a pan of warm water on the table too, for dipping. Make sure each person has a large, clean plate for rolling. I like to serve these rolls with two dipping sauces—a Cashew Nut Dipping Sauce from my friend Jeni and a traditional Vietnamese Dip (Nuoc Cham) made with fish sauce.

SERVES 6 AS AN APPETIZER, SNACK OR PART OF MULTICOURSE MEAL

One 12-oz (340-g) package rice paper wrappers
1 head soft, leafy green lettuce, leaves separated
1 cucumber, cut into matchsticks
2 carrots, cut into matchsticks
1 bell pepper, cut into matchsticks
1 big handful fresh mint
1 big handful fresh Thai basil or sweet Italian basil leaves
1 portion Cashew Nut Dipping Sauce (page 30), Peanut Dipping Sauce (page 30) or Vietnamese Dip (page 28)

LEMONGRASS PORK
1 lb (500 g) pork
1 lemongrass stalk, outer leaves peeled until you reach pale yellow leaves, bottom 3-in (7.5-cm) of stalk grated with rasp grater, or 1 teaspoon lime zest
2 cloves garlic, finely minced
2 teaspoons soy sauce
2 teaspoons fish sauce
1 teaspoon sugar

1 To prepare the Lemongrass Pork, slice the pork as thin as you possibly can. To make it easier to slice, place the pork in the freezer for 15 minutes to firm up. Or you can bribe your meat peeps at the butcher counter to slice it for you on their big, fancy machines.
2 In a bowl, combine the slice pork with the rest of the ingredients and marinate for 15 minutes at room temperature or overnight in the refrigerator.
3 In the meantime, prepare the vegetables and herbs for the rolls.
4 Heat a wok or frying pan until very hot. Add the marinated pork slices in a single layer. You may have to do this in a couple of batches. Fry for 1 to 2 minutes on each side, depending on how thin you've sliced your meat.
5 Have the cooked Lemongrass Pork, rice paper wrappers, vegetables and herbs ready on your work surface to roll, or arrange the ingredients on your dinner table and have everyone roll their own summer rolls. To assemble the summer rolls, follow the illustrated instructions on facing page. Serve with one or more of the dipping sauces.

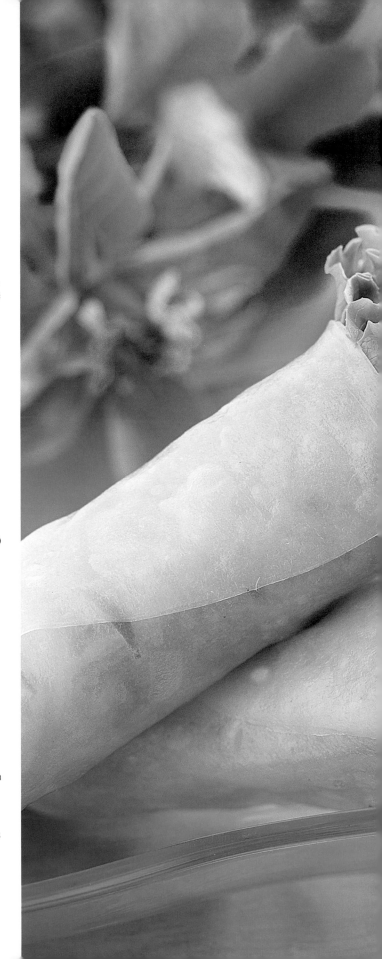

HOW TO ASSEMBLE SUMMER ROLLS

1 Fill a pie tin, a large shallow bowl or a deep plate with warm (not hot!) water. Dip the edge of a rice paper in the water and quickly use both hands to turn the rice paper so that each side can dip in the water for 2 seconds.

2 Lay the still-stiff rice paper on a clean, dry surface. Fold the rice paper in half. The paper should be pliable and may still be a bit stiff. If the rice paper is floppy, soggy and too slippery, try using cooler water or dipping the paper in the water for a shorter amount of time.

3 On the bottom half, lay your lettuce first to create a bed for the vegetables and juicy meat. Layer on your vegetables, meat and herbs. Do not overstuff! Each roll should only have 1 to 2 pieces of meat. If you are too greedy and put too much filling in the roll, they will be difficult to roll up!

4 Starting from the bottom, roll up. Tuck the ingredients in as you get that first turn to create a tighter roll. Don't suffocate the poor ingredients, but do make it nice and snug.

5 Continue rolling and you can make a slight tug back on the roll to make tighter. If your work surface is dry, tugging will be easy. Wipe your work surface dry before rolling your next roll.

NOTE: One of the biggest mistakes is soaking the rice paper in water that's too hot or soaking for too long. The rice paper should be dipped in the water for a few seconds, not soaked. The water should be warm, not hot. In fact, the rice paper should still be a bit stiff after dipping. By the time you've piled on your ingredients, the paper is just right for rolling.

Pork and Mango Potstickers

In college, my girlfriends and I would get together and have potsticker, or dumpling, parties. We'd set the filling ingredients in the middle of the table and we'd sit and fold dumplings. Hundreds of 'em! We would devour a big batch that evening and then divvy up and freeze the rest for a rainy or lazy day.

You'll want to buy the round dumpling wrappers, also called "potsticker" or "gyoza" wrappers. Square wonton wrappers are too thin to use for fried potstickers (though the same filling ingredients in this recipe make fabulous wontons (see page 61 on how to fold wontons).

Once you have the right type of wrapper, and all the ingredients at hand, making homemade dumplings take just four steps—chop, combine, wrap and cook!

SERVES 6 AS AN APPETIZER, SNACK OR PART OF
   A MULTICOURSE MEAL
$1/4$ head of medium cabbage
2 teaspoons salt
2 green onions (scallions)
$1/2$ lb (250 g) ground pork (or ground turkey)
$1^{1}/2$ tablespoons soy sauce
2 teaspoons rice wine (or dry sherry)
2 teaspoons rice vinegar
1 teaspoon sesame oil
$1/2$ mango, chopped
1 tablespoon cornstarch
Cornstarch paste: 2 tablespoons cornstarch plus $1/2$ cup
   (125 ml) water
1 package of round dumpling wrappers, defrosted and covered
   with a damp towel
High-heat cooking oil
$1/2$ cup (125 ml) Chinese Dipping Sauce (page 29)

1 To prepare the vegetables, finely shred the cabbage in your food processor. Place in a bowl and add the salt. Mix and let sit for 10 minutes. After 10 minutes, squeeze the water out of the cabbage. (You can just use your hands—take a fistful of cabbage and squeeze over the sink or put cabbage in cheesecloth and squeeze). Use a food processor to shred the green onions. You do not have to salt and squeeze the green onions, as they don't have much water content.
2 To make the filling, combine the ground pork, cabbage and green onions in a big bowl. Add the soy sauce, wine, rice vinegar, sesame oil, and stir to combine. Add the chopped mangoes. Stir in the 1 tablespoon of cornstarch to help the mixture hold together.
3 To wrap the potstickers, combine the ingredients for the cornstarch paste in a small bowl, stirring until the cornstarch is dissolved. You will use the paste to seal the dumplings. Take 1 dumpling wrapper, and spoon 1 heaping teaspoon of the filling mixture in the middle. Dip your finger in the cornstarch paste and go around the edges of the dumpling wrapper. Fold

TIPS FOR FREEZING: If you are freezing potstickers, do so BEFORE you cook them. Just lay the uncooked dumplings out and freeze them in a single layer (like on a baking sheet or plate). Once frozen, gather them up and bag them for storing in the freezer. If you don't freeze them in a single layer first, they'll all stick together and you'll have a massive lump of potsticker. To cook, add them to the pan while the potsticker is still frozen (do not defrost). Just add an extra minute and half of steaming time. They'll turn out perfect.

HOW TO SHAPE THE DUMPLINGS

To get a traditional crescent shaped potsticker, you'll fold, pleat and pinch only on one side of the wrapper. The reason the potstickers are folded this way is because the shape makes a flat bottom. The bottoms crisp up in the frying pan.

1 Spoon 1 heaping teaspoon of the filling onto a dumpling wrapper. Don't be tempted to overfill! Dip your finger into the cornstarch paste and "paint" all around the edges of the dumpling skin.

2 In the middle, pinch the top and bottom together, tightly.

3 Starting just left of the middle, use your left hand to bring the TOP portion of wrapper to pleat TOWARDS the middle. Pinch to secure that pleat. Move down just a bit, and do the pleating again. Repeat once more. You will have 3 pleats on each side, all pleats pointing towards the middle.

4 Now, it's time to do the right side. Do the same using only the top portion of wrapper. Pleat TOWARDS the middle, or to the left. Repeat 2 more times.

5 Finish by pinching the pleat all around one more time with your thumb and lower portion of your finger. Remember, any unsealed section will cause the potsticker to leak filling!

6 Ta-da!

THE SHORT-CUT METHOD

If the pleating sounds too difficult, you can just pinch the dumpling tight all around. This method won't produce a natural flat bottom, and won't be as stable as the crescent-shaped pleating method, but it is easier. You can also fry the dumplings on their sides for even greater crispy-crunch! After following step 1, you'll want to just pinch the rest of the dumpling closed. Use your thumb and the lower part of your index finger to squeeze tightly. Set the dumpling on the cutting board so that it stands on the surface and try to shape into a flat bottom. Make sure the dumpling is sealed.

the bottom part of wrapper up to meet the top. Crimp the edge and pinch tightly to seal. Shape dumplings further by placing them on a table or counter so they lay flat on the bottom. Crimped edges should be sticking up and on top. Keep wrapped dumplings covered with a slightly damp towel or plastic wrap.

4 To cook the potstickers, pour about 2 tablespoons of oil into a nonstick frying pan over medium heat. When hot but not smoking, carefully place the dumplings in frying pan, flat side down, not touching each other. Do not crowd too much or they will not brown. Fry the dumplings in batches for 2 to 3 minutes, until the bottoms are nicely browned. Add $1/4$ cup (65 ml) of water and immediately cover to start the steaming process. Steam for 3 to 4 minutes. Remove the lid and let the rest of the water boil off and re-crisp the bottoms, about 1 minute. Cut open one of the dumplings and make sure the inside meat is cooked. Before starting your next batch, wipe the frying pan clean before adding more cooking oil. Adjust amount of water and steam time for the next batch as needed.

5 Serve with the Chinese Dipping Sauce on the side.

Firecracker Shrimp

One of the very first food blogs I ever visited was Rice and Noodles, written by a very gorgeous Mae Gabriel who lives on Jersey Island just off the coast of France. (How exotic does that sound!?) It was Mae's breathtaking images that really inspired me to take food photography seriously. I always made sure that I visited Mae's blog AFTER I ate lunch, because whatever she cooked looked so scrumptious that I probably would have jumped on the next flight and showed up for lunch at her house. This is a recipe from Mae and it's become a regular at my dinner parties. But they rarely make it to the table, because guests stand in the kitchen, snagging the Firecracker Shrimp as they cool on the rack. The sweet chilli sauce used in this recipe is all sweet and no spicy. It's thick, glossy and makes the perfect marinade and dip for Firecracker Shrimp.

SERVES 4 TO 6 AS APPETIZER
1 tablespoon cornstarch or flour
$^1/_4$ cup (65 ml) water
24 medium tail-on shrimp, shelled (leave tail on) and deveined
$^1/_2$ teaspoon salt
Freshly ground black pepper
1 cup (250 ml) sweet chilli sauce, divided
12 eggroll or fresh spring roll wrappers, cut in half diagonally and covered with plastic wrap or a damp cloth
High-heat cooking oil for frying

1 In a small bowl, mix the cornstarch with the water to make a slurry.
2 Lay the shrimp flat on a cutting board and using a sharp paring knife, cut a few nicks on the inside curve of the shrimp. Be careful not to cut through the shrimp. Pat the shrimp very dry.
3 Season the shrimp with the salt and pepper. Pour $^1/_4$ cup (65 ml) of the sweet chilli sauce on a small plate. Hold the shrimp by its tail and dip both sides of the shrimp in the sweet chilli sauce. Avoid getting the tails wet (if the tail of the shrimp is wet with marinade, it will splatter in the hot oil). Let the shrimp marinate for 10 minutes at room temperature.
4 Use paper towels to pat the shrimp slightly, to soak up the extra marinade. Some of the sticky sweet chilli sauce should still be on the shrimp.
5 Roll the shrimp in the halved wrappers, following the instructions below.
6 In a wok, deep fryer or large sauté pan, add 1$^1/_2$ inches (3.75 cm) of oil and heat it to 375°F (190°C). Add the firecracker shrimp a few at a time to the oil and fry until golden brown on each side, about 3 minutes. Drain on a baking rack and serve with a side of sweet chilli sauce for dipping.

More Options
■ Dip in Sriracha chilli sauce, Sweet Chilli Sambal (page 26), Apricot Sweet Chilli Sauce (page 28) or Ginger Scallion (page 28).
■ Add a thin slice of mango with the shrimp with wrapping to make Firecracker Mango Shrimp.

ROLLING THE SHRIMP WRAPPER
1 Lay an eggroll or spring roll wrapper on a dry, clean surface as shown. Lay a shrimp with the tail sticking out.
2 Bring the left corner of the wrapper over the shrimp and begin rolling left to right. Make sure that you are rolling tightly. As you roll, bring the top corner of the wrapper down and over the shrimp. Again, make sure you leave no open pockets of air. Big air pockets and holes will allow oil to seep in.
3 Continue rolling towards the right. Dip your finger or a pasty brush into the cornstarch slurry and paint the final corner. Roll to seal. Lay the roll seam side down on a dry plate or tray. Repeat with the rest of the shrimp and wrappers. Keep all uncooked Firecracker Shrimp covered with plastic wrap or barely damp towel.

Mom's Famous Crispy Eggrolls

This is one of those recipes that is a little more time consuming to make, but I'm including this in the book because: 1) it's my Mom's recipe, 2) everyone who has tried them instantly declare they are the best they've ever had, and 3) you can make a big batch of them and freeze them. 4) You can fry a batch up in just 15 minutes, even when frozen! I usually call a couple of my girlfriends over and we have an eggrollin' party where we'll make a massive batch of them, enjoy them fresh that night and have enough for all to take home and freeze. If you are making these with friends, I'd suggest doubling the recipe so each person has some to take home to freeze. I promise you they will taste just as good fried after frozen and you will never taste better eggrolls than these. BUT. . . you must follow my Mama's rules (see facing page).

MAKES 50 EGGROLLS
50 Spring/Eggroll Wrappers (about 2
    packages), defrosted unopened at
    room temperature for 45 minutes or in
    the refrigerator overnight
1 tablespoon cornstarch (or flour) mixed
    with $^1/_4$ cup (65 ml) of cool water
High-heat cooking oil, for frying

GROUND PORK
1 lb (500 g) ground pork
1 tablespoon soy sauce
1 teaspoon cornstarch
$^1/_4$ teaspoon sugar
Freshly ground black pepper

VEGETABLES
$^1/_2$ head of cabbage (abt 9 ounces/275 g)
3 small carrots
6 fresh shitake mushrooms (or 25 g dried
    black mushrooms soaked overnight),
    stems discarded
1 tablespoon high-heat cooking oil
2 to 3 cloves garlic, finely minced
1 teaspoon grated fresh ginger (see
    Jaden's Ginger Tips, page 33)
1 tablespoon Chinese rice wine
2 teaspoons soy sauce
$^1/_2$ teaspoon sugar
$^1/_4$ teaspoon salt
1 teaspoon sesame oil
Freshly ground black pepper

1 Combine the ingredients for the Ground Pork in a bowl. Marinate at least 10 minutes.
2 In the meantime, prepare the Vegetables. Shred the cabbage and the carrots using your food processor or by hand. Slice the mushrooms into very thin strips (or you could use your food processer and pulse a few times to get a fine chop).
3 Set a wok or large frying pan over high heat. When hot, add 1 tablespoon of oil and swirl to coat. Add the garlic and ginger and stir fry until fragrant, about 15 seconds. Add the pork and stir-fry until no longer pink, about 2 minutes. Add the cabbage, carrots and the mushrooms and stir-fry for 1 minute, until the vegetables are softened. Add the rice wine, soy sauce, sugar, salt, sesame oil and black pepper. Continue to stir-fry for another minute. Scoop the pork and vegetable mixture onto a sheet pan and spread out to cool. Prop up one end of the baking sheet so that it tilts and will allow all the moisture to drain to one end. Let cool for 15 minutes.
4 Discard all of the accumulated juices. Use paper towels to blot the filling to rid of extra oil or juice. Now, we're ready to wrap!
5 Follow the illustrated instructions on facing page. As you complete the rolls, place them in a neat, single layer and covered with plastic wrap to prevent drying. If you want to stack the eggrolls, make sure you have layer of parchment paper in between the layers to prevent sticking. They can be fried immediately, frozen or refrigerated up to 4 hours until ready to fry.
6 To fry the eggrolls, fill a wok or pot with 2 inches (5 cm) of high-heat cooking oil. Heat the oil to 350°F (175°C) or until a cube of bread will fry to golden brown within 10 seconds. Gently slide in or lower the eggrolls, frying 4 to 6 at a time, turning occasionally until golden brown about $1^1/_2$ minutes. Place on wire rack to drain and cool.

> **NOTE: To fry frozen eggrolls, do not defrost the eggrolls—just add them to the oil frozen, frying 4 to 6 at a time in a wok, large sauté pan or deep fryer. Add an additional $1^1/_2$ minutes to the frying time when cooking from frozen state.**

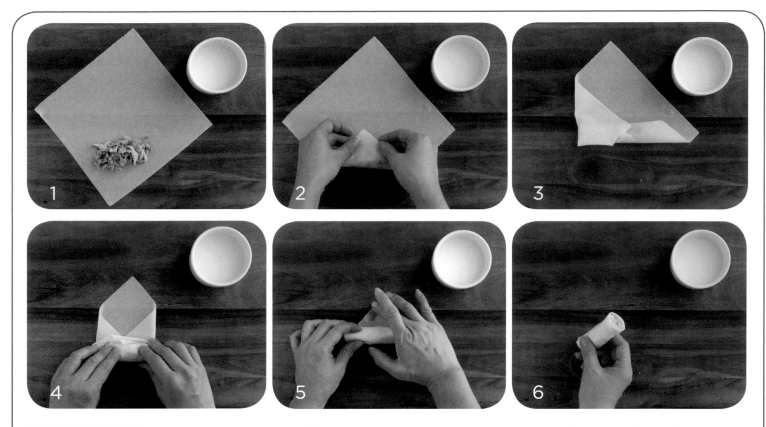

MAKING EGGROLLS

1 Lay the wrapper on a clean, dry surface as shown. Spoon just 1½ tablespoons of filling near the bottom corner. Resist the urge to over stuff with too much filling!

2 Lift the bottom corner up and begin roll-ing until you reach halfway up.

3 Fold over the left side, and then the right side towards the center.

4 Continue folding up with a tuck-roll-tuck-roll motion.

5 Dip your fingers into the cornstarch slurry and brush over the final top corner.

6 Finish up the roll and seal. Lay the eggroll seam side down on a dry plate or baking sheet. See how the roll is tight and there are no holes? Keep the eggrolls . . . covered with plastic wrap or a barely damp towel.

NOTES: MAMA'S RULES

#1: Your filling ingredients must be drained of excess moisture and cooled before rolling. Soggy, hot filling makes soggy eggrolls.

#2: Use the right kind of wrapper. The size I get is 8 x 8 inches (20 x 20 cm) around and come 25 wrappers to a pack-age. These wrappers are light, thin and fry up to a shatteringly crisp crunch. Oh yes, before I forget—"spring roll" and "eggroll" are interchangeable and there's no agreed-upon standard on which term means what dish. I call "spring rolls" the Vietnamese fresh, un-fried rolls (page 44) and "eggrolls" the deep-fried Chi-nese version. Sometimes my regular American grocery store will have "spring roll pasta sheets" that are in the refriger-ated produce section. Do not use those— they are way too thick! Let's just say that if it has Italian writing on the package, it's probably not the good stuff for Chinese eggrolls.

#3: Treat the wrapper right. You want to keep the wrappers covered with a damp towel at all times to prevent the edges from drying and cracking.

#4: Roll small and tight! Sloppy and loosely rolled eggrolls will break apart and allow oil to seep into the inside of the roll. Mama says baaaad. One time I was watching a celebrity chef on televi-sion making monster eggrolls the size of a cola can. Who in the heck can wrap their mouths around that thing? It looked hideous. Mama's eggrolls are elegant and skinny. Don't be too greedy and overstuff them! And roll them tight so that the fill-ing doesn't fall out while frying!

#5: Lay the rolled eggrolls neatly with a piece of parchment, foil or wax paper in between each layer if you are stacking them on top of each other. Keep them covered with plastic wrap or a towel to prevent drying. If you are freezing, freeze them like this first. Once frozen, you can gather them up and transfer them to a plastic freezer bag. If you roll them out and jumble them all together in a big pile, they'll eventually stick to each other and you'll tear the delicate skin trying to pry them apart.

VEGE-TALES:

Lately there have been a rash of recipes for sneaking healthy vegetables into dishes for kids—recipes like Carrot and Spinach Brownies, Cauliflower Banana Bread, Broccoli Gingerbread.

Like, totally. Gag me with an asparagus spear.

Do you even know how many flaxseed chicken nuggets my kids can slingshot across the room in 12.3 seconds with one hand tied behind their backs? The long-term effect of sneaking foods into your kids meals is the under appreciation of the taste of real vegetables. Plus, do you want kids to grow up with confusion over what mashed potatoes really taste like? When their school friends come over for supper, they'll wonder why the hot dogs have a green tinge and smell like the wrong end of a hippo. That, my friends, leads to worse things than not eating greens, like social anxiety, adult bedwetting and a plethora of disorders that require expensive medication.

If we're going to dupe our kids into eating vegetables, let's do it right.

There are a variety of tactics that I employ in the Steamy Kitchen household:

Bribery: "If you eat your broccoli, I'll give you an extra 50 cents for college."

Blatant Honesty: "See this picture of Uncle Jimmy? He's a wimp. He didn't eat his veggies."

Hostile Negotiations: "If you don't clean your plate, I'll whip Buzz Lightyear with a fishing pole and shock him with cattle prod."

Neuro-Linguistic Programming: "It's funny how much the more you try to resist the natural urge to eat Brussels sprouts, the more you keep wanting it, getting more and more excited about what you are tasting in your mouth at this very moment in time."

Exploiting Sibling Competitiveness: "If you eat your carrots, I'll love you way more than your brother."

Good Cop/Bad Cop: "Dude. If I were you, I'd just stuff those carrots in your mouth. Mom's coming and she's on her sixth straight day of PMS. Don't want to be on the receiving end of that monster."

Dr. Phil: "Are you eating what you're eating today because you want to eat it, or is it because it's what you think you were eating yesterday when you were trying to finish eating?"

Spontaneous Egomania: "SPINACH?! You can't handle the spinach! Son, I have a greater responsibility than you can possibly fathom. You weep for Cheetos and curse the alfalfa sprouts. I would rather you just said "thank you", and went on your way. Otherwise, I suggest that you pick up that spinach and eat it like a man. Either way, I don't care what you think you are entitled to." (You have to say that in Jack Nicholson's voice in *A Few Good Men*!)

The Wrath of God, Buddha and Santa: "THEY ARE ALL WATCHING YOU RIGHT NOW."

And my favorite technique of all, **Funny Food Names**. Like Furikake French Fries (I incorrectly pronounce it Fur-ee-kokky for giggles)—making you laugh so hard you don't notice you're eating seaweed.

Furikake French Fries

Furikake is a Japanese condiment that includes dried bonito flakes, seaweed, sesame seeds and other seasonings. You can find it at most Asian markets. While normally used to sprinkle on steamed rice, I sprinkled it on a fresh batch of french fries for a really cool sweet/salty hit that will have your kids eating vegetables from the sea—and liking it! Furikake comes in a small can with a pull-tab so you can shake out the furikake. (Heehee! I love saying that word!) There are many different flavors. And yes, it's a real word.

*DISCLAIMER: Yeah, I know this isn't a healthy recipe. Get your kids to like seaweed FIRST with French fries, THEN switch it up on them—sprinkle Furikake on steamed broccoli, spinach, tofu … whatever! But that is another technique called Bait and Switch. This double-technique is for the experienced only. Amateurs do not try.

SERVES 4 AS APPETIZER OR SNACK
One 1-lb (500-g) bag frozen French fries
2 tablespoons furikake seasoning
Salt to taste

Follow the directions on the bag of your frozen French fries. Be a good parent and bake 'em instead of frying. Bake until golden and crispy. While the french fries are still hot, season with the furikake seasoning and salt.

Other Options

■ If you want to make your own furikake, take a sheet of roasted seaweed (nori). To re-crisp the seaweed, toast it a few inches above an open flame or under a broiler until super-crisp but not burnt. It should only take a minute for each side. Crush the seaweed with your hands and add some salt and sesame seeds.

■ Furikake Popcorn—this stuff is awesome sprinkled on popcorn!

■ For more seasoning ideas for fries or popcorn, see Asian Flavored Salts (page 27).

Soups, Salads & Wraps

I think we were really spoiled as kids because we had soup every night for dinner. Mom always made sure of it! These days, with both Scott and I working full time, it's hard to tend to a simmering pot on the stove. Instead, I make stock (pages 31–32) in a slow cooker or pressure cooker and freeze batches of it so I have access to the good homemade stuff in a pinch. Otherwise, I'll buy packaged stock or broth at the store. I like the ones that are in the paper carton as opposed to the canned version (don't like the taste of tin). These soups are quick to prepare—with stock in the freezer or in a carton, the soups come together in minutes.

Salads are only fun if they have fab ingredients. I know, call me a salad geek, but something so healthy HAS to be fun to eat! That's why I love salad wraps. And the only reason that both my boys totally adore salads is because I make the salads fun to assemble and eat (and . . . okay, confession . . . some-times I let them top their salads off with crushed potato chips).

FAR LEFT TOP TO BOTTOM: At Diane Cu's gorgeous backyard; Andrew stalling—doesn't want to eat breakfast; at Jessica's, my local organic produce stand.

Lemongrass Chicken and Coconut Soup

This soup is a wonderful combo of two of my favorite Thai soups—Tom Yum and Tom Kha. It's a little hot, a little sour and the added coconut milk helps tame the spice.

Tom yum paste comes just like Thai curry pastes—either in a can, plastic tub or a pouch. It's incredibly easy to use and lasts for months if stored in the refrigerator.

I use fresh kaffir lime leaves, ginger and lemongrass in the recipe for extra freshness, but these ingredients are totally optional as the tom yum paste is pretty intense. Remember, you don't eat these herbs (they are used for flavoring the broth). Traditionally, these herbs are just left in the soup (you'll use your spoon to push them out of the way when you drink). And I prefer serving the soup this way, as the aromatics will continue to work their magic up while I enjoy the soup. But I'll let you choose whether or not you'd like to keep them in or discard them.

The number of chillies you use depends on the size and kind that you buy—generally the smaller and thinner the chilli pepper is, the hotter it will be. For my recipe, I've used jalapeno, as that gives the perfect amount of heat that I'm looking for and it's readily found in most markets in the U.S.

SERVES 4 AS PART OF MULTICOURSE MEAL

- 3 cups (750 ml) store-bought or home-made Mom's Chicken Stock (page 31)
- 1 thumb-sized piece of ginger, sliced into thin coins (see Jaden's Ginger Tips, page 33)
- 2 stalks lemongrass (use the bottom 6-in/15-cm of the stalk, smash with side of cleaver or cut in half lengthwise)
- 4 fresh kaffir lime leaves, torn in half
- 1 fresh chilli pepper of your choice, sliced
- 1 cup (250 ml) good quality coconut milk
- 3 tablespoons tom yum paste (or to taste), divided
- 1 tablespoon fish sauce
- 2 teaspoons sugar
- 6 oz (170 g) boneless, skinless chicken breast, thinly sliced
- 1 cup (70 g) straw mushrooms, rinsed, drained and sliced in half lengthwise
- 1½ tablespoons lime juice
- One small handful of fresh cilantro (coriander) leaves (about ¼ cup/12 g), for garnish

1 In a pot, add the stock, ginger, lemongrass, kaffir lime leaves and chilli pepper and bring to a boil. Once boiling, reduce the heat to low and simmer for 5 minutes. Stir in the coconut milk, half of the tom yum paste, the fish sauce and sugar, and let that return to a boil, still on low heat. Taste the soup and add the remaining tom yum paste as per your taste. If you'd like, use a skimmer to fish out the ginger, chilli, lemongrass and kaffir lime leaves and discard.

2 Turn the heat to high and add the chicken and mushrooms. When the soup returns to a boil, reduce the heat to low and simmer until the chicken is cooked through, about 4 minutes. Stir in the lime juice. Garnish with the fresh cilantro leaves and additional slices of chilli pepper, if you like.

Chicken and Corn Soup

Quick and Hearty Rice Soup

This is a quick from-scratch soup that you can make in 30 minutes. No canned broth, no artificial anything. Actually, it's more like a cross between Chinese *jook* (porridge) and a soup. And please, don't call it "joop". You can use any vegetables that you have. The firmer the vegetables, the thinner you have to slice them so they cook in 30 minutes. For this soup, you don't wash the rice, as we want all of that starch to thicken the soup. The more you stir the pot, the thicker the soup gets. You can also add ¹⁄₂ cup (110 g) of rice if you like the thicker *jook* style.

SERVES 4 FOR LUNCH OR AS PART OF MULTICOURSE MEAL

¹⁄₂ lb (250 g) ground beef
2 teaspoons soy sauce
1 teaspoon Chinese rice wine (or dry sherry)
Freshly ground black pepper to season the beef
Pinch of sugar
1 teaspoon high-heat cooking oil
4 cups (1 liter) water
¹⁄₄ cup (55 g) uncooked rice
1 tomato, cut into 8 wedges
1 carrot, shredded
¹⁄₄ cup (40 g) frozen peas
Salt or soy sauce to taste

1 In a bowl, mix together the beef with the soy sauce, wine, black pepper and sugar.
2 Set a medium pot over high heat. When the pot is hot, add the cooking oil and swirl to coat. Add the ground beef mixture and fry for 2 minutes, breaking up the beef as you go.
3 Pour in the water, rice, tomato and carrot and bring to a boil. When it reaches a boil, turn the heat to low, cover and simmer for 25 minutes. The rice should be fully cooked and soft. Add the frozen peas and cook for another minute. Taste and, if needed, add just ¹⁄₂ teaspoon of salt or soy sauce. You can always add more.

Chicken and Corn Soup

In this light soup, instead of cream, the natural milk of the corn serves to create this luscious soup. To extract the corn milk, you will grate one ear of corn on a box grater and squeeze out the milk hidden inside the kernels.

SERVES 4 AS PART OF MULTI-COURSE MEAL

3 egg whites (separate 1 into one bowl and the other 2 into another bowl)
2 teaspoons cornstarch
¹⁄₄ lb (115 g) ground chicken
2 ears fresh, sweet white or yellow corn
4 cups (1 liter) store-bought or homemade Mom's Chicken Stock (page 31)
¹⁄₄ cup (35 g) ¹⁄₄-in (6-mm)-diced Virginia ham, or any other salted, cured ham
Salt to taste
1 tablespoon chilli oil
2 tablespoons chopped green onions (scallions) or fresh cilantro (coriander), for garnish

1 In a large bowl, whisk 1 of the egg whites with the cornstarch. Add the ground chicken and stir vigorously with a wooden spoon or chopsticks until well combined.
2 On a cutting board, lay one of the ears of corn on its side and, with a serrated knife, cut off the kernels. Reserve BOTH the kernels and the cob.
3 In a large bowl, use the large holes of a box grater to grate the remaining ear of corn. Stand the empty cob upright in the bowl and use the back of a chef's knife to run up and down the spent corn cob, pressing to extract all of the corn pulp. Repeat on the other reserved cob. Over a fine meshed sieve, use your hands to squeeze all of the grated corn and pulp to extract the corn milk. Discard the spent corn and pulp, reserving the corn milk.
4 In a stockpot, bring the chicken stock to a boil over high heat. Add the corn milk and simmer 5 minutes. Add the ground chicken, corn kernels and ham and cook another 2 minutes, stirring to break up the chicken. Season with the salt. Remove from the heat and drizzle in the remaining 2 egg whites, stirring with a spoon to create long, thin trails of egg white. To serve, ladle the soup into bowls, drizzle with the chilli oil and garnish with green onions or fresh cilantro.

Quick and Hearty Rice Soup

Quick Vietnamese Chicken Pho

In my young, crazy, single days, after a night of clubbing in Hollywood, my friends and I would head over to a rinky-dink Vietnamese noodle shop to fill up on pho. Asian girly posters littered the walls and the same bad karaoke DVD played over and over. Thank goodness the steaming, hot, intoxicating bowl of pho drowned out the awful Chinglish rendition of "Baby Got Back". That soup was un-pho-king believable.

Here's my cheater version of this popular Vietnamese Chicken Noodle Soup, or *pho ga*. It takes 30 minutes from start to finish instead of the usual 3 hours. You can buy a package of pho ga spices for usually less than $2 at Asian markets. The single-use package has all the spices you'll need and a little mesh bag so that the spices stay in one place. Toasting these spices brings out the flavors.

SERVES 4

1 lb (500 g) dried rice noodles (about ¼-in/6-mm wide)

CHICKEN PHO BROTH
2 tablespoons whole coriander seeds
4 whole cloves
2 whole star anise
2 quarts (2 liters) store-bought or home-made Mom's Chicken Stock (page 31)
1 whole chicken breast (bone-in or boneless)
½ onion
One 3-in (7.5-cm) chunk of ginger, sliced and smashed with side of knife
1 to 2 tablespoons sugar
1 to 2 tablespoons fish sauce

ACCOMPANIMENTS
2 cups (200 g) bean sprouts, washed and tails pinched off
Fresh cilantro (coriander) tops (leaves and tender stems)
½ cup (170 g) shaved red onions
½ lime, cut into 4 wedges
Sriracha chilli sauce
Hoisin sauce
Sliced fresh chilli peppers of your choice

1 To make the Chicken Pho Broth, heat a frying pan over medium heat. Add the coriander seeds, cloves and star anise and toast until fragrant, about 3-4 minutes. Immediately spoon out the spices to avoid burning.
2 In a large pot, add all the ingredients (including the toasted spices) and bring to a boil. Reduce the heat to medium-low and let simmer for 20 minutes, skimming the surface frequently. Use tongs to remove the chicken breasts and shred the meat with your fingers, discarding the bone if you have used a bone-in breast.
3 Taste the broth and add more fish sauce or sugar, if needed. Strain the broth and discard the solids.
4 Prepare the noodles as per directions on the package.
5 Ladle the broth into bowls. Then divide the shredded chicken breast and the soft noodles evenly into each bowl.
6 Have the Accompaniments spread out at the table. Each person can customize their own bowl with these ingredients.

Ochazuke Rice with Crisp Salmon Skin and Nori

Ochazuke is a Japanese dish where hot green tea is poured over cooked rice. It's commonly topped with seaweed, pickled plums, salmon and even wasabi. You can get ready-made packets of Ochazuke seasonings at Japanese markets, but it's just as easy to brew some tea (I used a green tea teabag) and mix in instant dashi granules (see page 20 for information about dashi granules). If you don't have dashi granules, you can brew your tea in a light broth instead of plain water.

When I'm buying salmon, I kindly ask my fishmonger to pretty please skin the salmon fillet for me and wrap the skin separately. I'm paying for the whole thing anyway, skin and all, so why not use the tasty skin for Ochazuke? The salmon skin crisps up wonderfully under the broiler and it's the perfect topping for this popular Japanese dish. I'm more of a savory breakfast kinda gal, and this is what I have many mornings. Well, truth be told, it's also what I have for a midnight snack too! Anytime I have leftover rice in the fridge, you can be sure I'm enjoying warm, soothing ochazuke the next day. You can also spice it up with a dab of wasabi paste if you want.

SERVES 2 AS BREAKFAST, MIDNIGHT SNACK OR HANGOVER CURE

One 4 x 6-in (10 x 15-cm) piece salmon skin (uncooked and make sure it's scaled!)
Pinch of salt
4 cups (1 liter) freshly brewed hot green tea
1/2 teaspoon instant dashi granules
1 1/2 cups (240 g) cooked, leftover short-grain rice
2 tablespoons shredded seaweed nori

1 Season the salmon skin with salt and place on a sheet pan. Place the salmon skin 6 inches (15 cm) from top heating element and broil on high heat for 5 to 7 minutes. Keep a close watch to make sure you don't burn the salmon skin. Cut the crispy skin into strips.
2 Mix the brewed green tea with the instant dashi granules, and stir well. Divide the cooked rice in two medium serving bowls. Pour the green tea mixture over the rice. Top with the salmon skin and the shredded nori.

Crab and Pork Wonton Noodle Soup

Can I just tell you how adorable kids are when they cook, especially when it involves folding dumplings? I taught the boys how to make wontons when they were 4 and 5 years old and put them to work in the kitchen while I'm chillin' on the couch with a glass of wine. So yes, making wonton dumplings is so easy that little kidlets can do it.

While the recipe has two steps (making the wonton dumplings and then cooking the noodle soup) the wontons can be made ahead of time. Or bribe your kids to fold a big batch of wontons, freeze them and then you can have them anytime. Just add them frozen to your boiling broth.

You can also skip the whole idea of noodle soup and just boil the wontons in water, drain and eat them with your favorite soy dipping sauce or hot chilli sauce. (Any of these in the Basics chapter will pair well: Sweet Chilli Sambal, Ginger Scallion sauce, Chilli Garlic Sauce, Chinese Dipping Sauce, Sweet Soy Sauce for the kids or just even a squirt of Sriracha chilli sauce).

To freeze wontons (or any handmade dumpling): Okay, this is important. As you fold the wontons, lay them in a single layer on a plate or baking sheet. Freeze them just like this. Once the wontons are frozen, you can gather them up and put them in a freezer bag. If you try to dump the freshly folded wontons in a freezer bag and then freeze—they will all stick together and freeze into one big solid clump-o-dough. Not good.

To boil wontons in water to enjoy with a dipping sauce: If you just want to boil the wontons and eat them without the noodle soup, follow the same instructions as boiling with broth. You'll bring a pot of water to boil, add the wontons, and bring to boil again. Add 1 cup (250 ml) of cool water, return to a boil and repeat once more. Once it returns to a boil the last time, they are happy dumplings and are ready to eat! Drain and serve. By the way, are you curious as to why I didn't give you boiling instructions like, "boil 7 minutes"? Well, this method of boiling, adding water, boiling again, repeating is so reliable. Whether you are boiling 15 or 30 wontons, the instructions are the same. The more dumplings you have in the water or broth . . . the longer it takes to come to a boil, right? I love the Chinese method of self-timing.

SERVES 6
(MAKES ABOUT 50 TO 60 WONTONS)
8 cups (2 liters) store-bought or home-made Mom's Chicken Stock, Seafood, Pork or Vegetable Stock (pages 31–32)
Crab and Pork Wonton Dumplings (see recipe on this page)
8 oz (250 g) dried wonton noodles or 12 oz (350 g) fresh/frozen wonton noodles
1 lb (500 g) bok choy, leaves separated and washed well
1/3 cup (50 g) chopped green onions (scallions), for garnish
1/4 cup (65 ml) Chilli Garlic Sauce (page 29) to use as dipping (optional)

CRAB AND PORK WONTON DUMPLINGS
1/2 lb (250 g) ground pork
2 green onions (scallions), finely minced
1 tablespoon soy sauce
1 teaspoon rice vinegar
1 teaspoon cornstarch
1/4 teaspoon sugar
2 teaspoons grated fresh ginger
1/2 cup (100 g) chopped crabmeat, drained
1/4 teaspoon salt
Freshly ground black pepper to taste
1/2 teaspoon sesame oil
1 lb (500 g) wonton wrappers, covered with a barely damp towel
Cornstarch slurry: 1 tablespoon cornstarch dissolved in 1/4 cup (65 ml) cool water

1 To make the dumpling filling, combine the pork, green onions, soy sauce, rice vinegar, cornstarch and sugar in a large bowl. Mix well and set aside.
2 In a small bowl, squeeze the grated ginger pulp, extracting the juice into the bowl. Discard the spent ginger. Add the crabmeat, salt, pepper and sesame oil and stir gently to mix with the ginger juice.
3 When ready to wrap, add the crab mixture to the bowl with the ground pork mixture. Toss gently to mix. To wrap the wontons, see the illustrated instructions.

HOW TO WRAP WONTONS

1 Put a teaspoon of filling in the middle of a wrapper. With your finger or a pastry brush, apply some of the cornstarch slurry along all the edges.
2 Fold over to form a triangle, press to secure the edges, encasing the filling. Dab some of the cornstarch slurry on one tip of the triangle.
3 Bring two corners together and secure. Place on baking sheet and cover loosely with plastic wrap to prevent drying. Repeat with the remaining wrappers and filling. The wonton dumplings are ready for use in the soup or to be frozen for later use (see facing page on how to freeze the wontons). If you're using them later in the day, cover the baking sheet tightly with plastic wrap and refrigerate until ready to cook.

4 To make the soup, pour all but 2 cups (500 ml) of the stock into a large stockpot and bring to a boil. (The reserved stock should be room temperature or just slightly chilled.) Turn the heat to medium-high and add the wonton dumplings. Bring pot back to a gentle boil. When it reaches a boil, add 1 cup (250 ml) of the reserved stock. Bring back to a boil again and add the remaining 1 cup (250 ml) of reserved stock. Adding the broth a little at a time lets the wontons cook, but at a gentle heat. A rapid, rolling boil will tear the delicate wonton skins.
5 With the heat still on the pot (you still need to cook the noodles and bok choy), use a spider or sieve to scoop up the wontons and distribute among the serving bowls. Add the noodles and the bok choy to the pot and let simmer for 1½ minutes, until cooked through. Ladle the broth, noodles and bok choy into bowls. Garnish with the green onions and serve with the Chilli Garlic Sauce, if desired.

Crisp Fuji Apple and Crab Salad

I've always loved pairing seafood with fruit, and the combination of sea-salty crab with crisp apple was inspired by friend and food writer, Jennifer Jeffrey, and her co-author Andrea Froncillo of the famed The Stinking Rose restaurant in San Francisco. A Vietnamese-style dressing gives the salad a shot of spice and tang. When I buy pre-cooked crab meat, I like to toss it with a bit of ginger juice first, to freshen and wake up the flavors. Use a microplane grater to grate the fresh ginger then scoop up the mound of ginger with your fingers and squeeze directly into a bowl to release its juices. Discard the remaining spent pulp and toss the crab meat with the ginger juices.

SERVES 4 AS PART OF MULTICOURSE MEAL OR FOR LUNCH
- 1/2 lb (250 g) cooked fresh or canned crabmeat, drained
- 1 teaspoon grated fresh ginger (see Jaden's Ginger Tips, page 33)
- 1 crisp textured apple (Fuji or Granny Smith)
- 4 cups (350 g) mixed baby greens
- Salt and freshly ground black pepper to taste
- 2 tablespoons very thinly sliced fresh mint
- 1 teaspoon freshly squeezed lime juice

DRESSING
- 3 tablespoons fish sauce
- 2 tablespoons sugar
- 2 tablespoons fresh lime juice
- 6 tablespoons neutral-flavored oil (such as vegetable, canola, grapeseed)
- 1/4 teaspoon peeled and grated fresh ginger (see Jaden's Ginger Tips, page 33)
- 1 clove garlic, finely minced
- 1/4 to 1/2 teaspoon finely minced fresh chilli pepper (leave the seeds in if you like it hot)

1 In a small bowl, whisk together the ingredients for the Dressing.

2 In a large bowl, add the crabmeat. Use your fingers to squeeze the freshly grated ginger to release the ginger juices into the bowl with the crabmeat. Discard the spent ginger pulp. Gently mix the crabmeat with a fork.

3 Core the apple and cut into matchstick strips. Immediately add the apples to the crabmeat and toss lightly with the salt, pepper, mint and lime juice. Assemble plates by layering baby greens and topping with crab/apple mixture.

4 Use a teaspoon to drizzle some of the Dressing onto the salad until lightly coated. You should have some leftover Dressing. The Dressing will keep in the refrigerator for up to 1 week.

HOW TO CUT ACROSS THE GRAIN

Many cuts of beef are tough and fibrous because they contain muscles used often by the cow. Even though they are tough, cut from the muscular parts of the cow, like flank and skirt steak, have insane beefy flavor and are some of my favorite cuts. But if you know how to slice them across the grain, you'll end up with ribbons of tender beef. Take a look at your steak. Do you see the fibers running in one direction? Well, you want to slice your steak thinly, PERPENDICULAR to those fibers, so that you are cutting ACROSS the fibers or the grain.

1 Lay your steak so that the fibers run left to right, like in the photo.

2 Slice across the grain, as shown.

Thai Beef Salad Wraps

These lettuce wraps are so pretty on a platter! The steak is grilled to medium-rare and then thinly sliced and served warm on top of a cool, crisp lettuce wrap. You can also chop or tear the lettuce with your hands and serve it as a regular salad instead of a wrap. If you have chopped peanuts, you can add those too.

The pineapple juice sweetens and tenderizes the steak. Make sure you don't let the steak sit in the pineapple juice for more than 1 hour—otherwise it will break down the meat too much. You can also substitute with fresh orange juice. After grilling, when you are slicing the meat, slice ACROSS the grain to ensure you get tender cuts, especially if you are using flank or skirt steak.

SERVES 4 TO 6

1 lb (500 g) flank steak (you can also use top sirloin or skirt steak)
$\frac{1}{2}$ cup (125 ml) pineapple juice
Salt
1 tablespoon high-heat cooking oil
1 head leafy lettuce
1 large cucumber, thinly sliced
1 large tomato, sliced in half, watery seeds scooped out and sliced into thin wedges
$\frac{1}{4}$ red onion, very thinly sliced
Handful of fresh mint

DRESSING

$\frac{1}{2}$ to 1 teaspoon finely minced chilli pepper of your choice
1 clove garlic, finely minced
2 tablespoons minced fresh cilantro (coriander) stems
$1\frac{1}{2}$ tablespoons sugar
2 to 4 tablespoons fish sauce
5 tablespoons freshly squeezed lime juice (about 2 to 3 limes)

1 Marinate the flank steak in the pineapple juice for 30 minutes to 1 hour (no longer than 1 hour).

2 In the meantime, whisk together the ingredients for the Dressing. Start with 2 tablespoons of fish sauce and taste and add the rest as needed. To lessen the intensity of the Dressing, add 1 teaspoon of water.

3 Pat the steak very dry and season with salt. Set a large frying pan on high heat. When the pan is hot, pour in the oil and swirl to coat. Add the steak and grill to medium-rare, about 3 to 5 minutes each side, depending on thickness of your steak. Let rest on cutting board for 10 minutes and slice ACROSS the grain into thin, $\frac{1}{4}$-inch (6-mm) strips. (See illustrated instructions on page 62).

4 Assemble the salad wraps by filling each lettuce leaf with cucumbers, tomatoes, onions, a few slices of beef and top with fresh mint.

Baked Tofu Salad with Mustard Miso Dressing

While I looove deep fried tofu, it's not the most healthy thing to be putting in a salad. Thank goodness that baking tofu squares is easier and better for you! The texture is golden-crisp-crunchy on the outside, slightly chewy on the inside. I adapted the baked tofu recipe from Mark Bittman's *How to Cook Everything Vegetarian* and paired them with a tangy Miso Mustard Dressing. Make sure you buy firm or extra firm tofu that you find in the refrigerated section of the market.

To toast sesame seeds, add them to a frying pan (no oil) and turn the heat to medium. Stir continuously until toasted. It should only take a couple of minutes and will make a world of difference in taste.

SERVES 4 AS PART OF MULTICOURSE MEAL
One 14-oz (400-g) block firm or extra-firm tofu
2 teaspoons high-heat cooking oil
¼ teaspoon salt
4 handfuls lettuce leaves
4 radishes, thinly sliced
2 tablespoons toasted sesame seeds

(MAKES 1 CUP/250 ML)
MUSTARD MISO DRESSING
2 tablespoons miso (yellow, red or white)
1 teaspoon Dijon-style mustard
⅓ cup (80 ml) rice vinegar
2 tablespoons finely minced shallot or onion
1 tablespoon sugar
½ cup (125 ml) neutral-flavored oil (such as vegetable, canola, grapeseed)

1 Preheat the oven to 350°F (175°C).
2 Cut the tofu into ¾-inch (2-cm) cubes, and pat very dry with paper towels on all sides. Toss the tofu cubes gently with the oil and season with the salt. On a sheet pan, spread the tofu cubes out in a single layer. Bake for 45 minutes to 1 hour. The tofu should be golden brown and crisp on the outside, yet still soft in the middle. Remove to a baking rack and let cool.
3 In a bowl, use a whisk to combine the ingredients for the Mustard Miso Dressing. Set aside. You will have more than you need for this salad, but the dressing will keep for 1-2 weeks in the refrigerator.
4 In a large bowl, assemble the torn lettuce leaves, sliced radishes and tofu. Toss with 3 tablespoons of the Mustard Miso Dressing and sprinkle the sesame seeds on top. Serve immediately.

More Options
■ The tofu also makes a great snack on its own. Serve them with the Apricot Sweet Chilli Sauce (page 64).

Pomelo and Edamame Salad with Honey Ginger Vinaigrette

Pomelos are an Asian grapefruit, and they're sooo good! They come in sizes as small as a regular grapefruit and I've seen some as large as basketballs! The flavor is milder and less tart/bitter than grapefruit with a slight honeylike taste. The skin is spongy and thick and the membrane is very thick. You'll have to use a knife to cut through it. The easiest way to peel a pomelo is to cut through just the thick skin and section it like you would an orange. Peel apart the pomelo sections, and now peel away the membrane as well. Use your hands to tear away the juicy pomelo pulp and eat! The pomelo fruit is juicy and lush. Can I tell you a secret? I think that it's one of the sexiest fruits in the world.

Edamame are Japanese soybeans . . . you know, the green soybeans that you get sometimes at a Japanese restaurant. The outer shell is inedible (well, you can try, but it doesn't taste that great)—but once you squeeze open the shell, bright green shiny pods pop out! They are good for you and . . . um . . . they go great with beer! You can buy edamame already shelled and cooked in the refrigerated section at your regular grocery store and you can use them as it is. They are also found in the freezer section (for these, you'll just follow the instructions on the package to boil and then shell).

1 In a small bowl, whisk together the ingredients for the vinaigrette.
2 Toss the edamame pods, pomelo sections, baby greens and mint on a large platter and drizzle on about $1/4$ cup (65 ml) of the Honey Ginger Vinaigrette. Store the remaining vinaigrette in the refrigerator for up to 1 week.

> **TIP: Edamame tip: I often buy a bag of frozen shell-on edamame and store them in the freezer. Instead of boiling them in plain water, I like to boil them in a big spoonful of instant dashi granules (page 20) dissolved in boiling water.**
>
> **It seasons the edamame and no need for any additional salt.**

SERVES 4 AS PART OF MULTICOURSE MEAL
1 cup (150 g) shelled edamame pods
$1/2$ pomelo, peeled and separated into small bite-size sections
4 handfuls of mixed baby greens
Leaves from 1 sprig of fresh mint (and finely sliced, if you wish)

HONEY GINGER VINAIGRETTE
2 tablespoons honey
$1/2$ teaspoon grated fresh ginger
$1/4$ cup (65 ml) fresh orange juice or grapefruit juice
2 teaspoons freshly squeezed lime juice
6 tablespoons grapeseed oil, mild olive oil, vegetable or canola oil
Salt and freshly ground black pepper to taste

Miso Ramen with all the Trimmings

Outside of Japan, ramen didn't achieve cult status until the movie *Tampopo* came out in 1985. For a while, all I wanted to do was open a ramen noodle shop and it even spurred a two-week visit to Japan in search of the perfect bowl. (I didn't find it, but then again, I got distracted by a cute guy I met at the sushi bar.)

Even in college, at late night cramming sessions, I'd slurp down the 15-cent instant stuff. And yeah, I still eat that instant stuff—I still love it.

SERVES 4

4 eggs

10 oz (285 g) dried ramen noodles

1/2 cup (200 g) fresh or canned bamboo shoots, sliced

1/2 cup (170 g) fresh or canned corn kernels, drained

1/3 cup (80 g) defrosted frozen or fresh spinach

8 cups (2 liters) store-bought or homemade Meat or Vegetable Stock (pages 31 & 32)

2 teaspoons instant dashi granules (page 20)

1 tablespoon soy sauce, or to taste

4 tablespoons fresh miso paste

1 cup (100 g) fresh bean sprouts

2 green onions (scallions), finely chopped

4 teaspoons chilli oil (optional)

More Topping Options

Top with store bought barbeque cha-siu pork

Enoki mushrooms

Sliced Japanese fish cakes

Snow peas

Spinach leaves

Firm tofu, diced

1 Place the whole, un-cracked eggs in a medium pot and fill with water to cover eggs by 1 inch (2.5 cm). Turn the heat to high and when boiling, turn the heat to medium and let the eggs cook for 10 minutes. Promptly use a slotted spoon to remove the eggs and peel the egg under cold running water. Slice each egg in half.

2 Return the same pot of water to a boil. Add the ramen noodles and cook for 3 minutes, until the noodles are cooked through. Drain and rinse with cold water to stop the cooking.

3 Divide the noodles, hardboiled eggs, bamboo shoots, corn and spinach among 4 large serving bowls.

4 In a large pot, add the stock, instant dashi and soy sauce. Bring to a boil over high heat. Remove from the heat and stir in the miso. Taste the soup and add an additional 1 to 2 tablespoons of miso if you'd like. Ladle soup into each bowl. Top each bowl with fresh bean sprouts, green onions and a drizzle of chilli oil, if desired.

Healthy Chinese Chicken Wraps

I'm a savory salad gal, and my husband is crazy in love with the Chinese chicken salad at a big chain restaurant in town, which is doused with a fattening, sticky sweet honey mustard sauce. So, I had to create a recipe that lightened up the salad both in taste and calories. The verdict? He ate it all. This is a fantastic way to use up cooked leftover chicken and makes a light lunch. The dressing is made with yogurt instead of the usual mayonnaise, but still tastes luscious and creamy. You'll love the crunchy almond slivers, fresh celery, bursty grapes in this salad wrap. If you want, you can go my husband's route and use leftover cold fried chicken torn into pieces too!

SERVES 4 AS PART OF MULTICOURSE MEAL OR FOR LUNCH
4 wraps, thin flatbreads or tortillas

HONEY MUSTARD YOGURT VINAIGRETTE
3 tablespoons honey
1 tablespoon Dijon mustard
2 tablespoons plain non-fat yogurt
2 tablespoons rice vinegar (or substitute with white vinegar)
$1/2$ teaspoon sesame oil
Generous pinch of salt

CHINESE CHICKEN SALAD
$3/4$ lb (350 g) cooked chicken, cut into bite-size pieces
10 to 15 seedless grapes, halved
1 celery stalk, diced
3 tablespoons almond slivers or slices
$1/2$ teaspoon kosher salt
Freshly ground black pepper, to taste
$1/4$ teaspoon five spice powder
One large handful of watercress or arugula

1 In a small bowl, whisk together the ingredients for the Honey Mustard Yogurt Vinaigrette, and set aside.
2 In a large bowl, toss together the ingredients for the Chinese Chicken Salad with just enough vinaigrette to lightly coat.
3 Assemble the wraps, spooning additional vinaigrette into each wrap if desired.

Seafood

My dream home comes with tons of land for a veggie garden and a big pond for a backyard. Oh, and while I'm at it, how about a little boat for fishing and someone to come stock my big pond with giant, yummy fishes, squid, shrimp and clams. Hmmm . . . okay, maybe that wouldn't work well. But wouldn't it be cool to be able to catch fish for tonight's dinner? Earlier this year, I brought blogger friends David Lebovitz, Elise Bauer, Diane Cu, Deb Perelman and Matt Armendariz with me to Club Med in the Bahamas. One of our most memorable moments was fishing. We caught four giant 50-pound wahoos and two nasty toothed barracudas! Guess what we had for dinner?

FAR LEFT TOP TO BOTTOM: Yes, I caught that! A big wahoo in the Bahamas; Who's the fairest of them all?; Andrew eating breakfast in his Buzz Lightyear costume.

Mussels in Coconut Curry Broth

This is another one of those quick 15-minute meals that has become a favorite among my friends. It's slurptastic and I've never seen a bowl come back to the kitchen with anything other than empty mussel shells. When you buy mussels at the market, make sure your fishmonger hand-selects each mussel for you. The mussels should be closed or just slightly open (but should close when tapped). They should smell faintly of the sea. Once you get home, open the bag (gotta let the babies breathe). Grab two different-sized bowls, one that fits inside the other. Place the mussels in the smaller bowl. Fill the larger bowl with ice and put the smaller bowl inside, on top of the ice, and refrigerate. After cooking, discard any that are still closed or any with cracked shells.

> **TIP: Here are some ingredient tips—The noodles.** Mung bean noodles, which are white when dried and transparent when cooked, are gluten free and very healthy! They are also sometimes called vermicelli noodles, cellophane or glass noodles and they come in "skeins" or small bundles. Look at the ingredient list on the package—the only two ingredients should be mung bean and water. **The lemongrass.** If you don't have a stalk in your refrigerator, just take a lemon and use a vegetable peeler to peel several strips of the peel. **The stock.** The recipe calls for seafood stock, and generally you can find cartons of seafood stock or broth right next to the beef, chicken or vegetable stock/broth. I've also used vegetable stock with great success in this recipe. Beef and chicken would be too strong in flavor for the mussels. If you use vegetable stock, you can add a small bottle of clam juice (look in the canned seafood section) to the stock for additional seafood flavor. If you want to make seafood stock from scratch, see page 32.

SERVES 4 AS PART OF MULTICOURSE MEAL

2 lbs (1 kg) mussels
1 teaspoon high-heat cooking oil
½ cup (125 ml) Thai curry paste, divided
10 oz (300 ml) coconut milk, shake the can vigorously to mix the fat with the liquid before opening
3 stalks lemongrass, outer leaves peeled and bottom 6 in (15 cm) of stalk cut in half lengthwise, or 3 or 4 strips of lemon peel (yellow part only)
2½ cups (625 ml) store-bought or home-made Seafood Stock, page 32 (substitute with Vegetable Stock, page 31)
1½ tablespoons fish sauce
1 teaspoon sugar
3 small skeins (100 g) mung bean noodles, soaked in cold water for 5 minutes and drained
1 small handful fresh Thai basil or sweet Italian basil leaves
Juice of ½ lime

1 Scrub the mussels, remove any fibers from the shell and discard any with cracked shells and those that won't close when tapped gently.
2 Set a wok or large pot on medium heat and add the oil. When the oil is just beginning to shimmer, add three-quarters of the curry paste and fry for 15 seconds to release its flavors. Take care not to burn the curry paste. Pour in about ½ cup (125 ml) of the coconut milk and stir until the curry paste is completely dissolved. Add the lemongrass, stock, fish sauce, sugar and remaining coconut milk. Turn the heat to high and bring to a boil. Reduce the heat and simmer for 3 minutes. Taste the broth and if you want a spicier broth, add the remaining curry paste.
3 Turn the heat to high and add the mussels. Immediately cover with a tight fitting lid. When the broth returns to a boil, lower the heat and simmer for 3 minutes.
4 Remove the lid, push the mussels to one side, add the drained mung bean noodles and redistribute the mussels and simmer another minute uncovered. Stir in the basil leaves and the lime juice. Remove the lemongrass or the lemon peel before serving as they are meant to flavor the broth only.

SERVES 4 AS PART OF MULTICOURSE MEAL

1 tablespoon high-heat cooking oil
3 to 4 cloves garlic, finely minced
1 fresh or dried chilli pepper of your choice, minced
Generous pinch of salt
1 lb (500 g) raw shell-on shrimp with their tails, deveined (see below)
$\frac{1}{4}$ cup (65 ml) pilsner-style beer, preferably Tsingtao brand
2 green onions (scallions), minced

Set a wok over medium heat. When it just starts to get hot, add the oil and swirl to coat. Add the garlic, chilli pepper and salt and fry until fragrant, about 15 to 30 seconds. Add the shrimp and immediately begin tossing, using your spatula to scoop the oil all over the shrimp and bathe it in the garlicky oil. Pour the beer in and immediately cover. Steam the shrimp for 3 to 4 minutes, until cooked through. Toss in the green onions and mix well. Serve immediately.

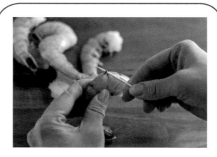

TIP: To devein a shell-on shrimp, use a toothpick and go in between the shell segment to fish out the black vein or digestive tract.

Beer Steamed Shrimp with Garlic

One of my childhood heroes was Martin Yan. I used to watch Martin on television, mesmerized by his thick Chinese accent and kung fu–esque knife skills. I got to finally meet the master chef himself in person a couple of years ago and yeah, it's really true, he can carve a whole chicken in 18 seconds! Martin is a big fan of steaming seafood in Tsingtao beer and I've used that technique here. The beer totally brings out the sweetness in the shrimp. This is a simple dish with few ingredients and I bet you could cook this, start to finish, in 15 minutes. Oh, another note: I always believe that the more I have to wrestle with my food, the better it tastes. Which is why I love shrimp with their shell-on, blue crab and crayfish. I figure the more work I have to do, the more I savor its flavor! And I think most Chinese will agree with me—we love eating with our hands and suckin' those shrimp shells! If you're not into that kind of thing, then go ahead and remove the shells before cooking.

Grilled Fish with Kabayaki Sauce

I spent my sixteenth birthday in Japan as an exchange student for the summer. Back then, I didn't appreciate the art and subtlety of sushi and it didn't help that the first time I had a sushi dinner, I thought that big green ball of wasabi was a delicious green tea ice cream. Ouch. Big searing ouch.

During those weeks in Japan, I gravitated towards the cooked stuff, especially Unagi-don—or Japanese grilled eel with a sweet soy glaze served over rice.

It's hard to find unagi outside Asian markets, plus I've just learned from Casson Trenor (www.sustainablesushi.net), a sushi sustainability expert, that wild unagi is on the brink of extinction and farmed unagi is a no-no for the environment (and your body). So, instead of unagi in this recipe, I've subsituted with a firm white fish. The sweet soy glaze, or "kabayaki sauce", is terribly addictive over fish and rice. My friend and fellow food writer, Amy Sherman, suggests using catfish fillets, as the texture is the most similar to unagi.

For the kabayaki sauce, make sure you're using "mirin" which is a sweet rice wine, and NOT the rice vinegar or Chinese rice wine. Serve this over short-grained rice.

SERVES 4 AS PART OF MULTICOURSE MEAL
1 tablespoon high-heat cooking oil
4 firm fish fillets, about 4 to 6 oz (125 to 175 g) each, patted very dry
6 cups (1 kg) steamed short-grained rice (page 129)
One small handful of dried or toasted seaweed shreds (Kizami Nori), for garnish
2 tablespoons thinly sliced green onion (scallion), for garnish

KABAYAKI SAUCE
½ cup (125 ml) soy sauce
½ cup (125 ml) mirin (Japanese sweet rice wine)
3 tablespoons sugar

1 In a small saucepot over medium high heat, stir together the Kabayaki Sauce ingredients. When the sauce begins to bubble, immediately turn the heat to low and let it simmer for 4 to 5 minutes, until thick enough to coat the back of the spoon. Be careful, as the sauce can easily thicken too much and you'll end up with a caramel! If it becomes too thick, whisk in a tablespoon of water at a time.

2 Set a large frying pan over high heat. When the pan is very hot, add the oil and swirl to coat pan. Lay the fish fillets in the pan, not touching each other. Fry for 2 minutes until the bottoms are browned. Brush the Kabayaki Sauce glaze on the fillets. Flip the fish over and brush the top of the other side. Fry for another minute or two, until the fish flakes easily and is cooked through.

3 Serve the fish over rice and pour additional Kabayaki Sauce over the fish. Top with seaweed shreds and green onions.

Mom's Chinese Steamed Fish

The moment I tell mom that I'm planning to come visit her, she pulls out her list. It's a list of dishes that I've tagged as my favorites, and this list has never changed in the past twelve years. Steamed fish Chinese style is always first, mainly because I could never get the flavors right when I cooked it myself. Every year, I'd bug mom about teaching me how to make this dish. And every year she brushes me off, saying, "aaahhh…too difficult…come home and eat!" Finally, I teased the secret recipe out of her last year and she revealed why she never taught me. She figured that the more I missed HER cooking, the more frequent the visits! Okay, so here are mom's secrets for making clean, fresh tasting steamed fish, just like the Chinese restaurants!

1) Buy fresh fish—well, duh. But I had to say it. Large Asian markets in big cities will have a fish tank brimming with live fish. You pick out what you want and the fishmonger will go fishin', do the dirty work and present you with a scaled, gutted and cleaned whole fish to take home. If you're dealing with already-still fish, you can either buy a whole fish or a large fillet. When buying whole fish, look at the eyes to determine freshness. Clear, protruding eyes means that it is likely to be fresh. Avoid fish with sunken, cloudy eyes. Touch and push down on the fish with your fingers. If it's stiff, firm and the skin bounces right back, it's good. If the fish is flaccid and the flesh is slow to bounce back, pass.

2) The biggest mistake I made before mom revealed her secret was that I steamed the fish and then served the fish with its steaming juices and herbs. The problem with this is that the juice in the pan is extremely fishy and the herbs already flavorless. After steaming, discard all the herbs and pan juices and serve the fish with a clean, fresh sauce and fresh herbs that have been "popped" in hot oil.

3) The last tip is to delicately steam the fish on medium heat. A high-rolling, harsh boil will tear apart the delicate flesh of the fish and finished dish will not look as pretty (plus you run the risk of over cooking the fish).

1 Clean your fish, pat dry. Season generously inside and out with the salt and pepper. Take half of (A) and stuff inside the fish.
2 Lay the other half of (A) in a shallow pan, this will be your "herb bed". If using fillets, just use all of (A) for the bed. Lay the fish on top of the bed. If the fish is too long, cut the fish in half. Pour the Chinese rice wine on top of the fish.
3 Add 2 inches (5 cm) of water to your large pot, cover and bring to a boil. When it is boiling, uncover and wipe the inside of the cover clean of any condensation (all this condensation will drip back down on your fish, diluting the flavor), put your fish pan inside, propping it up with a small inverted bowl. Steam the fish over medium heat (see Note for steaming times).
4 Prepare the aromatics: Towards the end of the steaming process, you'll want to start preparing the aromatics that garnish the finished dish. Take a microwave-safe bowl, add (B) and microwave for 30 seconds. Set aside. When the fish is done,

carefully lift the fish out onto a serving platter, discarding all of the cooked cilantro/ginger/green onions and the fish juice in the pan. Pour the hot (B) over the fish.
5 Now we'll work with (C): In a separate pan or wok, heat up the cooking oil until you see smoke. Add the ginger and green onions, fry for 10 seconds to "pop" the flavors. Pour the hot oil with the green onions and ginger over the fish. You'll hear a very satisfying sizzle!

SERVES 4 AS PART OF MULTICOURSE MEAL

1 lb (500 g) whole fish (or fillets 1-in/ 2.5-cm or thicker for the best results)
Salt and pepper
1½ tablespoons Chinese rice wine (or dry sherry) to pour on fish prior to steaming

(A)
4 green onions (scallions), cut into 3-in (7.5-cm) lengths
One 3-in (7.5-cm) piece fresh ginger, sliced into thin coins
1 small bunch of fresh cilantro (coriander)

(B)
2 tablespoons coarsely chopped fresh cilantro (coriander)
1 teaspoon sesame oil
2 tablespoons soy sauce
½ teaspoon sugar
Generous pinch of salt
¼ teaspoon white pepper (or black pepper)
1 fresh chili pepper of your choice, thinly sliced (optional)

(C)
2 tablespoons high-heat cooking oil
One 2-in (5-cm) piece fresh ginger, cut into thin slivers (use technique in Jaden's Ginger Tips, page 33, for using ginger as a condiment)
2 green onions (scallions), cut into 3-in (7.5-cm) lengths

SPECIAL EQUIPMENT
A shallow pan to hold the fish and a large pot or wok for steaming. (If you don't have a fancy steamer or steamer insert, invert a small, shallow bowl to use as a stand. I've also improvised with 3 shot glasses too!)

> **NOTE: Steaming Times**
> ■ **Whole fish 1 lb (500 g): check at 12 minutes, add 2 minutes for every ½ lb (250 g)**
> ■ **Fillets 1 inch (2.5 cm) and thicker: check at 10 minutes, add 2 minutes for every ½ inch (1.25 cm) or more thickness** ■ **Fillets less than 1 inch (2.5 cm): check at 7 minutes** ■ **Super thin fillets: check at 5 minutes**
> **Check to see if the fish is cooked through at the times indicated. Poke at the flesh near the top fin. If flesh flakes easily near the top fin, then it's done. If the flesh sticks together, then add 1 to 2 more minutes to cooking time. For fillets, just gently poke at the flesh at its thickest part. Also check to make sure you haven't run out of steaming water.**

Salt and Pepper Squid

I've always been a big squid fan, especially FRIED squid! I can eat an entire dish by myself, and if I ever were to open a movie theater, Salt and Pepper Squid would be served. Forget the popcorn! Squeeze just a bit of lime over the squid, and if you want, eat with a bite of fresh chilli pepper.

Try to find baby squid that has been cleaned for you. It saves you the hassle of removing the cartilage and the thin outer membrane. You can buy frozen uncooked squid—just defrost before using and pay very dry. Squid come in many different sizes. The ones that I like to use are smaller, with bodies about 4 inches (10 cm) long.

The combination of all-purpose flour with cornstarch creates a light and crisp coating for deep frying.

If you don't have a deep fryer, use your wok or a medium sauté pan. The smaller the diameter of pot that you use, the less oil you need but also the fewer squid you can fry in each batch. Which is why a wok is perfect! It's diameter is small at the bottom and gently tapers up. The secret to this dish is to use clean oil. Once you are done frying, let the oil cool and discard the oil.

SERVES 4 AS PART OF MULTICOURSE MEAL
High-heat cooking oil for frying
1 lb (500 g) uncooked squid, preferably about 4 inches (10 cm) long, cut into $^1/_2$-inch (1.25-cm) thick rings, leave small tentacles as they are
$^1/_2$ cup (50 g) all-purpose flour
$^1/_2$ cup (80 g) cornstarch
$1^1/_2$ tablespoons Sichuan Peppercorn Salt (page 27), plus extra for sprinkling over fried squid
1 lime, cut into wedges
Sliced fresh chilli peppers of your choice (optional)

1 In a wok or medium sauté pan, add enough oil to come up about $1^1/_2$ inches (3.75 cm). Set over high heat until the oil reaches 375°F (190°C) or when you flick a bit of flour, the flour sizzles on contact. Reduce the heat to medium to maintain the temperature. Have at the ready tongs and/or a spider and a sheet pan with a baking rack sitting on top to drain.
2 Rinse the squid in cool water and lay it flat on 2 layers of paper towels. Pat very dry with another 2 layers of paper towels.
3 Combine the flour, cornstarch and Sichuan Peppercorn Salt in a large bowl. Toss the squid in the bowl. When the oil is ready, use your tongs to grab a few pieces of squid, shaking off the excess flour mixture before lowering the squid into the oil. Deep-fry for about 60 to 90 seconds, or until lightly golden brown, and set on the rack to drain. Sprinkle some Sichuan Peppercorn Salt over the fried squid while hot. Repeat with the remaining squid. If the squid fries in less than 60 seconds, lower your heat. Serve with lime wedges and sliced chillies.

More Options
■ If you'd like a creamy dipping sauce, combine 1 cup (250 ml) of mayonnaise with 1 to 2 teaspoons Chilli Garlic Sauce or Sriracha chilli sauce and a pinch of sugar.
■ You can also use the Apricot Sweet Chilli Sauce (page 27), Sweet Chilli Sambal (page 26) or the Ginger Scallion sauce (page 28).
■ No Sichuan peppercorns? Combine 3 tablespoons kosher or fine sea salt with 2 teaspoons Chinese five spice powder.

Clams Sautéed in Garlic and Black Bean Sauce

Most of my friends have never had clams in shell other than in an Italian pasta dish. Oh, what they are missing! This shell-and-finger-suckin'licious dish is popular in Chinese restaurants.

Black bean sauce is the magic savory ingredient in this dish. Brands of black bean sauce and chilli garlic sauce differ in salt content. Taste as you thicken the sauce; you may also have to add an additional $^1/_4$ cup (65 ml) of light broth or stock to adjust.

You can use any type of clams, though I think the tiny ones taste sweeter. If you use larger clams, like the 2-inch (5-cm) or larger Cherrystone clams, you'll have to increase the cooking time. Take a peek and if not all the shells are opened, then steam an additional minute.

Have your fishmongers select your clams one by one. I know, it's a pain in the butt, but having even one bad clam in the lot can ruin a dish. The clamshells should be intact and should be tightly closed . . . unlike mussels whose shells may be slightly open, fresh clams should always have their mouths shut. Trust me, it's better that way. For tips on selecting and storing clams, see Shellfish Tips from John the Seafood Guy, page 39. The black bean sauce is great over rice so make sure you have plenty of rice to serve with this dish.

SERVES 4 AS PART OF MULTICOURSE MEAL

1$^1/_2$ lbs (750 g) Manila or Littleneck clams

2 teaspoons high-heat cooking oil

6 pinky-length whole dried chilli peppers, cut in half and most seeds discarded

1 clove garlic, finely minced

$^1/_2$ teaspoon grated fresh ginger (see Jaden's Ginger Tips, page 33)

3 tablespoons black bean sauce

3 teaspoons chilli garlic paste or sauce (substitute with any Asian chilli sauce)

1 cup (250 ml) store-bought or home-made light stock (Vegetable Stock or Seafood Stock, pages 31–32)

2 tablespoons Chinese rice wine (or dry sherry)

1 tablespoon minced chives, for garnish

1 Let the clams hang out in a big bowl filled with cool, fresh water for 20 minutes. This allows the clams to breathe in fresh water and expel any sand or grit. After 20 minutes, lift the clams out of the water (all the sand will have accumulated at bottom of the bowl). Now it's time to scrub the shells with a firm brush under cool running water. Discard any cracked and or opened shells.

2 In a wok or large sauté pan over medium-high heat, add the oil. When the oil is hot, add the dried chillies, garlic and ginger. Fry for 15 seconds, until fragrant. Add the black bean sauce and chilli paste and fry for another 30 seconds. Pour in the stock and wine. Turn the heat to high. When the mixture comes to a boil, immediately add the clams and cover.

3 Cook for 5 to 6 minutes until the clams open. Spoon out the clams, leaving the sauce in the wok. Discard any clams that did not open. Turn the heat to high and let the sauce thicken, about 1 minute. Taste the sauce, and add an additional $^1/_4$ cup (65 ml) of stock, if needed. Pour the sauce over the clams, sprinkle with chives and serve hot.

Coconut Shrimp

I had to choose just one recipe for you to try first in this book, this is it. In fact, this recipe is so simple that my kitchen-fearing friend, Jen, cooks this dish every time she wants to impress a date! (Oh my, she's gonna kill me for saying that!)

For this recipe, I'm using unsweetened shredded coconut found in health food stores and Asian and Indian markets. If you can't find it, use sweetened shredded coconut that you can find in your regular supermarket (look in the baking aisle) but omit the sugar in the recipe.

SERVES 4 AS PART OF MULTICOURSE MEAL

¼ cup (20 g) unsweetened shredded coconut
1 tablespoon high-heat cooking oil
1 lb (500 g) raw tail-on shrimp, deveined and patted really dry
2 tablespoons butter
4 green onions (scallions), cut into 2-in (5-cm) lengths
1 tablespoon finely minced garlic
3 tablespoons cognac (brandy or rum make good substitutes)
Generous pinch of salt
³/₄ teaspoon sugar (omit if you are using sweetened shredded coconut)

1 In a wok or frying pan over medium heat, add the coconut and toast until golden brown. This should only take about 3 to 4 minutes. Take care not to burn the coconut! Once the coconut is toasted, immediately remove to a plate to cool.

2 Wipe the wok or pan dry and set over high heat. When a bead of water instantly sizzles and evaporates upon contact, add the oil and swirl to coat. Add the shrimp to the wok, keeping them in a single layer. Fry for 1 minute, flip and fry an additional minute until almost cooked through. Remove from the wok, keeping as much oil in the wok as possible.

3 Turn the heat to medium, add the butter and, once the butter starts bubbling, add the green onion and garlic. Fry until fragrant, about 30 seconds. Pour in the cognac and add the salt and sugar. Stir and return the shrimp to the wok. Let the whole thing bubble and thicken just a bit—the sauce should lightly coat the shrimp. Remove from the heat, sprinkle in the toasted coconut and toss well.

More options

■ For a classic Malaysian Butter Shrimp dish, add 10 fresh curry leaves at the same time you are frying the shrimp. It will give an amazing warm lemony, sage-ish aroma. It's not the same as curry powder though.

Scallops with Tropical Fruit Salsa

This was the dish that really launched my food-writing career. Brian Ries, a food critic for a weekly paper called *Creative Loafing* contacted me for a story on "The $20 Showdown". The article featured five chefs, each contributing recipes for dinner for two, and only spending $20 in ingredients. Piece of cake, since usually I don't even spend $20 to feed my family of four!

After the story was published, *Creative Loafing* asked me to join them as their weekly food columnist. And they said I could write about anything I wanted! I was overcome with the joy of being published, but then that euphoria was quickly followed by "Oh crap, there's no "CRTL-Z button for the newspaper". That's probably the most difficult part of transitioning from blog to paper—there's certainly no morning-after delete function to erase anything embarrassing that I'd written! The Tropical Fruit Salsa is also great with tortilla chips, as a topping to grilled chicken, and to serve alongside your favorite fish or shrimp skewers. Use as much chilli powder in the Tropical Fruit Salsa as you want. I love the tingling sensation after the initial sweetness of the fruit. This is a great recipe to serve with Coconut Rice (page 130).

SERVES 4 AS PART OF MULTICOURSE MEAL
20 large scallops, preferably dry-packed
Generous pinch of salt or Citrus-Ginger Salt (page 27)
Freshly ground black pepper
1 tablespoon high-heat cooking oil

TROPICAL FRUIT SALSA
1 mango, diced
1/2 small papaya, diced
1/4 cup (40 g) diced red onion
2 tablespoons minced fresh mint
Pinch of Asian chilli powder or cayenne powder (or to your taste)
1 tablespoon lime juice
Generous pinch of salt or Citrus-Ginger Salt (page 27)
Freshly ground black pepper to taste

1 In a bowl, combine the ingredients for the Tropical Fruit Salsa. Gently toss and set aside.
2 Pat the scallops dry with a paper towel and season with the salt and pepper.
3 Set a large frying pan over high heat. When a bead of water sizzles and evaporates immediately upon contact, add the oil and swirl to coat. Carefully add the scallops. Make sure that the scallops do not touch each other—they should have a finger-width's space between them. Fry 1 1/2 to 2 minutes on each side. The scallops should have a golden brown crust and the interior should be just barely cooked through. Serve with the Tropical Fruit Salsa.

Tea Smoked Salmon with Cucumber Relish

Wok smoking is an age-old Chinese technique. Most popular is the tea-smoked chicken or duck, but salmon works wonderfully. The trick is to smoke the salmon low and slow as the gentle cooking creates an absolutely silky, feather-light texture. I learned this technique from Barbara Tropp, whose book, *The Modern Art of Chinese Cooking* has become my go-to resource when Mom's not available to give me her wisdom on the phone.

If you don't have a wok or pot big enough for the bamboo steamer, I highly recommend Helen Chen's Steamer Ring for about $5, which will let you use any stockpot with a bamboo steamer.

SERVES 4 AS PART OF MULTICOURSE MEAL
4 salmon fillets, about 6 oz (175 g) each
Generous pinch of salt
1 cup (210 g) uncooked rice
1 cup (70 g) black tea leaves
2 tablespoons Sichuan peppercorns
1 cup (200 g) sugar

SPECIAL EQUIPMENT
Bamboo steamer, wok and aluminum foil

CUCUMBER RELISH
1/2 cup (170 g) diced cucumber
1/2 cup (85 g) diced red bell pepper
1/2 cup (170 g) diced green apple
1 teaspoon minced fresh cilantro (coriander) or other fresh herb
2 teaspoons rice wine vinegar
Pinch of salt
Pinch of sugar

1 Season the salmon with the salt on both sides. Place the salmon pieces in a bamboo steamer. You should have no more than 2 to 3 pieces per steamer basket, as they should not be touching. If you crowd them too much, the steam and smoke will not be able to circulate.

2 Fold a large square of foil into quarters and place that on the bottom of the wok. This makes sure that the smoking ingredients do not burn. Next, line the wok with a large piece of foil. Pour the rice, tea leaves, Sichuan peppercorns and sugar in the middle of the aluminum foil.

3 Turn your heat to high and let the wok heat up. When you start seeing 3 to 4 thick, steady streams of smoke coming from the sides of the wok, it's ready. It should take about 8 to 10 minutes to heat up. Make sure that you get a good start on the smoke before adding the food, as we will be smoking on a low heat the rest of the way.

4 Once you start seeing bigger streams of smoke and can start smelling the wonderful aroma of the peppercorns and tea, turn the heat to low and place your bamboo steamer on top. Scrunch up more foil and place around the outside edge of the steamer to enclose the smoke so that it travels up and into the steamer, and does not escape out to the edge of wok.

5 Place the lid on the steamer and smoke on low for 10 minutes. Remove from the heat and let sit for another 10 minutes to finish cooking.

6 In a bowl, mix all of the ingredients for the Cucumber Relish. Serve the fillets with the Cucumber Relish on top.

More Options

■ If you're not up for smoking, I have another method of cooking salmon for you that will create the same slow-cooked, silky texture. Preheat the oven to 250°F (120°C). On a sheet pan, make a bed of orange slices from 2 oranges. Lay the salmon on the bed and slow-cook the salmon for 30 minutes. Discard the oranges and top the salmon with the Cucumber Relish. This is a must-try method. Though the salmon looks uncooked, trust me, it's fully cooked. The slow-cooking method preserves all of the natural flavors and colors of the fish.

SMOKING IN A STEAMER BASKET
1 Rice, tea leaves, Sichuan peppercorns and sugar are poured in the middle of the aluminum foil.

2 The salmon is placed in the steamer once big streams of smoke have begun to waft up.
3 Additional foil is scrunched up

and place around the edges of the steamer to keep smoke from escaping from around the edges of the wok.

Herb Crusted Fish with Sweet Chilli Sambal

For this dish any medium-firm to firm-fleshed fish fillet (say that 10 times fast!) will work beautifully. How about salmon, catfish, grouper or swordfish? Just shorten cooking time if you're using fish thinner than 1 inch (2.5 cm) thick. You'll find endless uses for this vibrant Thai Basil and Mint Oil. I like to use it as a finishing oil, drizzling it on just about any dish. Instead of discarding the spent herbs after straining them to make the oil, you'll slather them on the fish fillet. They create the most incredible herb crust that protects the fish from drying out while being pan-fried.

SERVES 4 AS PART OF MULTICOURSE MEAL
Four 6-oz (170-g) skinless, medium-firm fleshed fish fillets, about 1-in (2.5-cm) thick
Salt and freshly ground black pepper to season the fish
2 tablespoons herb puree (Thai Basil and Mint Oil, recipe below)
1 tablespoon high-heat cooking oil
2 tablespoons hot chilli sauce (or Sweet Chilli Sambal, page 26)

(MAKES 1 CUP/250 ML)
THAI BASIL AND MINT OIL
1¹/₂ cups (50 g) loosely packed fresh Thai basil leaves (discard stems)
1¹/₂ cups (50 g) loosely packed fresh mint (discard stems)
1 cup (250 ml) canola oil (or other neutral-flavored oil)
¹/₂ teaspoon salt

1 To prepare the Thai Basil and Mint Oil, have a colander and big bowl of ice water ready. Bring a medium pot of water to a boil. When boiling, add the basil and mint. When water returns to a boil, immediately drain the leaves and shock the leaves in the ice water. With your hands, squeeze all the water out of the herbs. You should be left with about ¹/₂ cup (100 g) of herbs.
2 In a blender or food processor, add the herbs, oil and salt and puree for 1¹/₂ minutes, until the mixture is well blended. In a fine mesh sieve over a bowl, strain the herb oil, using a rubber spatula to press out the oils from the herbs. Set the oil aside and reserve the pureed herbs for coating the salmon. You'll only use a few tablespoons of the Thai Basil and Mint Oil as a finishing oil on the fish. Store the oil in a glass jar in the refrigerator for about a week. Since the herbs are salted, go light on the salt when seasoning the fish fillets.
3 Pat the fish fillets very dry with paper towels. Lightly season the fish with salt and freshly ground black pepper. Spread 1 teaspoon of the herb puree on the top and the bottom of the fish fillet. Let it sit for 15 minutes at room temperature.
4 Heat a large frying pan on high heat, and when hot, add the oil. When the oil is hot, but not smoking, add the fish fillets, making sure that they do not touch each other. Cook for 2 minutes, flip. Turn the heat to medium and cook for 4 minutes, until the fish just cooked through (check the thickest part of the fish). Serve with the Thai Basil and Mint Oil drizzled on top (about 2 teaspoons per serving) and the hot chilli sauce on the side to taste.

More Options:
■ Any extra Thai Basil and Mint Oil can be stored in the refrigerator for about a week. You can toss it with cooked noodles for a great side dish. Toss with steamed vegetables and a squeeze of lime for a pop of flavor. Or you can add rice vinegar to taste and it becomes the most fabulous salad dressing in the world.

Asian Crab Cakes

These are the best crab cakes. Ever. I've got an eternal love affair with the ubiquitous Sriracha chilli sauce in the plastic bottle with green cap and a rooster on the front. "Sriracha" is too hard to say and spell, so my girlfriend Kelly calls it "rooster sauce" and you DO NOT want to know what our other naughty nickname for this sauce is (thanks Sarah of Tastespotting.com—you told me once and now it's stuck in my mind!). The crab cakes are super moist and the super light panko breadcrumbs gives it a fabulous crisp-crunch. The quality of crabmeat you use is important. I don't always have the time to hand-pick at a crab to harvest the meat (okay, truth be told, I do have the time BUT if you put a big 'ole pile of crabs in front of me and ask me to extract the meat into a bowl WITHOUT eating a bite, that would be total torture . . . a chunk of meat for the crab cakes, a big bite for me . . . one for the crab cakes, three bites for me . . .). I usually buy good quality crabmeat that comes refrigerated in a big 1-pound (500-g) tin or frozen in a pouch.

SERVES 4 AS PART OF MULTICOURSE MEAL
2 eggs
1 lb (500 g) good quality crabmeat
1 tomato, finely diced
1 green onion (scallion), finely minced
1 teaspoon grated fresh ginger (see Jaden's Ginger Tips, page 33)
Generous pinch of salt
Freshly ground black pepper to taste
2 teaspoons fish sauce
1 teaspoon freshly squeezed lime juice
1 to 3 teaspoons Asian chilli sauce (Sriracha preferred)
$1/4$ cup (30 g) plus 1 cup (120 g) panko breadcrumbs
2 tablespoons high-heat cooking oil
1 tomato, finely diced, for garnish
1 green onion (scallion), thinly sliced

SRIRACHA MAYO
1 tablespoon Sriracha chilli sauce (or any other Asian-style hot sauce)
1 teaspoon freshly squeezed lime juice
$1/2$ cup (125 ml) mayonnaise

1 In a large bowl, beat the eggs. Add the crabmeat, tomato, green onion, ginger, salt, black pepper, fish sauce, lime juice, hot chilli sauce and $1/4$ cup (30 g) of the panko breadcrumbs. Mix gently.
2 With your hands, gently form 8 equal-sized crab cakes. Do not squeeze too hard. It's easier if you form the crab cakes on a clean, flat surface and pat gently to form the cake.
3 Set a frying pan over medium-high heat. When it is very hot, add the cooking oil and swirl to coat.
4 On a plate, spread out the remaining 1 cup (120 g) of panko breadcrumbs. Using a small spatula, gently lift one of the crab cakes and set it on top of the breadcrumbs. Spoon some of the breadcrumbs on top of the cake and press gently to adhere. Immediately transfer the crab cake to the frying pan and bread the remaining crab cakes, each time transferring to the frying pan after breading. Sauté the crab cakes for 2 minutes on each side, until golden brown.
5 Prepare the Sriracha Mayo by combining the Sriracha, lime juice and mayonnaise in a small bowl. Stir well to blend. Top each crab cake with some of the Sriracha Mayo and top with diced tomato and thinly sliced green onions.

Meat

All my friends know that I simply love . . .
no . . . more like I'm infatuated with meat.
Yes, my vegan friends have tried very hard
to convert me, but I simply will not budge.
Simply seared peppered steaks on the grill
(by my husband, of course . . . I'm not
allowed to touch his grill), savory pan-fried
pork chops with a tangy, fruity sauce and
rich lamb spiced with a slathering of Asian
herbs. Yeah, I'm a meat-a-holic!

FAR LEFT TOP TO BOTTOM: Nathan kissing our very first broccoli from our garden; Why do I look so perky in the early morning? COFFEE; On set live at Tampa's CBS10 with hosts Marty and Dave during the early evening news.

Pork Chops with Plums and Sweet Spices

I had to make this dish three nights in a row in order to get a photo for this book. Not because I couldn't get the perfect shot, but because each time I made this dish its warming spices and juicy chops were just too much for my will power to resist a little bite here, a little bite there. Then, pretty soon, I was left with nothing to photograph but a pile of chop bones. This recipe is also a favorite of the group recipe testers for this cookbook! Serve with steamed rice.

SERVES 4 AS PART OF MULTICOURSE MEAL
4 pork chops, about ¹/₂ to ³/₄-in (1.25 to 2-cm) thick, patted dry with paper towels
Salt and freshly ground black pepper
1 tablespoon high-heat cooking oil
3 firm plums, cut into 6 wedges each (see Tip below)
4 whole star anise
1 teaspoon grated fresh ginger (see Jaden's Ginger Tips, page 33)
1 teaspoon whole pink peppercorns

SAUCE
1 tablespoon soy sauce
2 tablespoons sake (or dry white wine)
1 tablespoon brown sugar
¹/₂ teaspoon ground cinnamon
¹/₂ teaspoon ground coriander
1 teaspoon lime juice
3 tablespoons water

1 In a small bowl, combine the ingredients for the Sauce and set aside.
2 Season the pork chops on both sides with salt and pepper. Set a large frying pan over high heat. When hot, add the oil, swirling to coat. Lay the pork chops in the pan, bone pointing toward the middle. The chops should not be touching. Fry until the bottoms are nicely browned, about 4 to 5 minutes. Flip and cook for another 3 to 4 minutes until the center of the chops register 140°F (60°C). If you are using thicker pork chops, cover the pan with a lid, lower the heat to medium-high and let them finish cooking for another couple of minutes, or until they reach 140°F (60°C).
3 With tongs, remove the pork chops to a plate, leaving as much of the juices in the pan as possible. Cover the chops loosely with aluminum foil to keep warm.
4 Return the same pan to the stove on medium heat. When the pan is hot and the pan juices are beginning to sizzle, add the plums, star anise, ginger and pink peppercorns. Fry 30 seconds, until fragrant and add the Sauce mixture. Whisk and simmer on low heat for 2 minutes. Taste and adjust with additional lime or sugar if needed. The Sauce should taste tangy, sweet and warming from the spices. Pour over the pork chops and serve.

> **TIP:** Here's how to cut a whole plum into nice, even wedges: Lay your whole plum down on your cutting board, cleavage side up. Make a slice down ¹/₂ inch (1.25 cm) on either side of the plum cleavage. Then cut these "cheeks" further into wedges. This way, you're cutting around the seed instead of trying to pry it out.
> In case you're wondering, yes, there is a technical term for the plum's cleavage . . . it's called "meridian" but isn't it more fun to call it a cleavage???

Sweet and Sour Lychee Meatballs

During college, I snuck in a few appliances that weren't necessarily legal in my dorm room, but damn, did I eat well during nights of "stealth cooking". I had a little rice cooker, water boiler and a tiny electric stovetop burner. We indulged in instant ramen, steamed rice with unagi and one time I even attempted to make a sweet and sour dish from canned pineapples, ketchup and shrimp that I snuck out of the dining hall. Okay, so this is a sexier, more sophisticated version of sweet and sour, made with canned lychees. Normally, meatballs are deep-fried in sweet and sour dishes, but I've made it healthier by pan-frying the meatballs and then letting them simmer in the sauce. To save time, you can also purchase frozen pork or turkey meatballs and use those instead. In my house, anything sweet and sour must have rice to soak up the sauces!

SERVES 4 AS PART OF A MULTICOURSE MEAL
One 14-oz (400-g) can lychees, drained (reserve the juice for the sauce)
1 to 2 tablespoons high-heat cooking oil
1 red bell pepper, cut into 1-in (2.5-cm) chunks
1 green bell pepper, cut into 1-in (2.5-cm) chunks

SWEET-AND-SOUR SAUCE
$\frac{1}{4}$ cup (65 ml) juice from canned lychees
$\frac{1}{4}$ cup (65 ml) white vinegar
3 tablespoons brown sugar
2 teaspoons grated fresh ginger
$\frac{1}{4}$ cup (65 ml) ketchup
$\frac{1}{4}$ teaspoon salt

MEATBALLS
1 lb (500 g) ground pork
1 egg
$\frac{1}{4}$ teaspoon salt
1 tablespoon flour

1 Bring the Sweet-and-Sour Sauce ingredients to a boil in a saucepan, then let simmer over low heat for 5 minutes.
2 Cut each lychee in half, lengthwise.
3 Using a big spoon, combine the Meatballs ingredients in a bowl. The mixture

should be thick and very sticky. If not, add 1 teaspoon of flour. To form the Meatballs, put a good handful of the meat onto the palm of your hand and squeeze a ball of meat through your index finger and thumb (see photo). You may have to repeat this motion two or three times to shape the ball into a tight, compact and round meatball. Use a small spoon to scrape the Meatball off your hand and place on a plate. Try to keep all the Meatballs $1\frac{1}{2}$ inches (3.75 cm) in diameter to make sure they cook evenly.
4 In a large frying pan over medium-high heat, add just enough cooking oil to thinly coat the pan. When hot, add the Meatballs, making sure they do not touch each other. Fry 2 to 3 minutes, rotating the balls so that they become evenly browned. The middle of the Meatballs should still be uncooked, as we will finish cooking them in the sauce.
5 Add the red and green bell peppers and sliced lychees to the pan. Pour in the Sweet-and-Sour Sauce and cover with a tight-fitting lid. Let simmer over low heat for 4 to 5 minutes, until the Meatballs are cooked through. You may want to cut into one of the Meatballs to check for doneness.

More Options
■ Instead of ground pork, use ground turkey or chicken. Cut your simmer time to 1 to 2 minutes to avoid overcooking the meat.
■ How about pineapple, longan or rambutan instead of lychee?

Hoisin and Honey Glazed Baby Back Ribs

This is low and slow cooking at its finest. If you like fall-off-the-bone baby back ribs, you'll loooove this recipe. While it does take three hours to slow cook in the oven, it's only five minutes of active time—just stick 'em in the oven and set your timer. There's hardly any work involved—which is my kinda dish!

I must warn you though; this is not a dish you make when you're using your best table linens. The last time I made these ribs, Andrew and Nathan just sat at the dinner table and went full force devouring the sweet ribs. Nathan loved it so much that after his third rib, he turned to me and planted a sticky sloppy kiss right on my cheek.

SERVES 6 AS PART OF MULTICOURSE MEAL
5 lbs (2.25 kg) baby back ribs
Salt and freshly ground black pepper

(MAKES 1 CUP/250 ML)
HOISIN HONEY GLAZE
1 teaspoon high-heat cooking oil

3 cloves garlic, finely minced
1/2 cup (125 ml) hoisin sauce
1/2 cup (125 ml) honey
1 1/2 tablespoons dark soy sauce
1 teaspoon five spice powder
1 tablespoon chilli garlic sauce
2 teaspoons rice vinegar

1 Preheat the oven to 300°F (150°C).
2 With a knife or sharp kitchen shears, cut the ribs into sections with 5 or 6 ribs each (enough for a serving). Season the ribs on both sides with the salt and pepper. Place the ribs in a large Dutch oven or roasting pan (do not use a sheet pan—it's too shallow to hold in all the juices during roasting). You can stack ribs on top of each other, but try to crisscross them. Cover tightly with a lid or double layer of aluminum foil and slow roast for 3 hours (or up to 6 hours). Remove the ribs to a large sheet pan. Reserve any pan juice/drippings for another use (see More Options).
3 To make the Hoisin Honey Glaze, heat the oil in a saucepan over medium heat. Just when the oil starts to get hot, add the garlic and fry until fragrant, about 15 seconds. Add the remaining ingredients and simmer over medium-low heat for 10 to 15 minutes, until thickened and it coats the back of a spoon.
4 When the glaze is ready, turn the oven to broil and set the oven rack in the upper one-third position. Arrange the ribs in one layer on the sheet pan, meat side up. Generously spoon or brush the glaze on top of the ribs and broil for 3 minutes, until the glaze begins to bubble and caramelize. Keep an eye on the ribs to make sure you don't burn the glaze! Brush on additional glaze if you want before serving.

More Options

■ The pan drippings are so full of flavor! Here is a great idea from Michael Latham, one of my recipe testers: Refrigerate the pan drippings, then spoon off the layer of fat and discard. Strain the pan drippings in a fine-meshed sieve lined with cheesecloth. Freeze the strained drippings in an ice cube tray. Whenever a recipe calls for any kind of broth, use a cube for a rich, meaty flavor.
■ Add some of those pan drippings in the Miso Ramen soup (page 66).

Steak with Sweet Tomato Onion Sauce

This dish is a favorite oldie that I've had many times in western-style Hong Kong cafes in the U.S. The steak usually comes on a sizzling platter with a sweet and tangy tomato and onion sauce. Make sure you taste the sauce at the end of cooking to adjust the seasoning based on how acidic or sweet your tomatoes are. I love this dish with steamed Jasmine rice.

SERVES 4 AS PART OF MULTICOURSE MEAL
2 tablespoons high-heat cooking oil
Four 1 to 1¼-in (2.5 to 3-cm)-thick steaks (top sirloin, strip), set out at room temperature for 30 minutes prior to grilling
Salt and freshly ground black pepper
2 to 3 cloves garlic, finely minced
1 whole onion, sliced
3 tomatoes, cut into 6 to 8 wedges each

SWEET AND SOUR TOMATO SAUCE
1 tablespoon ketchup
1½ tablespoons rice vinegar or white vinegar
¼ cup (65 ml) water
2 tablespoons sugar
1 teaspoon soy sauce

1 In a small bowl, whisk together the ingredients for the Sweet and Sour Tomato Sauce.
2 Set a large frying pan over high heat. When a bead of water sizzles upon contact and immediately evaporates, add 1 tablespoon of the oil to the pan and let the oil heat up. You want the pan super hot to get the best sear as possible on the steaks.
3 While the pan is heating, brush the remaining 1 tablespoon of oil on each side of the steaks. Season the steaks with salt and pepper and carefully lay them in the hot pan, not touching each other. Cook for 3 to 4 minutes on each side or until they reach your desired level of doneness. Instant read thermometer should read 120°F (50°C) at the center of the steak for medium-rare. Remove the steaks to a plate and tent loosely with aluminum foil.
4 Return the frying pan to medium heat. You should still have some oil left in the pan. Add the garlic and onion slices and cook for 2 minutes. Push the garlic and onion slices to one side of the pan and add the tomato wedges. Cook the tomatoes 1 minute. Add the Sweet and Sour Tomato Sauce and simmer until slightly thickened and the tomatoes and onions are nicely coated with the sauce.
5 Now you'll have to taste and adjust. How sweet and how sour is a personal preference, plus your tomato may be juicy sweet or a bit acidic (make sure you taste a bit of the tomato too).
* Too puckery? Add ½ teaspoon of sugar.
* Not sour enough? Add ¼ teaspoon of rice vinegar.
* Need a little more salt? Add ¼ teaspoon of soy sauce.
* Sweet and sour too strong? Add 1 tablespoon water.
6 Pour the sauce mixture on top of the steaks and serve.

More Options
■ If you're not a fan of beef, try this sauce over cauliflower "steaks". Slice a head of cauliflower into ¾-inch (2-cm)-thick slices so that they resemble big, thick, roundish slabs. Cut enough for one slab per person. Season and pan-fry each side for 2 minutes (you might have to use 2 frying pans) in a bit of cooking oil until golden brown. Bake at 250°F (120°C) for 10 minutes until the center can be pierced easily with a fork. Remove, tent and make the Sweet and Sour Tomato Sauce to pour over.
■ I also really love this sauce on top of a piece of firm, grilled fish like tuna steaks.

Grilled Steak with Balsamic Teriyaki

This is a KILLER steak sauce or marinade! This recipe was inspired by a local Japanese restaurant called Vizen in Sarasota. The chef wouldn't reveal his super-secret recipe (which is totally fine, I respect that), so I spent many hours experimenting with ingredients to get as close as possible to their balsamic teriyaki. No need to use the super-aged good stuff, a mid-grade bottle of balsamic will do, as we will be simmering it and reducing it by half, which thickens and concentrates the flavors. For this recipe, I've used my favorite cut of beef, the skirt steak, and marinated it for a couple of hours before grilling. If you don't have the time to marinate, you can also simply season steak with salt and pepper, grill it to your liking and pour the sauce over just before serving. Of course, you don't have to use skirt steak. We are meat lovers, and I've made this sauce to serve with flank, sirloin, strip and rib eye too. When cooking with skirt or flank steak, the most important thing to remember is to slice the meat ACROSS the grain. See tips on page 62. This recipe is great with the Mashed Potatoes with Miso (page 121).

SERVES 4 AS PART OF MULTICOURSE MEAL
1 lb (500 g) skirt steak (or other steak of your choice)
2 tablespoons high-heat cooking oil (if cooking in frying pan)

MAKES ABOUT $^3/_4$ CUP (185 ML)
BALSAMIC TERIYAKI SAUCE
1$^1/_2$ tablespoons unsalted butter
1 shallot, minced
2 cloves garlic, finely minced
1 cup (250 ml) balsamic vinegar
2 teaspoons sugar
$^1/_4$ cup (65 ml) store-bought or home-made Beef, Chicken or Vegetable Stock (pages 31–32)
2 tablespoons soy sauce
1 tablespoon mirin (sweet rice wine)

1 To make the Balsamic Teriyaki Sauce, add the butter to a saucepot and set over medium-low heat. When the butter just starts to bubble, add the shallots and the garlic and cook for 3 minutes or until the aromatics are soft. Watch to make sure you don't burn the shallots or garlic.
2 Pour the balsamic vinegar in and bring to a boil. When boiling, immediately turn the heat to medium-low and simmer, uncovered, for 15 minutes, or until reduced by half. The balsamic should be thick, glossy and coat the back of a spoon. Add the sugar, stock, soy sauce and mirin. Stir well and bring to a boil. When it reaches a boil, immediately turn the heat to low and let simmer for 5 minutes. Let cool and reserve $^1/_2$ cup of the sauce for marinating and the remaining $^1/_4$ cup for serving.
3 If you're marinating the steak before grilling it, place the steak and just $^1/_2$ cup (125 ml) of sauce in a large sealable plastic bag. Marinate 2 hours or overnight in the refrigerator. Thirty minutes prior to

grilling, remove steak from refrigerator and let it sit at room temperature. Discard the marinade and pat the steak very dry.
4 Grilling Outdoors. If you're grilling outdoors on your barbeque grill (my preferred method), preheat the grill for direct grilling over high heat. **Grilling in Pan on Stovetop.** If you're cooking the steak on the stovetop, set a large frying pan or griddle over high heat. When a bead of water sizzles and evaporates upon contact, add the oil and swirl to coat.
5 Add the steak to the hot grill or pan in one layer. The pieces should not be touching. Cook for 3 to 5 minutes on each side for medium-rare. Skirt steak varies in thickness, so you might want to add the thicker pieces to the grill or pan first and give them an extra minute head start.
6 Let the grilled skirt steak rest for 5 minutes, then cut ACROSS the grain for ultimate tenderness. Pour the remaining $^1/_4$ cup (65 ml) of the Balsamic Teriyaki Sauce over the meat.

Korean BBQ-style Burgers

Korean BBQ is traditionally cooked with paper-thin slices of rib eye beef and marinated short ribs. This burger brings the same marinade into a party-friendly burger, inspired by friend Sarah Gim, founder of the popular food porn site, Tastespotting.com. If you're hungry and bored, do not…I repeat…do not visit Tastespotting. Whatever you have in the refrigerator will not look half as interesting as some of these reader-submitted food pics. When you eat Korean BBQ, you'll have about a dozen or so "banchan" or little side dishes of kimchi, seaweed, vegetables and tofu. It's fun to do the same for these burgers. Lay out the "banchan burger bar" on the table and let your guests create their own! The simple, Quick Cucumber Carrot Pickle is a wonderfully tangy burger topping.

MAKES FOUR $^{1}/_{3}$-LB (150-G) BURGERS
1$^{1}/_{2}$ lbs (750 g) ground beef
3 tablespoons finely minced garlic
3 tablespoons grated fresh ginger
2$^{1}/_{2}$ tablespoons soy sauce
2$^{1}/_{2}$ tablespoons brown sugar
3 tablespoons finely minced green onion
   (scallion)
2 teaspoons sesame seeds
Freshly ground black pepper to season
   the beef
2 teaspoons high-heat cooking oil (if grilling on stovetop)
4 burger buns

BANCHAN BURGER BAR
Tomato slices
Lettuce
Quick Cucumber Carrot Pickle (recipe
   below)
Kimchi
Ketchup
Sriracha chilli sauce
Hot mustard

QUICK CUCUMBER CARROT PICKLE
1 cup (150 g) matchstick cut carrots
1 cup (150 g) matchstick cut cucumber
$^{1}/_{2}$ teaspoon sesame seeds
4 teaspoons rice vinegar
$^{1}/_{2}$ teaspoon sugar

1 In a bowl, mix the ground beef with the garlic, ginger, soy sauce, brown sugar, green onion, sesame seeds and black pepper. Form into 4 equal-sized patties. For best results, form a slight indentation in the middle of the patty and shape them just under 1 inch (2.5 cm) thick as they will puff up during grilling, especially in the middle. Let rest for 15 minutes at room temperature.

2 In the meantime prepare the Quick Cucumber Carrot Pickle. In a small bowl, toss the carrots, cucumber and sesame seeds with the rice vinegar and sugar.

3 Assemble the condiments and garnishes of your choice for the Banchan Burger Bar.

4 Preheat the barbecue grill for direct grilling over high heat.

5 If you are cooking on the stovetop, set a large grill pan or frying pan over high heat. When a bead of water sizzles upon contact and evaporates, add the cooking oil. Place the patties on the hot grill or frying pan, not touching each other. Cook the patties 5 to 7 minutes on each side for medium (internal temperature of 150°F/65°C). Serve with the banchan burger toppings.

Vietnamese Banh Mi Sandwich

When I first met Todd and Diane of WhiteonRiceCouple.com, I knew instantly that we must have been eating buddies from another lifetime. They gifted me a massive basketful of fresh jackfruit, mangosteen, tangerines and blood oranges!

My boys and I feasted on Banh Xeo, a super crisp crepe made with mung beans and rice flour and played in their lush garden. This recipe for Vietnamese Grilled Beef Hoagies, or Banh Mi, is inspired by this young, generous couple. It's a favorite of my husband, who is mad about anything beef, especially sandwiches.

This Banh Mi has layers upon layers of flavors and textures, the thin, caramelized slices of grilled beef, sweet-sour Vietnamese pickled carrots and daikon and then the soft, sweet shallots. If you can, buy your meat pre-sliced or ask your butcher to slice it on their super fancy slicer. It just makes it so much easier! You can also get a frozen package of unseasoned beef for cheese steak or unseasoned thin-sliced rib eye that an Asian market normally sells for Korean bulgogi.

MAKES 4 SANDWICHES

1 tablespoon finely minced garlic
1 tablespoon fish sauce
1 tablespoon soy sauce
1 teaspoon sugar
½ teaspoon freshly ground black pepper
2 tablespoons high-heat cooking oil, plus more as needed, divided
1 lb (500 g) sirloin, top round or rib eye, as thinly sliced as possible
5 shallots, thinly sliced (or substitute with 1 onion)
Four 8-in (20-cm) hoagie rolls or baguette sections
8 large pieces leafy green lettuce
1 portion Carrot Daikon Pickle (page 31)
4 sprigs fresh cilantro (coriander)

1 In a bowl, whisk together the garlic, fish sauce, soy sauce, sugar, black pepper and 1 tablespoon of the oil. Add the beef slices and mix well to coat each slice. Marinate at room temperature for 30 minutes or overnight in the refrigerator.
2 Set a large frying pan or grill pan over high heat. When the pan is hot, pour in 1 tablespoon of the oil and swirl to coat the pan. You'll be cooking the beef in batches—how many batches depends on how big your pan is.
3 Add the beef slices, laying them flat

and in a single layer. Fry for 30 seconds to 1 minute, depending on how thin your beef is sliced. Flip and fry the other side 30 seconds to 1 minute. The edges of the beef should be just slightly charred, but the cooking time should be kept to a minimum to avoid overcooking the meat. Pour any juices left in the pan into a small bowl. Fry additional batches of meat slices in the same way, adding a touch more oil if necessary, and reserving the pan juices.
4 Return the pan to the stovetop on high

heat. Add a touch more cooking oil and when hot, add the sliced shallots. Fry for 30 seconds, until just softened, mopping up any remaining pan juices and caramelized bits during the frying.
5 To assemble the sandwiches, slice the hoagie rolls or baguettes in half lengthwise. Brush each side of the rolls with some of the pan juices. To each sandwich, add a layer of lettuce, then add some grilled beef, Carrot Daikon Pickle, grilled shallots and then a sprig of fresh cilantro.

Beef Satay with Peanut Dipping Sauce

This is a great party food, as eating food on sticks is always fun and easy. I like to use very thinly sliced beef and cook over high heat. The satay sears quickly, and allows me to get on with partying with my friends instead of slaving away in the kitchen. Cool, crisp cucumber slices and dipping sauce is a traditional accompaniment to satay. Serve with Coconut Rice (page 130).

1 Combine all the Satay Marinade ingredients in a large sealable plastic bag. Add the beef strips and seal, pressing as much air out of the bag as possible. Marinate the steak 30 minutes to overnight.

2 If you are using an outdoor grill, preheat the grill to high, direct heat. Skewer the steak strips onto the bamboo skewers, weaving them back and forth up the strip. Straighten the strips out along the skewer just a bit, so that it will cook evenly. If you are cooking indoors with a frying pan or grill pan, preheat the pan over high heat.

3 Grill the satay 1 to 2 minutes on each side, depending on the thickness of your beef. If your strips are thicker than $1/4$ inch (6 mm), add an additional minute to each side. Serve with cucumber slices and Peanut Dipping Sauce or the Cashew Nut Dipping Sauce on the side.

> **NOTE: If you don't have lemongrass, you can leave it out or substitute with $1/2$ teaspoon grated lime zest. To use lemongrass, cut away the tops of the stalk (we're only using the bottom 6 inches (15 cm) of the stalk). Peel away the outer leaves until you get to pale yellow leaves, which will become difficult to peel away. Thinly slice the stalk—I'm talking about as thin as possible. Separate the rings with your fingers and set aside for use in the marinade.**

SERVES 4 TO 6 AS PART OF MULTICOURSE MEAL

1 lb (500 g) flank steak or sirloin, sliced into $1/4$-in (6-mm) thin, long strips across the grain (For instructions on how to cut the beef across the grain, see page 62)

20 bamboo skewers (at least 7 in/18 cm long), soaked in water for 15 minutes

2 whole cucumbers, sliced into $1/4$-in (6-mm) coins

Peanut Dipping Sauce (page 30) or Cashew Nut Dipping Sauce (page 30)

SATAY MARINADE

1 teaspoon ground coriander

1 tablespoon thinly sliced lemongrass (see Note)

2 tablespoons minced shallots (about 1 shallot)

2 cloves garlic, finely minced

1 teaspoon grated fresh ginger (see Jaden's Ginger Tips, page 33)

1 tablespoon cooking oil

2 tablespoons soy sauce

1 tablespoon brown sugar

Chinese Beef Broccoli

I can't remember the last time I went to a restaurant and ordered Broccoli Beef. Love the dish, but there's nothing I detest more than goopy brown sauce that normally drags this dish down at most Chinese restaurants.

I want my broccoli to be tender-crisp and taste like broccoli, not just covered in thick sauce. My tip is to steam the broccoli separate and to use a minimal amount of cornstarch (it's only in the steak marinade). We'll simmer the sauce to let it thicken naturally.

But what about the flavor? The secret ingredient to the absolute best Broccoli Beef is Chinese black vinegar, which adds a mellow sweet tang. If you don't have Chinese black vinegar, substitute with good, dark balsamic vinegar.

Don't forget the steamed Jasmine rice with this dish!

SERVES 4 AS PART OF MULTICOURSE MEAL

1 lb (500 g) top sirloin or flank steak, thinly sliced into 1/8-in (3-mm)-thick strips
1 1/2 lbs (750 g) broccoli, cut into bite-size florets
1 tablespoon high-heat cooking oil
1 tablespoon minced garlic

BEEF MARINADE

1 1/2 teaspoons soy sauce
1 teaspoon cornstarch
1/2 teaspoon cooking oil
Freshly ground black pepper to season the beef

STIR-FRY SAUCE

3 tablespoons oyster sauce
2 teaspoons Chinese rice wine (or dry sherry)
2 teaspoons Chinese black vinegar (or balsamic vinegar)

1 In a bowl, combine the ingredients for the Beef Marinade. Add the beef and let marinate for 10 minutes at room temperature.
2 In a small bowl, mix together the ingredients for the Stir-fry Sauce.
3 In a wok or large sauté pan, add 1 inch (2.5 cm) of water and bring to a boil. Add the broccoli and cover to steam for 3 minutes. The broccoli should be bright green, crisp tender and you should be able to pierce the stem with a fork. Drain.
4 Discard the water in the pan and dry the pan well. Set the pan over high heat and when hot, add the high-heat cooking oil and swirl to coat. Add the garlic and fry for 15 to 30 seconds, until fragrant. Add the steak strips, keeping them in one layer and fry 30 seconds. Flip the strips and fry the other side.
5 Pour in the Stir-fry Sauce and stir to combine. Simmer until the sauce is thick enough to coat the back of a spoon, about 30 seconds. Add the cooked broccoli back into the pan and toss to coat well.

More Options
■ Use the broccoli stems to make the Broccoli Stem Pickle (page 30).
■ To keep this dish vegetarian, replace the beef with fresh, thick, meaty shitake mushrooms (cut in half) or even sliced portobello mushrooms.

Grilled Lamb Chops with Asian Pesto

The first time I made this dish, I was sooo excited that I ran circles in the kitchen! I love having a few dishes in my repertoire that is so freakin' easy that my younger brother could handle (just kidding, he's actually a pretty good cook . . . and he's single and get this, he's a DOCTOR. Yeah. I'm totally accepting bids for his phone number!) If you want those fancy grill marks, first of all get a pan that has grill indentations. (Or grill outdoors on your BBQ grill). After pre-heating your grill pan or barbecue grill, lay the chops so that the bone points to ten o'clock. Grill 1½ minutes, then rotate the chops (do not flip) so that the bone points to two o'clock. After another 1½ minutes, flip and do the same thing—lay them at ten o'clock, grill and then rotate to two o'clock. These chops go great with Mashed Potatoes with Miso (page 121).

SERVES 4 AS PART OF MULTICOURSE MEAL
2 lbs (1 kg) lamb chops (about 4 chops per person)
¹/₂ cup (125 ml) Asian Pesto (see page 31)

1 If the lamb chops come in a rack, cut apart the lamb chops between the bones into even pieces. Marinate the lamb chops in half of the Asian Pesto at room temperature for 15 minutes or overnight in refrigerator. Reserve the other half of the Asian Pesto.
2 Heat a large frying pan or grill pan on high heat. When very hot, add the lamb chops to the pan. Grill 3 minutes per side for medium rare.
3 To serve, spoon some of the reserved Asian Pesto on top of each of the lamb chops.

P.S. My bro is sooo going to be mad at me for this!

Chicken

I'm still a pretty frugal shopper. Nothing thrills me more than to find a chic outfit at 70 percent discount on the clearance rack! When it comes to chicken, I look for deals too (no, not the clearance rack) but pound for pound, buying a whole chicken is a way better deal as I can create at least three meals out of one chicken for my family of four!
1) a good stir-fry with the breasts,
2) Thai curry chicken with the thighs, and
3) chicken noodle soup with the bones.
And I always buy organic chicken these days. Not only is it good for you, the clean taste and silky texture makes a big difference!

FAR LEFT TOP TO BOTTOM: I'm a one-button princess! I love my rice cooker, can't live without it; Kids off to school; A little beach vacay for me and Scott.

Chicken Skewers with Honey and Turmeric

One of my very first friends that I made through blogging was Bee of Rasamalaysia.com and she gave me this recipe to include in the book. Bee marinates chicken wings in a Malaysian combination of turmeric and honey. I've made skewers from her recipe, perfect for the outdoor grill. Turmeric is a relative of the ginger, and the powder is a deep, bright golden-yellow that gives Indian and Southeast Asian dishes a majestic glow. Recent research found something that Ayurvedic medicine has known all along . . . that turmeric has incredible medical benefits.

I use the tops of green onions, minced, in much of my cooking, but my absolute favorite part are the bottoms grilled. Once grilled, they turn so sweet and mild. I took the hint from traditional Japanese yakitori and added the sweet green onion bottoms to these skewers.

1 In a large bowl, whisk together the ginger, honey, soy sauce, turmeric powder, Asian chilli powder and orange juice. Add the chicken and mix well to coat. Marinate in the refrigerator 30 minutes to overnight.
2 Twenty minutes prior to cooking, set the chicken at room temperature to take off the chill and soak the bamboo skewers in water so that the skewers don't burn on the grill.
3 Cut the green onion bottoms into 1 1/2-inch (3.75-cm) lengths. Skewer the chicken and green onion pieces, alternating each.
4 Preheat the grill to medium-high heat. If possible, leave one section of your grill on low heat. Grill on medium-high, 2 minutes each side and then move the skewers to the low heat to finish cooking, covered, for another 2 minutes. Watch the skewers, as the sugars in the honey and orange juice may caramelize fast!

SERVES 4 AS PART OF MULTICOURSE MEAL
1 teaspoon grated fresh ginger (see Jaden's Ginger Tips, page 33)
1 tablespoon honey
1 tablespoon soy sauce
1/4 teaspoon turmeric powder
1/4 teaspoon Asian chilli powder or ground red pepper (cayenne powder)
1 tablespoon freshly squeezed orange juice
1 lb (500 g) boneless chicken breast or thigh meat, cut into 1-in (2.5-cm) cubes
6 green onions (scallions), bottom 6 in (15 cm) only
12 bamboo skewers

Maridel's Chicken Adobo

I admit, I haven't cooked a lot of Filipino dishes in my kitchen. But it's not because I don't like Filipino food, quite the contrary. In San Francisco, I just lived two exits away from a plethora of Filipino restaurants, where a lunch buffet was only $4.99! How can you beat that? So I asked my Filipino sister-in-law, Maridel, for her family's adobo recipe.

Adobo is the national dish of the Philippines and refers to the combination of vinegar, soy sauce, garlic, bay leaves and peppercorn. You can adobo pretty much anything from short ribs to beans. Unlike traditional western cooking, the meat is browned in oil after simmering, not before. I like to use skin-on dark meat for the adobo as it won't dry out during the long simmering time. You can skip the browning if you run out of time. Serve with steamed rice.

SERVES 4 AS PART OF MULTICOURSE MEAL
1½ lbs (750 g) skin-on chicken legs and thighs
2 tablespoons high-heat cooking oil

ADOBO SAUCE
⅓ cup (80 ml) cider vinegar (or white vinegar)
¼ cup (65 ml) soy sauce
3 cloves garlic, minced
2 bay leaves
1 teaspoon black peppercorns
1 tablespoon sugar
½ cup (125 ml) water

1 In a large bowl, whisk together the ingredients for the Adobo Sauce. Add the chicken and mix to coat well. Marinate 2 hours to overnight in the refrigerator.
2 In a large, heavy bottomed pot on medium-high heat, add the chicken and the marinade. Bring to a boil and turn the heat to low. Cover and simmer for 20 to 30 minutes, stirring the pot halfway through to redistribute the sauce and chicken.
3 Using tongs, remove the chicken to a dish. Keep the Adobo Sauce on the stovetop and turn the heat to high to let the sauce thicken for 5 minutes. Use a spoon to skim off some of the oil that may be on the surface of the sauce.
4 Set a frying pan over high heat. When hot, add the oil. Pat the chicken skin dry with paper towels and carefully add the pieces skin-side down to the pan. Careful, if your chicken skin is not dry, it may splatter. Fry for 2 minutes until the skin is crisp and a wonderful golden brown. Alternatively, you can place the chicken skin-side up (pat dry first) on a sheet pan. Set the oven rack to the top level and broil for 3 minutes until the skin is nice and crisp.
5 Pour the Adobo Sauce over the chicken and serve over rice.

Hainanese Chicken Rice

This is one of Mom's signature dishes. If you like pure, silky, moist chicken, there's no better way to cook it than this recipe. The Ginger Scallion condiment is essential to this dish. Because the chicken is gently poached, the condiment provides that explosion of flavor—that zing—that makes this dish come alive. This dish can be served warm, room temperature or even slightly chilled. If you've ever had this popular Singaporean hawker stall dish, this is my quick variation of it.

Mom usually cooks this dish with a whole chicken, but using boneless chicken pieces shortens the cooking time to make this a 30-minute dish.

Don't throw out the poaching liquid! Season with salt to taste and serve as a warming soup with your meal. If you have time to cook the rice AFTER the chicken steeps, use the flavorful poaching liquid in place of water in the steamed rice recipe.

SERVES 4 AS PART OF MULTICOURSE MEAL

1 cup (250 ml) store-bought or home-made Mom's Chicken Stock (page 31)
2 tablespoons Chinese rice wine (or dry sherry)
4 cloves garlic, whole, smashed
One 2-in (5-cm) piece of ginger, sliced into 4 to 6 coins, and each coin whacked with the side of knife
3 green onions (scallions), cut into 3-in (7.5-cm) lengths
Salt to taste
4 boneless chicken pieces with skin on (breasts, thighs or a combo)
1 teaspoon sesame oil
1 portion Ginger Scallion sauce (page 28)
1 portion Steamed Rice (page 129)

1 In a large pot (with a tight-fitting lid), add the stock, wine, garlic, ginger, green onions, salt and chicken pieces and pour enough water into the pot to cover the chicken by 1 inch (2.5 cm). Turn the heat to high and bring the broth to a boil. Once it reaches a boil, immediately turn the heat to low and let simmer for 3 minutes. Skim the surface. Cover with a tight fitting lid and turn the heat off. Let the chicken steep in the hot broth for 20 minutes.

2 While the chicken steeps, cook the rice and prep all the ingredients for the Ginger Scallion sauce and have it at the ready. (Prep, but do not heat up the oil for the sauce yet. You'll finish the sauce just before serving).

3 Check the chicken for doneness by poking the thickest part with a chopstick or paring knife. If juices run clear, it's done! Remove the chicken, plunge in an ice bath, pat dry, brush all over with the sesame oil and let cool at room temperature.

4 With a small fine-meshed strainer or ladle, remove the garlic, ginger and green onions from the broth. Skim the surface of the broth if necessary. Taste and season with additional salt, if needed. The remaining broth is served as soup (or, if you have time, used in place of water to cook the rice).

5 Serve with the Ginger Scallion sauce, rice and the soup.

More Options

■ If you are going to cook this with a whole chicken (use a small 3 1/2-lb/1.6-kg chicken), like the traditional Hainan Chicken, double the amount of chicken broth. To the pot, add the whole chicken, chicken broth, wine, ginger, green onion, garlic and salt. Bring to a boil, then turn the heat to low and simmer the chicken for 15 minutes. Turn off the heat and let steep for 40 minutes. Check doneness. Plunge the whole chicken in ice water bath, pat dry, then brush with sesame oil all over. Let cool enough to handle. Use some of the poaching broth in place of water to cook the rice (page 129) and the remaining poaching broth as soup. Carve the chicken and serve with the Ginger Scallion sauce, flavorful rice and soup.

Pan-fried Mango Chicken

It amazes some of my friends that I can whip, whirr and stir up a meal with whatever I can find in the kitchen or farmer's market. It's not that I have countless recipes memorized—oh, quite the contrary. The talent comes from nothing more than learning just a handful of cooking methods and then adapting them to the ingredients you have on hand.

This pan-frying technique originally comes from chef and author Nigel Slater. I use his basic formula for chicken and add my own touches with curry powder and luscious mango chunks. The garlic mellows out and softens during the cooking, and the perfect bite is a bit of mango, a bit of garlic and juicy chicken. You can purchase a whole chicken, carve it yourself and save the bones for soup (page 31). But if you're too chicken to carve it yourself, buy already cut-up chicken. If you'd like to use boneless pieces, cut the cooking time by a few minutes.

SERVES 4 AS PART OF MULTICOURSE MEAL
1 tablespoon high-heat cooking oil
One whole chicken (about 3$\frac{1}{2}$ lbs/1.6 kg), cut into 8 pieces (leave skin on)
1 teaspoon curry powder
Salt and freshly ground black pepper
2 tablespoons butter
10 cloves garlic, peeled and left whole
1 cup (250 ml) store-bought or home-made Vegetable or Mom's Chicken Stock (pages 31–32)
2 teaspoons rice vinegar
1 mango, peeled and cut into 1-in (2.5-cm) chunks
2 tablespoons minced fresh mint

1 Drizzle the oil all over the chicken and season with the curry powder, salt and pepper.
2 Heat a large sauté pan over high heat and add the butter. When the pan is hot and the butter is bubbling, add the chicken pieces to the pan, skin side down. Fry until the skin turns a golden brown. Add the garlic cloves to the pan, filling in the space between the chicken pieces. Turn the heat to medium-low and cover with a tight-fitting lid.
3 Cook for 15 minutes, then flip the chicken. Cover again and cook an additional 15 to 20 minutes until the chicken is cooked through and no longer pink near the bone.
4 Use tongs to remove the chicken to a platter and tent loosely with aluminum foil to keep warm. Tilt the pan and spoon out some of the fat. Turn the heat to high, pour in the stock and rice vinegar and, with a wooden spoon or spatula, scrape the yummy bits off the bottom of the pan.
5 Add the mango chunks and fresh mint to the pan and let cook for 1 minute. Taste the sauce and season with additional salt if needed. Pour over the chicken pieces and serve with Steamed Rice (page 129).

Thai Coconut Chicken Curry

I call Thai curry my "emergency hurricane food" because in Florida, every year right around late August, we start getting some nasty hurricanes. I always like to keep a ton of food on hand, just in case I have an urge to host a dinner party in the middle of emergency evacuation. When our area is instructed to hunker down for the storm, guess whose house everyone comes to? Most of the ingredients in my Thai curry are from canned goods, like curry paste, coconut milk, baby corn and bamboo shoots. You can even skip the chicken altogether and substitute canned straw mushrooms.

How much curry paste to use is totally up to you. I prefer a spicier curry, so I use 4 ounces (125 g) of Maesri brand curry paste. My advice is if this is your first time making curry and you are spice-shy, start with half of the amount. You can always whisk in more later. If you find that you've added too much curry paste, just add a bit more coconut milk or water if you need to dilute. It's a good idea to read the instructions on your can of paste if you are using a different brand.

To enhance the canned curry paste, I add fish sauce, sugar, Thai basil and kaffir lime leaves, but that's totally optional. The more "enhancers" you add to the curry, the better tasting it will be. For tips on coconut milk, see page 20.

SERVES 5 TO 7 (WHEN SERVED WITH RICE)

4 oz (125 g) Thai curry paste

4 cups (1 liter) coconut milk, divided

1 tablespoon fish sauce

1 teaspoon sugar

3 fresh kaffir lime leaves, torn (optional)

6 oz (175 g) skinless, boneless chicken, cut into thin, bite-size pieces

One 8-oz (250-g) fresh or canned sliced bamboo shoots

One 15-oz (430-g) can baby corn, cut in half lengthwise

1/2 red onion, sliced

1/2 cup (12 g) loosely packed fresh Thai basil or sweet Italian basil leaves

1 Add the curry paste to a medium pot and turn the heat to medium-low. As the pot heats up, the curry paste will begin to fry, release its oils and become fragrant. It's best to keep the heat fairly low as you are doing this—otherwise you may burn the curry paste.

2 When the pot is hot and the curry paste is fragrant, pour in half of the coconut milk and turn the heat to high. Whisk until the curry paste has dissolved into the coconut milk. Pour in the remaining coconut milk, fish sauce, sugar and kaffir lime leaves. Bring the curry to a gentle boil and then add the chicken slices, bamboo shoots, baby corn and red onion. Stir well and simmer for 3 to 5 minutes, until the chicken has been cooked through. Timing depends on how thin you've sliced your chicken. Turn off the heat, stir in the basil leaves and serve with steamed Jasmine rice (page 129).

Thai-style Chicken in Sweet Chilli Sauce

Despite its name, sweet chilli sauce is not spicy at all—it's sweet with just a teeniest tiniest tinge of heat. The sauce is gorgeous with bits of chilli floating in the sauce. The kids like to dip French fries and chicken nuggets in it! If you don't have kaffir lime leaves, just leave them out of the recipe. The rest of the dish has so many different flavors that I promise you won't miss it!

1 In a large bowl, make the cornstarch slurry by stirring together 2 teaspoons of soy sauce and cornstarch until the cornstarch has dissolved. Add the chicken and toss to coat well. Marinate for 10 minutes at room temperature.

2 Set a wok or large frying pan over high heat. When a bead of water sizzles and evaporates upon contact, add the oil and swirl to coat. Add the chicken slices in one layer and cook for 2 minutes, flipping halfway. Remove the chicken from the wok, keeping as much oil in the pan as possible. The interior of the chicken will still be raw (it will get added back into the wok to finish cooking).

3 Lower the heat to medium and add the shallots, kaffir lime leaves and garlic. Stir-fry for 30 seconds. Add the red and yellow bell peppers and stir-fry for 1 minute, until the peppers are softened, but still have a nice crunch to them. Pour in the fish sauce, soy sauce and sweet chilli sauce and stir well. Add the chicken pieces back to the pan and let the entire thing simmer for 2 minutes. The chicken should have finished cooking (cut into a piece and check) and the sauce should be glossy and thickened. Turn off the heat and stir in the fresh basil leaves.

SERVES 4 (WHEN SERVED WITH RICE)

Cornstarch slurry: 2 teaspoons soy sauce plus ½ teaspoon cornstarch

1 lb (500 g) boneless chicken, sliced into thin, pinky sized pieces

1 tablespoon high-heat cooking oil

3 shallots, sliced thinly

2 fresh kaffir lime leaves, sliced into thin slivers (optional)

2 cloves garlic, minced

1 red bell pepper, thinly sliced

1 yellow bell pepper, thinly sliced

2 teaspoons fish sauce

2 tablespoons soy sauce

¼ cup (65 ml) sweet chilli sauce

1 small handful fresh Thai basil or sweet Italian basil leaves (about ¼ cup/12 g)

Baked Crispy Chicken with Citrus Teriyaki Sauce

Look how crunchy crispy the coating on the chicken is! Ya think I fried it? Nope! I've lightened the traditional dish by baking the chicken instead, a technique that I've adapted from the cool cats at *Cooks Illustrated*. The chicken is coated with Japanese panko, which are marvelously flakey and feather light breadcrumbs.

The Citrus Teriyaki Dipping Sauce is light, tangy and perfect for dipping. My kids like it when I cut up the strips for them, and they eat them like chicken fingers. Serve these with steamed rice or Mashed Potatoes with Miso (page 121).

SERVES 4 AS PART OF MULTICOURSE MEAL
½ cup (50 g) all-purpose flour
2 eggs
1 cup (120 g) panko breadcrumbs
1 lb (500 g) boneless, skinless chicken
    breasts
Salt and freshly ground black pepper
Nonstick cooking spray

CITRUS TERIYAKI DIPPING SAUCE
3 tablespoons soy sauce
3 tablespoons orange juice
3 tablespoons sake
3 tablespoons sugar
3 tablespoons mirin

1 In a saucepot, bring all ingredients for the Citrus Teriyaki Dipping Sauce to a boil. Turn the heat to low and let simmer for 6 minutes until slightly thickened.
2 Preheat the oven to 475°F (245°C).
3 Line up 3 shallow bowls. Put the flour in the first bowl, the eggs in the second (and beat with fork), and the panko in the third bowl. Also have nearby a sheet pan with a baking rack placed in it.

4 Pound each chicken breast to a ¼ to ½-inch (6 mm to 12-mm) thickness. Season each piece of chicken on both sides with salt and pepper.
5 You'll work with one piece of chicken at a time. Lightly dredge a piece in the flour on both sides. Then dip in the beaten eggs, making sure that you coat the entire piece. Then, pat in the panko, pressing gently to adhere the crumbs. While the chicken is still in the shallow bowl with the panko, spray the topside with cooking spray. Place the chicken piece onto the baking rack with the side you've just sprayed facing down. Then spray the other side with cooking spray. Repeat with the remaining chicken pieces.
6 Bake for 15 minutes, until the chicken is cooked through. Let the chicken rest for 5 minutes, then cut into several pieces. To serve, lay a bed of shredded lettuce on a plate, top with the sliced chicken pieces and serve with the Citrus Teriyaki Dipping Sauce.

Sweet and Sour Chicken

This dish is for my husband, Scott, who totally digs the standard Chinese take-out. The only time we eat out at Chinese restaurants is if we're visiting Mom and Dad in Los Angeles for some authentic dim sum fare. But at home in Florida, I'd just rather make simple Chinese dishes at home than to spend money on so-so take-out. But after 2 years of living in Florida, Scott started showing interest in shopping and offered to take me to the mall several times. What kind of wife would I be if I didn't take up on his kind offer?

And then it hit me. He wanted to take me to the mall because he was craving Panda Express, a Chinese fast food chain located in malls and airports. I'd be in the dressing room, shimmying into some fancy jeans and Scott would sneak off, order Sweet and Sour Chicken or Orange Chicken and scoff it down. Ahhh . . . my American husband was craving the Chinese-American classics that I never really cooked at home. Serve over steamed rice.

SERVES 4 AS PART OF MULTICOURSE MEAL

1 egg white
2 teaspoons cornstarch
$^1/_2$ teaspoon salt, divided
1 lb (500 g) boneless and skinless chicken thighs or breasts, cut into 1-in (2.5-cm) chunks
One 10-oz (300-g) can pineapple chunks (reserve the juice)
1 teaspoon grated fresh ginger (see Jaden's Ginger Tips, page 33)
$^1/_4$ cup (65 ml) white vinegar
$^1/_4$ cup (65 ml) ketchup
2 to 3 tablespoons brown sugar
2 tablespoons high-heat cooking oil, divided
1 red bell pepper, cut into 1-in (2.5-cm) chunks
1 yellow bell pepper, cut into 1-in (2.5-cm) chunks

1 In a bowl, whisk together the egg white, cornstarch and $^1/_4$ teaspoon of the salt. Add the chicken pieces and stir to coat evenly. Let sit for 15 minutes at room temperature or up to overnight in the refrigerator.

2 In the meantime, whisk together $^1/_4$ cup (65 ml) the reserved pineapple juice, ginger, vinegar, ketchup, brown sugar and the remaining $^1/_4$ teaspoon of salt.

3 Set a wok or large sauté pan over high heat. When a bead of water instantly sizzles and evaporates, pour in 1 tablespoon of the oil and swirl to coat. Add the red and yellow bell peppers and cook for 2 minutes. Remove from the wok onto a plate. Wipe the wok or pan dry.

4 Return the wok to the stove on high heat. When a bead of water instantly sizzles and evaporates, pour in the remaining 1 tablespoon of oil and swirl to coat. Add the chicken, spreading it out in one layer. Let the chicken fry, untouched for 1 minute, until the bottoms are browned. Flip and fry the other side the same for 1 minute. The chicken should still be pinkish in the middle.

5 Add the cooked bell peppers, pineapple chunks and the pineapple juice mixture. Let simmer for 1 to 2 minutes, until the chicken is cooked through.

Stir-Fried Chicken with Roasted Eggplant

This is a healthier, lighter version of the Chinese classic. The eggplant is a porous vegetable, and like a sponge, soaks up a lot of oil when fried. Roasting the eggplants first creates a very delicate, silky texture. Find the slender lilac or violet Asian eggplant, as they are sweeter and less bitter than the round, bulbous globe variety. Choose a firm, heavy eggplant with no wrinkles. Make sure that you pierce the eggplant several times to let the steam escape. Failure to do so will result in an exploding eggplant in your oven! (Trust me . . . it's a pain in the butt to clean!)

Most of the time, you'll see eggplant sliced on the diagonal, but since we're roasting it whole, it's difficult to slice once it's cooked. I thought I'd have a little fun cutting the eggplant the way I learned in Japan, with a bamboo skewer. You'll get strands and ribbons of silky eggplant. Lay the eggplant on its side, hold by the cap and insert a bamboo skewer or toothpick just under the cap and slide to the end. Rotate and just keep doing that all around. You can cut off the cap and discard, but my kids loved the way it looked just like this.

3 to 4 Asian eggplants, about 5 oz (150 g) each
1 teaspoon sesame oil
6 oz (175 g) ground chicken
1 tablespoon Chinese rice wine (or dry sherry)
1 tablespoon Chinese black vinegar (or good quality balsamic vinegar)
1½ tablespoons soy sauce
½ teaspoon sugar
¼ cup (65 ml) store-bought or home-made Vegetable or Mom's Chicken Stock (pages 31–32) or water
1 tablespoon high-heat cooking oil
2 cloves garlic, finely minced
1 teaspoon grated fresh ginger
1 green onion (scallion), thinly sliced on the diagonal

1 Preheat the oven to 450°F (230°C).
2 With a fork, pierce the eggplant several times all around to let the steam escape. Arrange the eggplants on a sheet pan and roast for 20 to 25 minutes, depending on the thickness of the eggplant. The skin should be wrinkly and you should be able to pierce it very easily with a fork. Remove and let cool on a rack. When the eggplant is cool enough to handle, brush the eggplants with the sesame oil. Hold the eggplant by the cap and insert a bamboo skewer or toothpick right under the cap and slide down to create long strands. Cut the cap off and discard if you'd like.
3 Spread the ground chicken out onto a cutting board. Use your cleaver or chef's knife to rat-tat-tat chop and mince the ground chicken further. Ground chicken has little fat, and mincing will help loosen up and create a lighter texture.
4 In a small bowl, mix together the wine, black vinegar, soy sauce, sugar and stock or water.
5 Set a wok or large sauté pan over high heat. When a bead of water sizzles upon contact and evaporates, add the cooking oil, swirl to coat. Add the garlic and ginger and cook until fragrant, about 15-30 seconds. Add the chicken and stir-fry until almost cooked through, about 3 minutes. Pour in the rice wine mixture and add the cooked eggplant. Cook for 1 minute. Scatter green onions on top.

CHICKEN

Veg, Tofu & Eggs

My brother lives waaaayy over there in California and, since he's a doctor and I'm an obsessed, sleep-deprived blogger, we get along just fine via instant messaging. Since I've been writing this book, we've been chatting online about our early food memories and stories growing up. When we were little, I was a fast and furious chopstick weasel, able to grab, tweeze and tease the tiniest bit of food morsel. And back then, neither my brother nor I were hot on veggies, and when I caught his eyes away from his plate, I'd quick-as-flash fling my veggies onto his plate. I finally fessed up to him via instant messaging tonight. Oh boy is he pissed at me!

FAR LEFT FROM TOP TO BOTTOM: Celery is cheap, plentiful and flavors many of my soups; Scott, me, Mom and Dad—celebrating my 8/8/08 birthday in Vegas (yeah, that's a tiara I'm wearing on my birthday!); Japanese shimeji mushrooms.

Garlicky Tofu and Spinach

If Popeye were Asian, he'd surely include tofu in his diet! That canned spinach has got to go, though. Who even eats canned spinach anymore when fresh is so easy to cook? Well I guess ripping off the bottom stems of the spinach and peeling back the plastic off the tub of tofu just doesn't have the same cartoon appeal as popping open a can of spinach with his bare hands.

My Garlicky Tofu and Spinach stir-fry includes a light sauce that gently coats the tofu. Try not to move the tofu too much in the pan, or it will crumble and break.

SERVES 4 AS PART OF MULTICOURSE MEAL

1½ tablespoons soy sauce
1 teaspoon cornstarch
2 tablespoons water
1 teaspoon sesame oil
1 generous dash of ground white pepper
   (or black pepper)
1 generous dash of sugar

1 tablespoon high-heat cooking oil
3 cloves garlic, finely minced
½ lb (250 g) fresh spinach, washed and
   trimmed
Generous pinch of salt
One 16-oz (500 g) block firm or medium-
   firm tofu, cut into 1-in (2.5-cm) cubes

1 In a small bowl, mix together the soy sauce, cornstarch, water, sesame oil, pepper and sugar.

2 In a wok or large frying pan, add the cooking oil and the garlic and turn the heat to medium-high. Let the oil and garlic warm up in the oil and when the oil is hot and the garlic is fragrant, add the spinach to the pan and immediately start stir-frying to mix the garlicky oil all over the spinach. Sprinkle the salt over the spinach and fry for 30 seconds.

3 Add the tofu cubes and pour the soy sauce mixture all over. Turn the heat to low, cover the wok and let cook for 1 minute.

Pan-fried Tofu with Dark Sweet Soy Sauce

This is the perfect tofu dish to make for tofu-virgins because of the crisp-crunchy texture of the tofu paired with a richly colored sweet and slightly spicy sauce. When I'm making this for the kids, I'll leave out the chilli garlic sauce and they will happily eat as much as I put on their plates.

Use firm tofu for this recipe; anything softer will be more difficult to pan-fry. You'll also press the tofu between large plates or cutting boards to extract the water, which will make the tofu even more firm and its texture more hearty.

Those cute green onion curls are easy to make. Use a knife or kitchen shears to cut the green onion lengthwise into super thin strips. Let them soak in icy-cold water for 10 minutes and then drain.

SERVES 4 AS PART OF MULTICOURSE MEAL
2 tablespoons Chinese dark soy sauce
2 tablespoons honey
1 teaspoon rice vinegar
1 teaspoon sambal oelek (or other chilli garlic hot sauce)
One 14-oz (400-g) block firm tofu
2 tablespoons high-heat cooking oil
1 tablespoon minced garlic
1 fresh chilli of your choice, sliced (optional)
1 green onion (scallion), sliced or chopped

1 In a small bowl, combine the soy sauce, honey, rice vinegar and sambal oelek. Mix together and set aside.

2 Cut the block of tofu into $\frac{1}{2}$-inch (1.25-cm)-thick slices. Place 3 layers of paper towels on a clean, dry work surface. Arrange 3 of the tofu slices on the paper towels and fold the towels over, pressing down to squeeze some of the water out of the tofu. Repeat with the remaining slices.

3 Set a large frying pan over high heat until a bead of water sizzle upon contact and evaporates. Pour enough oil to just coat the surface of the pan. Add the tofu slices to the pan, not touching each other. You might have to fry in two batches. Fry the tofu until the bottom is golden brown, about 2 to 3 minutes. Tofu slices should release themselves from the pan when they're ready. Carefully flip the tofu, away from you (the tofu may splatter) and fry the other side. Remove from the pan and drain on a rack or a paper towel.

4 Drain all but 1 teaspoon of cooking oil from the pan and return to medium heat. When the pan is hot, add the garlic and fry until fragrant, about 15 to 30 seconds. Pour in the soy sauce mixture and let simmer for 30 seconds to thicken slightly. Pour this sauce over the tofu. Top with fresh chilli and green onion.

VEGETABLES, TOFU & EGGS

111

Spicy Korean Tofu Stew

This is the best cold-weather dish ever and I make many variations of this stew depending on what I have on hand. Traditionally, this is a blow-your-socks-off spicy dish that will have even your eyelashes sweating. But you can adjust your spice level as you wish. If you can't find Korean chilli flakes, you can use regular chilli flakes in their place.

If you're vegetarian, skip the beef altogether and use a medley of mushrooms. When I'm in a seafood mood, I add shrimp and clams to the stew at the same time that I crack in the egg. Serve with steamed rice (preferably short-grained).

SERVES 4 (SERVE WITH RICE)

1 tablespoon high-heat cooking oil
3 cloves garlic, finely minced
1/2 lb (250 g) very thinly sliced beef
4 cups (1 liter) homemade or store-bought Vegetable, Beef, Pork or Chicken Stock (pages 31–32)
4 to 8 fresh shitake mushrooms
2 to 3 tablespoons Korean chilli flakes
1 tablespoon soy sauce
One 18-oz (550-g) block or tube of silken tofu, cut into large cubes
4 eggs
1 teaspoon sesame oil
2 green onions (scallions), sliced on the diagonal into 2-in (5-cm) lengths

1 Set a pot over medium-high heat. When hot, add the cooking oil and swirl to coat. Add the garlic and fry until fragrant, about 30 seconds. Add the beef slices and fry for 1 minute until browned. Pour in the stock, add the shitake mushrooms, chilli flakes and soy sauce. Turn the heat to high and bring to a boil.
2 Carefully add the tofu and return the stew to a rolling boil. Taste the stew and add additional chilli flakes or soy sauce if needed. Crack the eggs into the pot and let the eggs cook until the egg whites are white but the yolk still runny. Turn off heat, drizzle with the sesame oil and finish with the sliced green onions. Serve in bowls on top of the rice.

Green Beans with Preserved White Radish

Chinese love pickled and preserved vegetables, especially to eat in congee (rice porridge) or to stir-fry with vegetables. In this recipe we're using preserved white radish, or daikon, that is salted and dried. In China, this is called "lo bak gon".

The preserved radish is sweet, salty and has a slightly chewy crunch. Just a little bit of it will flavor an entire dish.

Each brand of pickled vegetables is seasoned differently, some are saltier than others, which is why you'll taste-test towards the end of the stir-fry and then add more soy sauce if needed.

SERVES 4
1 lb (500 g) green beans
2 tablespoons dried preserved radish
1 tablespoon high-heat cooking oil
2 cloves garlic, finely minced
2 teaspoons soy sauce
Pinch of sugar
$^1/_2$ teaspoon sesame oil

1 Fill a medium pot halfway with water and bring to a boil. Add the green beans and parboil for 6 minutes. Drain and rinse immediately with cold water. Drain thoroughly.
2 In a small bowl, add the preserved radish and cover with cold water. Swirl around for 30 seconds to wash the excess salt off. Drain and squeeze as much water out of the radish as possible.
3 Set a wok or large frying pan over high heat. When the wok is hot, add the cooking oil and swirl to coat. Add the preserved radish and garlic. Stir-fry until the garlic is fragrant, about 15 to 30 seconds.
4 Add the green beans and fry for 2 minutes. Add the soy sauce, sugar and sesame oil. Pick up a piece of green bean and a little of the radish and taste. You're looking for two things: to make sure the green beans are cooked through and tender-crisp and to taste for correct seasoning. If needed add an additional teaspoon of soy sauce.

Japanese Mushrooms Baked in Soy Sake Butter

Fresh mushrooms get a Japanese touch with this recipe. Cooking mushrooms can't get any easier than in aluminum foil! I like to use a combination of fresh shitake and enoki mushrooms. Use whatever fresh mushrooms your market carries—even non-Asian mushrooms are awesome cooked this way. Make sure that your mushrooms are relatively the same size (thinly sliced) so that they are cooked through at the same time.

If you don't have sake, you can substitute with a dry white wine or just leave it out. I've even done this with a splash of Japanese beer (and of course drinking the rest!). Shichimi Togarashi is one of the coolest Japanese spice mixtures. It includes chilli powder, orange peel, sesame seeds, ginger, seaweed and Japanese pepper. I sprinkle it on udon and soba noodle soups, steamed vegetables and of course these mushrooms. If you can't find it at your stores, try a blend of Asian chilli powder and sesame seeds.

SERVES 4 AS SIDE DISH

1/2 lb (250 g) fresh mushrooms, tough stems trimmed and cut into 1/8-in (3-mm) slices (see Tip below for preparation of enoki mushrooms)
2 tablespoons soy sauce
2 teaspoons sake (or dry white wine)
1 tablespoon mirin
1 1/2 tablespoons butter, cut into 3 pieces
1/2 teaspoon Shichimi Togarashi (or Asian chilli powder)
Aluminum foil

1 Lay out a long piece of aluminum foil, about 36 x 12 inches (90 x 30 cm). If you're using thin foil, it's best to double or even triple up to prevent ripping. Lay all the mushrooms in the center of the foil. Pour the soy, sake and mirin over the mushrooms, and lay the butter pieces on top. Fold up the foil so that the mushrooms are securely enclosed and the liquids do not spill out.

2 To cook the mushrooms directly on a gas stovetop, turn one of your burners to its lowest setting. Place the entire packet on the grate, right above the flame. Cook for 5 to 7 minutes until the foil packet is puffy and you can hear the sauce bubbling away. To cook the mushrooms under an oven broiler, place the oven rack about 8 inches (20 cm) from the heating element. Turn the broiler to high and broil for 5 to 7 minutes.

3 When the mushrooms are done, make a crisscross slit on the top of the packet, sprinkle with the Shichimi Togarashi and serve.

More Options:

■ If you forget to pick up aluminum foil at the store, you can also make this recipe in a frying pan. Heat a large frying pan over high heat. When hot, add the butter to melt. Add the mushrooms and fry for 3 minutes. Add the soy, sake, mirin and simmer for 2 to 3 minutes until cooked through. Sprinkle with Shichimi Togarashi and serve.

> **TIP: If you are using enoki mushrooms, cut the tough ends off and with your fingers, separate the bunches into several smaller bunches.**

Simple Baby Bok Choy and Snow Peas

Baby bok choy and snow peas only take a couple of minutes to cook, and steaming them in a light broth makes the dish so much better. Instead of heating up your wok or pan hot first, you'll warm up the oil WITH the garlic and ginger. As the oil heats up, it gently fries the aromatics, releasing its flavors into the oils. Basically, you're infusing the oil with as much flavor as you can prior to adding and frying the vegetable. This method will also prevent you from burning your garlic and ginger too! Once the oil heats up enough to add the vegetables, you'll toss the vegetables and roll 'em around in the beautiful garlicky-gingery oil to coat every single leaf. A splash of light stock or water will create enough steam to cook the vegetables.

SERVES 4

1 tablespoon high-heat cooking oil
2 cloves garlic, finely minced
1 teaspoon grated fresh ginger (see Jaden's Ginger Tips, page 33)
3/4 lb (350 g) baby bok choy, leaves separated
1/2 lb (250 g) snow peas
1/2 cup (125 ml) store-bought or homemade Mom's Chicken Stock or Vegetable Stock (page 31) or water
2 tablespoons oyster sauce
1/2 teaspoon sesame oil

1 Add the cooking oil, garlic and ginger into a wok or large frying pan. Turn the heat to medium-high. As the oil heats up, the garlic and ginger will sizzle and infuse the oil with flavor. When the oil is hot (be careful not to burn the garlic and ginger) add the bok choy and the snow peas. Immediately toss to coat the vegetables in the garlic, ginger and oil.
2 Stir-fry for 30 seconds. Add the stock or water and oyster sauce and bring to a boil. Cover and cook for 1 to 2 minutes until the bok choy is crisp-tender at the stem. Drizzle on the sesame oil and serve.

Tofu and Clams in a Light Miso Broth

I call this my zen-meal. Every aspect of this dish is soothing, from the mindful scrubbing of the clams, to my knife effortlessly gliding through the silken tofu, and even gentle stirring to melt the miso in the broth. It's clean, simple and you never feel stuffed after having a bowl! It's a perfect dish to make after a stressful day.

The silky soft tofu and feather-light enoki mushrooms are perfect just the way they are. They do not need to be boiled, but are simply warmed through in the broth. The type of Japanese noodles I like to use are called *hiyamugi*, sort of a cross between somen (thin) and udon (thick), but as always, use what you can find or have in your pantry.

You can use any type of miso you prefer—the white (shiro) miso is more delicate while the darker misos will be saltier and heavier.

SERVES 4 AS A LIGHT LUNCH OR HEARTY FIRST COURSE

12 oz (350 g) soft silken tofu, cut into 1-in (2.5-cm) cubes
¼ lb (125 g) fresh enoki mushrooms
8 cups (2 liters) water
2 teaspoons instant dashi granules
4 oz (125 g) dried Japanese noodles (soba, hiyamugi or somen)
24 small clams, such as littlenecks, scrubbed
3 tablespoons miso (any type)

1 Have 4 separate serving bowls ready, near the stove. Divide the tofu cubes and the enoki mushrooms among the bowls.
2 In a medium pot, combine the water and the dashi granules and bring to a boil. Add the dried noodles to the pot and cook according to package instructions. Use a pair of tongs or chopsticks to remove the noodles, reserving the broth in the pot. Divide the noodles among the bowls.
3 Return the dashi broth to a boil over medium heat and add the clams. When the clams open wide, about 3 minutes, remove the clams and add them to the bowls. Discard any that do not open. Turn off the heat and whisk in the miso. Taste and whisk in more miso if desired. Quickly ladle the hot miso broth into each bowl and serve.

Asparagus and Crab with a Light Ginger Sauce

Mom makes this dish a lot at home, either with broccoli or asparagus. She uses pre-cooked, packaged crabmeat. Mom taught me a few tricks about using pre-cooked crab-meat from the market. If you're using canned crabmeat, drain and discard the water in the can first. If using frozen crabmeat, defrost then lightly squeeze to get some of the excess water. Delicately toss the crabmeat with a little ginger juice, lemon juice and a dash of fish sauce. This will help give some flavor back to the crabmeat. Of course, if you have fresh crabmeat, even better! There's a lot of meat in a big snow crab leg, so sometimes I just buy one leg and pick the meat out of it to use in this dish.

1 Working over a bowl, use your fingers to squeeze the grated fresh ginger to release its juice. You should get about $^1/_2$ to $^3/_4$ teaspoon of ginger juice. Add the fish sauce, if using, lemon juice and crabmeat. Gently mix.

2 In a wok or large sauté pan, add the stock, sugar, salt and pepper. Bring to a boil. Add the asparagus and immediately cover. Steam on medium heat for 2 minutes, or until crisp-tender. Use a pair of tongs to remove the asparagus to a plate, leaving the broth in the pan. Drizzle the sesame oil over the asparagus.

3 Return the pan with the broth to the stove on low heat. Bring to a simmer and add the crabmeat mixture. Return to a simmer. Stir in the cornstarch slurry and let thicken, about 15 seconds. Taste the broth, and season with additional salt if needed. Pour over the asparagus.

SERVES 4

One 1-in (2.5-cm) piece of ginger, grated (see Jaden's Ginger Tips, page 33)

$^1/_2$ teaspoon fish sauce (optional)

$^1/_2$ teaspoon freshly squeezed lemon juice

6 oz (175 g) cooked crabmeat

$^3/_4$ cup (185 ml) store-bought or home-made Vegetable Stock or Seafood Stock (pages 31–32)

$^1/_4$ teaspoon sugar

Generous pinch of salt

$^1/_4$ teaspoon ground white pepper

1 lb (500 g) asparagus, ends trimmed

$^1/_2$ teaspoon sesame oil

Cornstarch slurry: $^1/_2$ teaspoon cornstarch dissolved in 1 tablespoon cool water

Three Pea
Stir-fry

My family loves peas every which way except for canned. What better way to please all than to stir-fry a combination of sugar snap, snow peas and shelled peas? Sometimes I'll stand in the kitchen and just eat them straight out of the wok.

The peas cook at different times, so I add the sugar snap peas first. At my markets, fresh shelled peas are hard to find, so I often grab a bag of frozen peas. No need to defrost—just add them frozen right into the wok!

SERVES 4 AS SIDE DISH
1/2 lb (250 g) sugar snap peas
1/2 lb (250 g) snow peas
1/2 lb (250 g) shelled peas (fresh or
  frozen)
1 teaspoon high-heat cooking oil
2 cloves garlic, finely minced
2 tablespoons soy sauce
Pinch of sugar
2 teaspoons sesame seeds

1 Wash all the peas. Snap and peel away the tough fiber that runs along the side of the sugar snap peas.
2 Set a wok or large sauté pan over medium-high heat. When hot, add the oil and swirl to coat. Add the garlic and fry until fragrant, about 30 seconds. Add the sugar snap peas and fry for 30 seconds. Add the snow peas and the shelled peas, and fry for 30 seconds. Add the soy sauce and sugar. Toss and cook until the peas are tender-crisp or to your liking, about 1 minute. Sprinkle with the sesame seeds.

More Options
■ Add some sliced fresh shitake mushrooms—just toss them in when you're frying the sugar snap peas.
■ If you've got a package of Chinese sausage (see page 19), take 1 sausage, dice it into 1/4-inch (6-mm) cubes and add them to the hot pan to fry for 1 minute before you add the garlic.

Fried Eggs with Tomato and Chinese Chives

In my backyard, I have a mini-garden with just a few of my favorite plants—tomatoes, Asian herbs, a kaffir lime tree and a variety of lettuces. When tomato season is in full swing, I'm always looking for different ways to cook them. Here's a super-easy side dish that combines the sweet/salty oyster sauce with perfectly ripe tomatoes.

Traditionally in this dish, the eggs are scrambled along with the tomatoes, but I find that cooking them together leaves you with soggy eggs and mushy tomatoes. By cooking them separately, you'll get a crispy edge (my kids favorite part), glorious runny yolk, and tomatoes that still hold their shape with just a slight char where flesh meets the pan.

SERVES 4 AS PART OF MULTICOURSE MEAL
2 tablespoons oyster sauce
2 tablespoons water
2 tablespoons high-heat cooking oil
3 large eggs, cracked into a bowl, keeping yolks intact
1 ripe tomato, sliced into wedges
1 small bunch Chinese chives, cut into 2-in (5-cm) lengths (see More Options for substitution ideas)

1 In a small bowl, whisk together the oyster sauce and water and set aside.
2 Set a large frying pan (nonstick is best) over high heat. When a bead of water sizzles upon contact and evaporates, add the oil and swirl to coat. Turn the heat to medium and add the eggs. Fry until the edges are crisp, the egg whites firm but the yolks still runny (sunny side up). If you want, you can tilt the pan and use a long handled spoon to spoon up some of the cooking oil and pour it on top of the eggs to cook them more quickly.
3 Carefully slide the eggs onto a plate, keeping as much oil in the pan as possible and return the pan to the stovetop on high heat. There should still be some oil left in the pan. Add the tomato wedges and the chives to the pan and let fry until the tomatoes are just warmed through and the chives wilted. Spoon the tomatoes and chives on top of the eggs. Return the same pan to the stovetop on medium heat and pour in the oyster sauce and water mixture. Let the sauce simmer for 30 seconds and drizzle on top of the dish.

More Options
If you don't have access to Chinese chives, you really can use any type of vegetable—green onions, regular chives, any herbs (sprinkle the fresh herbs, uncooked over finished dish), celery thinly sliced on the diagonal, sliced bamboo shoots, sliced red bell pepper, sliced mushrooms . . . be creative and use up the leftover bits of vegetables in your refrigerator!
■ You can also drizzle ¹⁄₂ teaspoon of sesame oil on top of the finished dish if desired.

Mashed Potatoes with Miso

My husband surprised me with a trip to Las Vegas for my 08/08/08 birthday (yes, I am really that lucky to have a birthday like that!). We had the best splurge meal ever at a restaurant called Japonaise in the Mirage casino—Kobe Rib Eye with Miso Mashed Potatoes. While Kobe beef is pretty pricey to cook at home, the potatoes are totally do-able. Here's my version of those creamy, dreamy potatoes. Of course, you don't have to use truffle oil. Any good extra virgin olive oil will be just fine.

I like cooking with shiro miso (white) but any kind of miso will work. Just know that the darker the miso, the stronger the flavor and saltier as well. Start with 2 tablespoons and you can always whisk in more.

SERVES 4 AS PART OF MULTICOURSE MEAL
2 lb (1 kg) Yukon gold potatoes (or Russet), scrubbed
4 tablespoons butter
2 cloves garlic, finely minced
2 tablespoons miso
1 cup (250 ml) whole or skim milk
Drizzle of truffle oil or good extra virgin olive oil
1 teaspoon minced chives

1 Place the potatoes in a saucepan and cover by 1 inch (2.5 cm) of water. Turn the heat to high and bring the water to a boil. Reduce heat to medium-low and simmer for about 20 to 30 minutes, until you can easily slip a paring knife in and out through the middle. Drain.
2 Peel the potatoes. For the creamiest texture, pass the potatoes through a ricer or food mill into a bowl. Alternatively, you can use a handheld potato masher or just smash with a fork.
3 In the same saucepan, heat the butter and the garlic over medium heat. Once the butter starts bubbling and the garlic is fragrant, whisk in the miso until it is completely incorporated into the butter. Whisk in about $3/4$ cup (185 ml) of the milk. Add the potatoes and stir. Add more milk, a little at a time, until you get the consistency that you want.
4 Finish with just a little drizzle of truffle oil or extra virgin olive oil and sprinkle on the chives.

Quick Omelette with Shrimp and Peas

My brother, Jay, always requests this dish each time he goes home to visit our parents, who live about an hour away from him. Luckily, it's a snap to make and only takes about 15 minutes from start to finish. The shrimp are split in half lengthwise, to make them easier to eat in one bite, and to allow me to stretch just a handful of shrimp to feed four as a side dish. Call me cheap, but hey it really works!

Cooking the shrimp separately from the eggs and makes them light and springy instead of being buried and heavy inside the egg.

1 In a bowl, combine the shrimp with the salt, cornstarch, sugar and ¹⁄₂ teaspoon of the sesame oil.

2 In a separate small bowl, combine the soy sauce, oyster sauce, water and remaining ¹⁄₂ teaspoon of sesame oil.

3 Set a wok or frying pan over high heat. When a bead of water sizzles and evaporates upon contact, add 1 tablespoon of the cooking oil and swirl to coat. Add the shrimp to the wok, keeping them in one layer. Stir-fry for 1 minute, until cooked through. Dish the shrimp out onto a plate, keeping as much oil in the pan as possible.

4 Return the pan to medium-high heat and when hot add the remaining 1 tablespoon of cooking oil. Pour the beaten eggs into the pan and gently scramble and fry until the edges are firming up but the middle is still runny. Add the peas to the top of the eggs and continue to fry. Pour the soy sauce mixture over the eggs and when the eggs are set, turn off the heat. Dish onto the serving plate and spoon the cooked shrimp over the top. Sprinkle on the minced cilantro.

SERVES 4 AS PART OF MULTICOURSE MEAL

¹⁄₄ lb (125 g) raw shrimp, cut in half lengthwise

Generous pinch of salt

¹⁄₂ teaspoon cornstarch

Pinch of sugar

1 teaspoon sesame oil, divided

1 teaspoon soy sauce

1 teaspoon oyster sauce

1 teaspoon water

2 tablespoons high-heat cooking oil, divided

4 eggs, beaten

¹⁄₂ cup (80 g) frozen or fresh peas

A few sprigs of fresh cilantro (coriander), minced

Asian Style Brussels Sprouts

Here's an Asian take on Brussels sprouts that highlights the salty, sweet, spicy and slightly sour flavor combination that's very typical of Vietnamese cooking. I've shredded them like cabbage and quickly stir-fried them in my wok. The Brussels sprouts still retain their fresh crunch and the Vietnamese seasonings really bring out the best of these little vegetables.

1 Trim the tough stalk end off the Brussels sprouts and thinly slice. You can also use a food processor with a shredder attachment to slice them if you'd like.
2 Set a wok or large sauté pan over high heat. When a bead of water sizzles upon contact and evaporates immediately, add the cooking oil and swirl to coat. Add the red onion and chilli slices and fry for 30 seconds. Add the garlic and fry another 30 seconds, taking care not to burn the garlic.
3 Add the Brussels sprouts and stir well to mix all the ingredients together. Spread the Brussels sprouts all over the surface of the wok to let it heat up and cook for 1 minute. Add the lime juice, fish sauce, sugar and salt and stir vigorously until all the seasonings are mixed throughout. The Brussels sprouts should be slightly soft at the leafy ends, but still retain a good crunch.
4 Taste and adjust with additional fish sauce if it needs a little more saltiness or a pinch more of sugar if the Brussels sprouts are slightly bitter.

SERVES 4 AS PART OF MULTICOURSE MEAL
1 lb (500 g) Brussels sprouts
1½ tablespoons high-heat cooking oil
½ red onion, thinly sliced
1 fresh chilli of your choice, thinly sliced
2 cloves garlic, finely minced
1½ teaspoons freshly squeezed lime juice
1½ teaspoons fish sauce (substitute with 1 tablespoon soy sauce)
½ teaspoon sugar
Generous pinch of salt

Chinese Broccoli with Oyster Sauce and Roasted Garlic

I will choose Chinese broccoli (gai-lan) over regular broccoli any day! But you've gotta make sure that you're getting fresh, young Chinese broccoli otherwise they can be tough and bitter. I've included tips (see facing page) on how to buy it.

As with many Chinese stir-fry dishes, the ginger in this dish is cut into ⅛-inch (3-mm) coins—the large pieces gently infuse the cooking oil and aren't necessarily meant for eating. When we cook family-style, my Mom just leaves the ginger coins in the finished dish, and we just push them out of the way when we eat. You can remove them prior to serving if you'd like. The whole garlic also infuses the cooking oil and after roasting, it becomes soft and yummy sweet. Sometimes, I double the amount of garlic cloves because I just love eating them and they are the "treats" in the dish!

SERVES 4

1 lb (500 g) of Chinese broccoli (gai lan) (see More Options below)
¼ cup (65 ml) store-bought or homemade Vegetable Stock (page 31)
1 tablespoon Chinese rice wine (or dry sherry)
½ teaspoon sugar
1½ tablespoons high-heat cooking oil
5 to 8 whole garlic cloves, peeled and gently smashed but left intact
One 1-in (2.5-cm) piece fresh ginger, cut into ⅛-in (3-mm) coins and smashed with side of cleaver
3 tablespoons oyster sauce
½ teaspoon sesame oil

1 Wash the Chinese broccoli and trim 1 inch (2.5 cm) from the ends of the stalk and discard. In a small bowl, mix together the stock, wine and sugar and set aside.

2 Heat a wok or large sauté pan on medium-low heat. Add the cooking oil, and when the oil is just starting to get hot (the garlic should sizzle slightly upon contact), add the garlic cloves and ginger coins and let them fry until golden brown on all sides. Be careful not to burn them; you just want to brown them on all sides. This should take about 2 minutes.

3 Turn the heat to high then add the Chinese broccoli. Use your spatula to scoop up the oil so that every stalk has been bathed with the ginger and garlic–infused oil.

4 Pour the stock mixture into the wok and immediately cover with a tight-fitting lid. Turn the heat to medium and let the vegetable steam for 3 to 4 minutes, until the stalks can be easily pierced with a paring knife or fork.

5 Remove the Chinese broccoli to a plate, leaving any remaining stock mixture in the wok. Pick out and discard the ginger coins. To the wok, add the oyster sauce and sesame oil and bubble and thicken on high heat for 1 minute. Pour the sauce mixture over the Chinese broccoli and serve.

More Options
■ You can use this same recipe to cook yu choy (Chinese spinach), bok choy or even regular broccoli. Just decrease your steam time to 2 minutes, as these are thinner vegetables.

THE STEAMY KITCHEN COOKBOOK

124

TIP: HOW TO BUY CHINESE BROCCOLI

Chinese broccoli are sold in bunches, so select a bunch and look at the ends of the stalk. If they are dry, crusty and shriveled. Don't buy it. The center of the stalk should be a creamy, milky, pale white, almost translucent color. If you see a dried, solid white circle in the middle of the stalk, it probably means the vegetable is a little old. It still could be good—look at the leaves and the buds for more clues to how fresh it is. The flower buds should be tight and compact—there should be buds and maybe just a couple of open flowers. The tiny tight buds are the most tender part of the broccoli, but lots and lots of open flowers means the stalk is older and past its prime for eating and it will be bitter and chewy. Why is this so important? If the Chinese broccoli is old, you'll really taste the bitterness and the vegetable will be tough and stringy.

PO-PO'S LOVING GESTURES

Some of the most loving gestures of a Chinese mom are expressed at the dinner table. Growing up, our family was never really the kissy-kissy, "I love you", emotionally expressive type. Sometimes it was because of the language barrier (my mom didn't speak much English and my brother and I "lost" our Cantonese growing up in North Platte, Nebraska) and sometimes because the older Chinese culture's expressions of love were more stiff and subdued. We are a much different family now. In the past few years, my brother and I have been able to really, deeply connect with our parents. We finally understand the hardship that our parents went through and the decisions that they made in the past . . . things that as children we so easily concluded, "that's not fair" or "they don't love me". It's such a comforting and belonging feeling to really see my mom, dad and brother as exactly who they are, cherishing all the wonderful love and accepting all their wonderful quirks. When we were little, my mom used to show her love every single night at the dinner table. Her chopsticks would quickly dart from dish to dish, picking out the best parts for my brother, my dad and me. The plump cheeks of the steamed fish, a perfect dark meat nugget from the soy sauce chicken, the giant red claw from the crab, the hidden fleck of salted fish, and the young tender flower buds from the Chinese "gai-lan" Broccoli. Now that I'm a mother of two little ones, I find myself doing the same thing, picking through the dish to find the best, most tender parts of each dish for my children. These days, "Po-Po's" (grandmother) chopsticks go to grandchildren's plates, not mine anymore. That's the most loving gesture of a Chinese Po-Po.

Rice & Noodles

Whoever invented the no-carb diet never tried my famous fried rice. I don't think I've ever met a fellow Asian who could swear off rice and noodles! On the weekends, Mom would make a big plate of fried noodles that we'd chow down for lunch. Any leftovers would carry forward for dinnertime . . . but rarely did we ever have any left because my brother Jay and I would sneak a little plate here and there for an afternoon snack!

FAR LEFT TOP TO BOTTOM: Oh yes, I do love my instant ramen! This was Nathan's first experience of this treat. I was blowing the hot noodles for him; Andrew probably wondering where he can hide his scrambled eggs; Po-Po (grandmother in Cantonese) and the boys.

Perfect Shrimp Fried Rice

How could I write a cookbook without giving props to my friend Elise, the genius behind the highly popular SimplyRecipes.com? When I first started blogging for a living, Elise was my superstar, guiding me through the murky world of marketing and giving me advice on better site design. So, when she accepted me to be a guest writer for SimplyRecipes.com, I was totally thrilled!

   Perfect Shrimp Fried Rice was the first recipe that I contributed and it won rave reviews on her site. Phew, I passed the test and now I'm a monthly writer for her site.

**SERVES 4 TO 6 AS PART OF MULTICOURSE
   MEAL**
4 cups (600 g) leftover, previously chilled
   cooked rice
1/2 lb (250 g) small raw shrimp, shelled
   and deveined
1/4 teaspoon salt
Freshly ground black pepper to taste
1/2 teaspoon cornstarch

2 tablespoons high-heat cooking oil,
   divided
3 eggs, beaten
2 green onions (scallions), minced
2 teaspoons fish sauce or 1 tablespoon
   soy sauce
3/4 cup (120 g) frozen peas and carrots,
   defrosted
1 teaspoon sesame oil

1 Gently separate the rice grains with a fork, taking care not to smush the delicate grains. In a bowl, toss the shrimp with the salt, pepper and cornstarch. Let marinate for 10 minutes at room temperature.

2 Set a wok or large sauté pan on high heat. When the wok is hot enough for a bead of water to instantly sizzle and evaporate, add 1 tablespoon of the cooking oil and swirl to coat the wok. Add the shrimp, quickly spreading it out around the cooking surface area so that they are not overlapping. Let fry, untouched for 30 seconds. Flip over and let the other side fry for 30 seconds, or until almost cooked through. Remove the shrimp from the wok to a plate, leaving as much oil in the wok as possible.

3 Turn the heat to medium and let the wok heat up again. Add the eggs, stirring in a quick motion to scramble the eggs. When the eggs are almost cooked through (they should still be slightly runny in the middle), dish out of the wok into the same plate with the cooked shrimp.

4 Use paper towels to wipe the same wok clean and return it to high heat. Add the remaining 1 tablespoon of cooking oil, swirling to coat. When the oil is hot, add the green onions and fry until fragrant, about 15 to 30 seconds. Add the rice and stir well to mix in the green onions throughout. Spread the rice all around the wok surface area and let the rice heat up, untouched until you hear the bottoms of the grains sizzle, about 1 minute. Use a spatula to toss the rice, again spreading the rice out over the surface of wok and let cook for 1 minute.

5 Drizzle the fish sauce (or soy sauce) all around the rice and toss. Add the peas and carrots, the cooked eggs, partially cooked shrimp and sesame oil, tossing to mix the rice evenly with all the ingredients. Repeat the tossing, spreading and 1-minute frying until each and every grain of rice is heated through. Taste and adjust with additional soy sauce if needed.

Steamed Rice

The first embarrassing moment in my cooking career was two years ago when I spent the afternoon with a local food critic, Brian Ries. We shopped together and he came back with me into the kitchen to interview, watch me cook and sample Seared Scallops with Mango and Melon with Coconut Rice. All was fine except for one thing. All my life, I've been spoiled by my rice cooker. I didn't know how to make rice without it. The water measurements, timing and technique are totally different. I mean. . . I've never ventured outside of the-one-finger-push-button-technique.

I know. I'm spoiled, sheltered and stupid. I undercooked my rice and watched him chew chew chew gulp cough. He was brave and polite—but I think I saw him pop a couple of Tums behind my back. How could I, a Chinese cook, mess up RICE of all things?!?! That's totally sacrilegious and I might as well be disowned by my "peeps".

"Ahhhh . . . Jaden-grasshoppa . . . Confucious, Buddha and Jackie Chan all very much upset. We meditate and pray for your awakening". Well, after that afternoon, I made rice in a pot, on the stovetop for the next two months straight. I call this Rice, Unplugged.

MAKES 6 CUPS RICE (1 KG)/SERVES 4 TO 6
2 cups (420 g) uncooked rice (long-grain or short-grain rice)
2¹/₂ cups (625 ml) cool water

1 Place the rice grains in a pot. Wash the rice, swishing it with your hands. Drain and repeat 3 more times until the water is no longer milky. This helps remove excess starch and clean the grains.
2 Fill the pot with the cool water and the washed rice. Turn the heat to high. When the water near the edge of the pot starts bubbling, cover the pot and reduce the heat to low. Cook for 15 minutes.
3 Turn off the heat and keep covered! Let it sit with lid on for 5 minutes to complete the steaming. Fluff with a fork after done.

Chinese Sausage with Rice and Sweet Soy Sauce

I've never seen anyone shuffle rice into their mouths faster than my kids when I make this dish. Well, I guess I did too when I was little and my mom cooked this rice! The white rice is steamed with a few whole Chinese sausages. The result is smoky, savory-sweet flavored rice that's truly addictive. There are a few different varieties of Chinese sausages—some with liver, some made with chicken, but I like the regular pork intensely marbled with delicious fat the best. See page 19 for information on Chinese sausage.

SERVES 4 TO 6 AS PART OF MULTICOURSE MEAL
2¹/₂ cups (625 ml) cool water
2 cups (420 g) uncooked rice (I prefer jasmine, a fragrant long-grain rice),washed and drained well (see step 1 of making Steamed Rice, recipe on this page)
4 Chinese sausages
¹/₄ cup (65 ml) Sweet Soy Sauce (page 30) plus more for the table

1 Fill the pot with the cool water and the washed rice. Snuggle the sausages in the rice grains. Turn the heat to high. When the water near the edge of the pot starts bubbling, cover the pot and reduce the heat to low. Cook for 15 minutes.
2 Turn off heat and keep covered! Let it sit with the lid on for 5 minutes to finish the steaming process. Remove the sausages (careful, they are hot!) and slice then on the diagonal into ¹/₄-inch (6-mm)-thick pieces. Arrange the sausages on top of the rice and drizzle the Sweet Soy Sauce on top. Have the extra Sweet Soy Sauce at the table for drizzling.

Coconut Rice

This rice is made with long-grained rice (I prefer jasmine) and is cooked with good quality coconut milk. It's sticky, slightly sweet and you will love it! Topping the coconut rice with toasted coconut flakes is entirely optional, but makes it extra special!

SERVES 4 TO 6 AS SIDE DISH
1 tablespoon butter
1 tablespoon brown sugar
1 teaspoon sea or kosher salt (or ½ teaspoon table salt)
2 cups (420 g) uncooked jasmine rice, washed and drained well (see step 1 of making Steamed Rice, page 129)
1½ cups (375 ml) good, thick coconut milk (shake can to mix well before opening)
1½ cups (375 ml) water
¼ cup (20 g) sweetened coconut flakes

1 Heat the butter a medium, heavy saucepan over medium heat. When the butter is melted, add the brown sugar and salt, and stir until dissolved. Turn the heat to high, add the rice and stir until all the grains are coated evenly.

2 Add the coconut milk and water. Stir. When boiling, immediately cover with a tight-fitting lid, turn the heat to medium-low and simmer undisturbed for 20 minutes. Remove the pot from the heat but do not open the lid. Really, no peeping! Let sit for 10 minutes.

3 While the rice is simmering, toast the coconut flakes on a dry frying pan over medium high heat. Stir frequently to avoid burning, remove from the pan as soon as the coconut is golden brown, about 2 minutes. Sprinkle the toasted coconut flakes on the rice.

FRIED RICE SECRETS

Mushy fried rice is evil! And it's probably the number one complaint people have about making fried rice at home, "Why can't my fried rice be fluffy like the restaurants?" Okay, so I'm going to give you the three secrets to making fluffy, flavorful fried rice.

USE PREVIOUSLY CHILLED LEFTOVER RICE
To get the perfect fried rice, you'll want to use yesterday's rice as it's had a chance to dry out a bit in the refrigerator. The heat of the pan and the liquid seasoning (soy sauce) will re-steam and hydrate the leftover rice. If you try to use freshly cooked, hot rice (like I did years ago) you'll end up with too much moisture in the rice and will make a heavy mess in the pan.

HIGH HEAT IS ESSENTIAL
But high heat doesn't mean that you need super high BTU's or a gas stove. All it takes is a bit of patience to let your pan or wok heat up. The high heat ensures that whatever ingredients you put into the pan get fried quickly and that each grain of rice gets hot to the core. So when is it hot enough? When the grains of rice practically dance off the wok.

DON'T TOUCH
A common mistake of stir-frying is to constantly poke, prod, turn and flip every second. In a restaurant kitchen where flames are so powerful they can singe your brows, chefs have to keep things moving. But in home kitchens, our stovetops need a little more time to do their work to heat up and cook our food. If you keep poking at the rice, the grains will break, release more starch and turn the entire thing goopy. It will never have a chance to fry correctly . . . not enough "wok time" as my Mom likes to say. The best thing is to do is to spread out the rice, use the entire cooking surface of the pan and just leave it alone. Put your spatula down and back away from the stove for a minute. Give the rice a chance to heat up. Then flip, toss and redistribute the rice, again spreading it out and leaving it alone to cook another side.

FRY THE INGREDIENTS SEPARATELY
Fried rice has many different ingredients, and in my home it's usually just a mixture of whatever vegetables, meats or seafood I can scrounge up from the refrigerator or freezer. But whatever the ingredients, you want to make sure that you can taste each individual one. To do this, you've got to fry your meat, seafood or vegetables first, one by one, and remove from the wok or pan when they're 80 percent cooked through and then toss them back in toward the end of the stir-fry to finish cooking. If you try to fry all of the ingredients at the same time in the same pan, they'll all compete for "wok time" and everything will end up tasting exactly the same!

USE WHAT YOU'VE GOT ON HAND
Oh, and one more tip—you really don't need to be exact on the measurement of the ingredients. If you only have three cups of leftover rice instead of four, just use a little less soy sauce. And if you have a few mushrooms in the fridge, throw them in! Once you get the technique of making fried rice using the secrets above, you can improvise and make up your own recipe, utilizing whatever is in your refrigerator.

Chinese Sausage Fried Rice

This fried rice recipe is my "signature" fried rice—the one that I'm always making at home and one day if I morph into my next life form, this is the dish that I want to be known for. When I have new guests over at my home for dinner, this fried rice is definitely on the menu. And guess what? It's also one of the very first dishes my Mom taught me. The two secrets (boy, I have a lot of secrets, don't I?) to the flavor of this fried rice is Lap Cheong (Chinese sausage) and fish sauce . . . oh, sweet fish sauce. It is my magical ingredient! Fish sauce is salty-sweet, a taste that I just cannot describe. Pungent in its smell, it mellows out like the sea once it's cooked. The sauce is used sparingly, and if you've ever had Thai or Vietnamese food, chances are 80 percent of the dishes you've had have fish sauce in the ingredients list. You can substitute with soy sauce if you don't have fish sauce.

Chinese sausage or Lap Cheong is cured, so it lasts for a long time, like Italian sausage. Since it keeps so well, it's always a staple in my home, because it transforms plain, leftover rice into the best restaurant style fried rice ever. All the marbled fat in the sausage is liquid gold—this is what you'll be frying your rice in! (Note: see page 19 for use and storage information on Chinese sausage and page 21 for information on fish sauce.)

SERVES 4 TO 6 AS PART OF MULTICOURSE MEAL

4 cups (600 g) leftover, previously chilled cooked rice
1 teaspoon high-heat cooking oil
2 eggs, beaten
2 links Chinese sausage, diced
2 green onions (scallions), minced
1 teaspoon soy sauce
2 teaspoons rice wine
2 teaspoons fish sauce (or substitute with soy sauce)
Freshly ground black pepper to taste

1 Gently separate the rice grains with a fork, taking care not to smush them.
2 In a wok or large pan over medium heat, add the oil and swirl to coat. When the oil is hot, add the eggs and quickly stir. Cook until they are almost set. The eggs should still be slightly runny in the middle. Remove the eggs to a bowl and wipe the wok clean with paper towels.
3 Set the wok over medium-low heat. When the wok warms, add the Chinese sausage and let the fat render for about 2 minutes. Take care not to burn the sausage! If it starts to darken too quickly, turn the heat to low. Remove the sausage to the same bowl as the eggs, leaving as much of the sausage fat in the wok as possible. You should have about 1 tablespoon of sausage fat in the wok. If you don't, add enough cooking oil to the wok to equal about 1 tablespoon. Swirl to coat the wok and turn the heat to high.
4 When the oil is very hot, add the green onions and stir-fry for 15 seconds. Add the cooked rice, breaking up any additional clumps with your spatula. Spread the rice all around the wok surface area and let the rice heat up, untouched, until you hear the bottoms of the grains sizzle, about 1 minute. Use the spatula to toss the rice, again spreading the rice out over the surface of the wok and let cook for 1 minute.
5 Add the soy sauce, rice wine, fish sauce, pepper, egg and the Chinese sausage to the wok, tossing to mix the rice evenly with the ingredients. Break up any clumps of rice and egg with your spatula. Repeat the tossing, spreading and 1-minute frying until each and every grain of rice is heated through. Taste and adjust with additional soy sauce if needed.

Korean Kimchi Fried Rice

I've got to admit, this is my hangover meal! Instead of scrambling the egg inside the rice, I fry the egg separately until the edges are ruffled, lacy and super crisp. On those mornings when I need that extra kick in the pants to get started, the fiery kimchi sure does its job!

For this fried rice, I prefer short-grain (sometimes labeled Sushi Rice) rice that's traditional in Korean and Japanese cooking. The short-grained rice is stickier and fuller, so making sure that it is at least day-old is important, as the refrigeration dries out the rice, making it perfect for fried rice. But what I do is keep a bag of cooked rice in the freezer, so that I can make Kimchi Fried Rice anytime. If you can't find short-grained rice, just use medium- or long-grained rice.

During the final moments of cooking, you'll taste the rice and adjust seasonings, as each batch of kimchi is very different. If you want a red-hot kick-in-the-pants fried rice, add more kimchi and kimchi juice. No kimchi juice in your jar? Just leave it out or substitute a teaspoon of white vinegar and a teaspoon of hot chilli sauce.

SERVES 4-6 AS PART OF MULTICOURSE MEAL

4 cups (600 g) leftover, previously chilled cooked rice (preferably short-grain)

2 tablespoons high-heat cooking oil, divided

$\frac{1}{2}$ cup (85 g) diced red bell pepper

$\frac{1}{4}$ cup (15 g) chopped green onion (scallion)

1 tablespoon finely minced garlic

Chopped kimchi (as much as you want)

1 tablespoon soy sauce

1 to 3 teaspoons kimchi juice

$\frac{1}{2}$ teaspoon salt

4 eggs

1 With a fork, gently separate the grains of rice, taking care not to smush the delicate grains.

2 Set a wok or large sauté pan over high heat. When hot, add 1 tablespoon of the oil and swirl to coat. Add the bell pepper and green onion and fry for 15 seconds. Add the garlic and fry for another 30 seconds.

3 Add the rice, toss with all the ingredients, and spread the mixture out all over the cooking surface. Let fry, untouched for 1 minute. Add the kimchi, soy sauce, kimchi juice and salt. Toss very well to mix all ingredients. Again, spread the rice out all over the cooking surface and let fry, untouched for 1 minute. Repeat the tossing, spreading and 1-minute frying until each and every grain of rice is heated through. Taste and adjust with additional soy sauce if needed.

4 Dish out the fried rice, rinse the wok and dry thoroughly. Return the wok to high heat. When the wok is hot, add the remaining 1 tablespoon of oil and swirl to coat. Crack the eggs into the wok and let fry for 1 minute. Then turn the heat to medium-low and continue to fry the eggs until the whites are completely set and the yolks still runny.

5 Top each portion of fried rice with an egg and garnish with additional kimchi if desired.

Simple Ginger and Green Onion Fried Rice

When steaming rice for a meal, I cook way more than I need for that evening, mainly because of what I can fry with it the next day. Even when my fridge is almost bare, I always have a nub of ginger and a few stalks of green onions in the vegetable drawer to fry up with rice. In less than 5 minutes, I have a side dish way more exciting than just leftover steamed rice.

1 Gently separate the rice grains with a fork, taking care not to smush the delicate grains.
2 Set a wok or large sauté pan over medium-high heat and add the oil. When the oil is just starting to get hot, add the green onions and ginger. Let cook until fragrant, about 30 seconds.
3 Turn the heat to high and immediately add the rice. Stir well to incorporate the green onion mixture throughout the rice. Spread the rice all around the wok surface area and let the rice heat up, untouched, until you hear the bottoms of the grains sizzle. Use the spatula to toss the rice, again spreading the rice out over the surface of the wok and let cook for 1 minute.
4 Add the wine, soy sauce and pepper and toss well. Repeat the tossing, spreading and 1-minute frying until each and every grain of rice is heated through.

SERVES 4-6 AS PART OF MULTICOURSE MEAL
4 cups (600 g) leftover, previously chilled cooked rice
2 tablespoons high-heat cooking oil
$\frac{1}{2}$ cup (30 g) minced green onions (scallions)
1 tablespoon grated fresh ginger (see Jaden's Ginger Tips, pg 33)
1 teaspoon Chinese rice wine (or dry sherry)
1 tablespoon soy sauce
Freshly ground black pepper to taste

RICE & NOODLES

Garlic Butter Noodles

If you're a doctor, nutritionist, health nut or my mom, please turn the page and pick another recipe.

These noodles are majorly addictive and I alone can eat an entire plate meant for four. It's my comfort food—how can you go wrong with garlic, butter and sugar?

If you don't have Chinese egg noodles, feel free to just use regular spaghetti noodles. I promise, it will be just as delicious. This is one of the most popular recipes on SteamyKitchen.com!.

SERVES 4 AS AN ACCOMPANIMENT TO OTHER HIGH-CALORIE, IRRESPONSIBLE FOODS

7 oz (200 g) dry egg noodles
3 tablespoons butter
$\frac{1}{2}$ cup (30 g) chopped green onion (scallion)
3 cloves garlic, finely minced
2 tablespoons brown sugar
1 teaspoon Maggi Sauce (or soy sauce)
1 tablespoon oyster sauce

1 Bring a large pot of water to a boil and cook the noodles according to the package instructions. Drain the noodles and wipe the pot clean. Return the pot to medium-high heat and add the butter. When the butter is sizzling and bubbling a bit, add the green onion and the garlic. Fry for 1 minute until very fragrant, be careful not to let the garlic burn.

2 Add the brown sugar, Maggi Sauce and oyster sauce and stir well to mix everything evenly. Add the noodles and toss vigorously to get the good stuff evenly distributed throughout the noodles. Dish out into a large bowl, grab a pair of chopsticks, hide in the closet and enjoy.

More Options

■ Use this recipe as a base for adding other ingredients. Try frying a handful of sliced fresh shitake mushrooms with the green onions.

■ To make Garlic Shrimp Noodles, fry $\frac{1}{2}$ lb (250 g) shrimp in the sizzling butter, keeping them in single layer, 1 minute each side or until cooked through. Dish the shrimp out of the wok onto a clean plate, keeping as much butter in wok as possible. Proceed with frying the green onions, garlic and noodles. Add the sauce and then toss in the cooked shrimp.

Korean Jap Chae Noodles with Beef

The type of noodle used in this dish, known as *Chap Chae* in Korea, is made from sweet potato starch and becomes translucent when cooked, which is how they got their English name, "glass noodles". They are gluten free and are wonderfully springy and light. I must warn you that once cooked, these noodles are the perfect consistency for a fun food fight. You can use any type of fresh mushrooms, like shitake or even the standard button mushroom, but traditionally, dried wood ear mushrooms, found in most Asian markets, are used. Just rehydrate the dried wood ear mushrooms in hot water for 15 minutes, drain and they'll be ready for your stir-fry. I love making this dish in the summertime, because you can serve these noodles at room temperature or even slightly chilled.

1 In a bowl, combine the soy sauce and the brown sugar. Set aside. If you're using dried wood ear mushrooms, soak the mushrooms in very hot water for 15 minutes to rehydrate. Then remove the tough stems.

2 Bring a large pot of water to a boil. Add the glass noodles and cook for 5 minutes. Immediately drain and rinse the noodles with cool water until they are just warm to the touch. Drain well and toss with the sesame oil. Use kitchen shears to cut the noodle strands to 8-inch (20-cm) lengths, if desired, to make them easier to cook and eat.

3 Set a wok or large sauté pan over high heat. When a bead of water sizzles and evaporates upon contact, add the cooking oil and swirl to coat. Add the onion, garlic, green onions and the beef slices, spreading out in one layer. Stir-fry for 30 seconds to 1 minute, or until the beef slices are just slightly pink in the middle. Add the carrots, the spinach leaves and mushrooms. Stir-fry until the carrots are softened, about 1 minute.

4 Pour the soy and brown sugar mixture into the wok. Add the noodles and toss continuously until the noodles are warmed through. Do not overcook the noodles—they should be springy but easy to bite into. Sprinkle on the sesame seeds.

SERVES 4 AS PART OF MULTICOURSE MEAL

2 tablespoons soy sauce
1¹/₂ teaspoons brown sugar
3 oz (85 g) sliced fresh shitake mushrooms or ¹/₂ oz (15 g) dried wood ear mushrooms
8 oz (250 g) dried Korean glass noodles
2 teaspoons sesame oil
2 tablespoons high-heat cooking oil
¹/₂ cup (30 g) thinly sliced onion
2 cloves garlic, finely minced
3 green onions (scallions), cut into 1-in (2.5-cm) lengths
6 oz (175 g) thinly sliced sirloin beef (or flank if cut across grain, page 62)
1 carrot, cut into matchsticks
¹/₄ lb (125 g) spinach leaves
1 tablespoon sesame seeds

Quick Noodle Stir-Fry

Most people think that the boxed mac-'n-cheese is a shortcut fast food. But, if you think about it, the stuff really isn't that convenient. It takes nine minutes to boil water (eleven if you watch), fourteen to cook the mac and two to reconstitute the "cheese". Twenty-five minutes for 580 grams of sodium and forty-nine grams of carbs? I can give you a better fast food. My 15-minute Quick Noodle Stir-Fry is actually healthy and it comes with real vegetables. The secret is in the type of noodles that we use here. These are fresh Chinese egg noodles that are found in the refrigerator or freezer and are boiled for less than two minutes! Just like fresh homemade pasta—you don't really need to cook the noodles more than a couple of minutes. I like keeping a couple of packs in my freezer for emergency noodle snacking or for a lazy dinner. They can be thick with a nice bite like the ones I've used in the photograph, or really thin and labeled "wonton" noodles. Just make sure you read the package directions for cooking times. You can even drop these noodles frozen into the boiling water—no need to defrost.

SERVES 4 AS PART OF MULTICOURSE MEAL
12 oz (350 g) fresh Chinese egg noodles (either refrigerated or frozen)
1 teaspoon sesame oil
2 teaspoons high-heat cooking oil
2 teaspoons finely minced garlic
One bunch, about 1 in (2.5 cm) around, Chinese chives
2 carrots, thinly sliced or shredded
2 tablespoons oyster sauce
1 teaspoon Maggi Sauce (substitute with soy sauce)
1 tablespoon Chinese rice wine (or dry sherry)
1 cup (100 g) fresh bean sprouts

1 Bring a medium pot of water to boil. Remove the egg noodles from the packaging. Separate the strands with your fingers (if using refrigerated). Add the noodles to the boiling water. Use long chopsticks or tongs to jiggle and separate the noodles as they are cooking. Your cooking time depends on how thick and wide your noodles are. If you're using thin, wonton noodles, 1 minute is sufficient for refrigerated and 2 minutes for frozen. For thicker noodles, like I have used, 2 minutes for fresh and 3 minutes for frozen.

2 When the noodles are cooked, drain them and, with your chopsticks or tongs, lift and toss them well with the sesame oil to prevent sticking for 30 seconds. The tossing will help cool the noodles as well as mix the sesame oil throughout the strands.

3 In a wok or large sauté pan over high heat, add the cooking oil. When the oil is just starting to get hot, add the garlic and fry until fragrant, about 15 seconds. Add the chives and fry until just softened, about 1 minute. Toss in the carrots and fry 30 seconds. Pour in the oyster sauce, Maggi Sauce and wine and stir well. Add the noodles and toss! toss! toss! When the noodles are heated and cooked through, your dish is done! Taste and adjust with more Maggi Sauce if needed. Toss with the bean sprouts and serve.

More Options:
■ If you'd like to add some protein to this dish, try some shelled edamame (Japanese soybean pods). You can find them in most grocery stores in the freezer section. Some come shelled and precooked. Others come with the shell-on. You'll need to boil these for a bit and then shell them, popping out the smooth, green soybean. After the noodles are done boiling, don't dump out the water just yet. Add the frozen edamame to the boiling water and follow the package instructions. Drain, shell, if needed, and toss them into the noodle dish at the end.

■ If you don't have access to fresh or frozen egg noodles, use dried egg noodles. Just follow the instructions on the package for boiling time.

Shrimp Pad Thai

My friend Ou, who just had a baby, is the wonderful gal who taught me how to make Pad Thai. Back home in Thailand, Ou usually makes Pad Thai by taste and when she came over for a cooking play date (eye roll . . . yes, I know that sounded lame), I followed her like a hawk with a measuring spoon and scale. She thought I was nuts! The difficult part about creating a Pad Thai recipe is that the main ingredients that make up the sauce are so incredibly hard to standardize, as each brand of fish sauce tastes different and tamarind paste too. This I learned from Pim of the famed ChezPim.com. (You'll also find a great recipe for Pad Thai on her site as well.) You can make Pad Thai sauce from scratch, but I've found time and time again that the most consistent results come when we start with jarred pad thai paste, which we build more layers of flavor upon. A key to good Pad Thai is perfectly cooked noodles, which means noodles that are NOT overcooked. If you overcook the noodles, even by just a couple of minutes, you'll end up with a goopy, soggy, clumpy mess.

1 In a large bowl, soak the rice noodles in hot water (not boiling, just hot straight from tap) for 10 to 15 minutes.
2 Combine the ingredients for the Pad Thai Sauce in a bowl.
3 Check back on the noodles. The noodles are sufficiently soaked when they are flexible but still a bit stiff. Drain them and set aside.
4 In a wok or large sauté pan over high heat, add just 1 tablespoon of the oil. When the oil is very hot, add the beaten eggs and swirl gently while it sets. Use your spatula to scramble the eggs and then remove from the wok.
5 Wipe the wok down with clean paper towels. Return the heat to high and add the remaining 2 tablespoons of oil. When the oil is very hot, add the shrimp and fry 1 minute, until cooked halfway through. Push the shrimp to one side or up the sides of the wok. To an empty area of the wok, add the garlic and green onions and stir-fry 15 to 30 seconds until fragrant. Add the drained noodles, the cooked eggs and the Pad Thai Sauce. Toss until all ingredients are well combined. Cover the wok and let simmer until the noodles are soft and cooked through, about 1 to 2 minutes. Check at the 1-minute mark and if the noodles are still a bit stiff, cover and cook another minute. The noodles should have soaked up a lot of the sauce, and you should taste a combination of sweet, salty, a little heat and a zing of tartness. Serve with the fresh bean sprouts, lime wedges and chopped peanuts at the table.

Other Options
■ Add some sliced baked, firm tofu (not the soft, white, uncooked tofu—it would be too delicate and crumble).
■ Substitute garlic chives or Chinese chives for the green onions.

SERVES 4 TO 6
PAD THAI SAUCE
4 tablespoons pad thai paste
2 teaspoons tamarind paste/concentrate
3 tablespoons fish sauce
3 teaspoons sugar
$^2/_3$ cup (160 ml) water
2 to 4 teaspoons Asian chilli sauce (preferably Sriracha) or 1 to 2 teaspoons Asian chilli powder or ground red pepper

PAD THAI NOODLES
8 oz (250 g) dried rice noodles (medium thickness)
3 tablespoons high-heat cooking oil
2 eggs, slightly beaten
1 lb (500 g) peeled, deveined raw shrimp
1 tablespoon finely minced garlic
4 green onions (scallions), cut into lengths
1 cup (100 g) fresh bean sprouts
1 lime, cut into 8 wedges
$^1/_2$ cup (80 g) coarsely chopped unsalted dry roasted peanuts

Sweets & Libations

I think stress level worldwide be greatly reduced if we made sweets and libations
something to enjoy and savor in between EACH
meal instead of just at the end of the day.
Okay, so much for my diet! I'm not much of a
baker (honestly I'm just not that great at
baking) so most of my sweets are frozen con-
coctions and easy-to-whip-up desserts.

Life is Sweet! (and sometimes highly caloric,
but that's okay, right?!)

FAR LEFT TOP TO BOTTOM: Oh how I love my Viet Iced Coffee!; Taking a time
out and enjoying a treat from friend Lori who owns We Take The Cake bakery;
MiMi (grandmother) with the boys enjoying a little dessert-disguised-as-breakfast.

MAKES 1^1/$_2$ PINTS (430 G)
2 large Asian pears
^{1}/$_4$ teaspoon freshly squeezed lemon juice
1 tablespoon finely grated fresh ginger
   (make sure you use a microplane grater,
   see page 33)
1^1/$_2$ cups (375 g) Greek-style plain yogurt,
   store-bought or homemade (page 146)
^{1}/$_2$ cup (100 g) sugar
Generous pinch of fine sea salt
1 tablespoon pink peppercorns, crushed

SPECIAL EQUIPMENT
Ice cream maker (remember to freeze
   your insert if you have one)

1 Peel and chop the pears into small
^{1}/$_2$-inch (1.25-cm) chunks. Toss with the
lemon juice to prevent browning. In a
blender, combine the pears and ginger
and puree until smooth. You may have
to use a tablespoon of water to get the
pears moving.
2 In a large bowl, combine the pear-gin-
ger puree with the yogurt, sugar and salt.
Refrigerate for 1 hour.
3 Churn the mixture in your ice cream
maker, following manufacturer's
instructions.
4 Top the frozen yogurt with the crushed
pink peppercorns.

> **NOTE: Because the pears are wa-
> tery, if you're making homemade
> Greek-style yogurt, make sure that
> the yogurt is drained well. When
> drained, the yogurt should be the
> consistency of very thick sour
> cream.**

Asian Pear Frozen Yogurt

This frozen yogurt flavor is a tribute to a Korean dessert called "Baesuk", which is
Asian pears poached in a sweet, gingery soup. The pears are studded with black peppercorns and it's a wonderful, cooling dessert after a full Korean feast. Inspiration for
this creation came from Jon, author of the blog, Evil Jungle Prince. Jon's blog is full of
Korean recipes, especially homemade kimchi recipes. Instead of black peppercorns,
I've used the pink variety. But in fact, the two are not related at all! The pink peppercorn is a berry and it's delicately sweet with a berrylike taste on the tip of your tongue
and a faint peppery finish at the end. Sheesh. I sound like I'm describing wine!

   The best way to describe Asian pears is that it's like a cross between an apple and a
pear. But if you can't find it in the stores, substitute with one pear of any variety and
one firm, crisp apple, like a fuji apple.

Tapioca Pearls with Sweet Coconut and Honeydew

Mom makes this cool, coco-nutty and soothing treat during the summer, when it's sticky-hot outside. It's a restorative and refreshing dessert after a big meal. But sometimes, we'll eat this during the middle of the afternoon for a cool-me-down treat!

Tapioca pearls are dried tapioca balls found at Asian markets. There are many different sizes. For this dessert, I like using the smallest size, about 1.5 millimeters in diameter. The larger ones are great in Bubble "Boba" Tea (page 149). Serve this chilled. Mango and papaya are also great in this dessert.

SERVES 8

3 cups (750 ml) water
1½ cups (300 g) sugar
1 cup (250 ml) whole milk
2 cups (500 ml) unsweetened coconut milk
⅔ cup (115 g) small dried tapioca pearls
2 cups (320 g) ½-in (1.25-cm)-cubed honeydew melon

1 In a medium pot, bring the water and sugar to a boil. When boiling, turn the heat to low and stir in the milk. When the mixture returns to a boil, turn off the heat and stir in the coconut milk. Make sure that you are not boiling the coconut milk (which would make it oily). Remove from the heat and let cool to room temperature.

2 Soak the tapioca pearls in cold water for 20 minutes exactly. The pearls will expand and turn bright white. Drain. In a medium pot, add about 4 cups (1 liter) of water and bring to a boil. In the meantime, have a fine-meshed sieve ready at the sink. When the water boils, turn off the heat and add the drained tapioca pearls and stir constantly for 1½ minutes. If you are using pearls larger than 1 millimeter, cook an additional 30 seconds or until the pearls are translucent with a very small white center. Bite into a tapioca pearl; it should be soft but not goopy.

3 Immediately drain the tapioca in the fine-mesh sieve and run cold water through the sieve to stop the tapioca pearls from cooking further. Swish with your hands to make sure that the pearls at the bottom of the sieve have a chance to cool down. Drain and add to coconut milk mixture. Chill the entire mixture for at least 2 hours or up to 3 days.

4 To serve, ladle the sweet coconut milk into a bowl and spoon in the cubed, fresh honeydew.

NOTE: Do not combine the honeydew and the coconut milk until just before serving. Storing the honeydew and the coconut milk together in the same container makes the honeydew bitter.

Grilled Pineapple with Chocolate Coconut Rum Sauce

The only time I let Scott be in charge of dessert is when MY pineapple is grilled on HIS barbecue grill. And, like our marriage, what results is smoky, juicy, tangy and sexy. Okay, I snuck the sexy in. But wait! If you drizzle chocolate coconut rum on that pineapple....now THAT'S SEXY!!

SERVES 4 (2 SKEWERS PER PERSON)
½ cup (75 g) sweetened coconut flakes
1 whole fresh pineapple, cored, peeled and cut into 8 long wedges
8 long bamboo skewers, soaked in water at least 30 minutes

CHOCOLATE COCONUT RUM SAUCE
3 tablespoons unsalted butter
4 oz (125 g) milk or dark chocolate, broken into small pieces
¼ cup (65 ml) coconut milk (or substitute with whole or skim milk)
2 tablespoons coconut rum
Pinch of sea salt

1 To make the Chocolate Coconut Rum Sauce, melt the butter in a small saucepan over medium heat. Gradually add the chocolate pieces and whisk continuously until melted. Add the coconut milk and whisk until combined. Remove from the heat and stir in the rum and sea salt.
2 In a dry, nonstick frying pan over medium heat, add the coconut flakes and toast until just golden brown at the edges, stirring constantly. Remove to a plate to cool.
3 Skewer the pineapple wedges on the bamboo skewers.
4 Preheat a grill, griddle pan or large frying pan on high heat. When hot, grill the pineapple wedges for 5 to 6 minutes until nicely caramelized, flipping once halfway. Serve with some drizzled Chocolate Coconut Rum Sauce and a sprinkling of the toasted coconut.

Fresh Starfruit and Mango with Chilli and Mint

I'm not big on sweets after dinner (mid-day sugar craving is another story). Asians generally eat fresh fruit that's cleansing and refreshing for the body. If you've never had fruit with sea salt, you've just gotta try it. The sea salt lets the sweetness of the fruit really sing, especially on tropical fruits!

I love using my mortar and pestle to make the chilli salt—pounding and releasing the oils of the chilli flavor the sea salt. If you enjoy the heat, use more intense chillies, like Thai bird's-eye or Serrano, but if you prefer the incredible flavor and just a slight zing, remove the seeds and the ribs of the chilli before pounding . . . or go for a bigger, milder chilli like Anaheim. Start with a little bit of fresh chilli in your mortar—taste—and you can always add more.

Normally when choosing mangoes, I'll go for the ripe ones, but in this case, green is good too. It's slightly sour and crunchy, perfect with salt. The star fruit is juicy, light and so pretty on a plate. Garnish the dessert with a chiffonade of fresh mint.

Definitely use good sea salt. Regular table salt is too harsh and salty. You could use kosher salt too, if you don't have sea salt. But I much rather prefer the freshness oceany taste of sea salt for fruit. If you don't have a mortar, you can chop your chilli finely and just mix with the salt, using the back of the spoon to crush and release the oils as your mix.

SERVES 4
1 tablespoon sea salt (use less if your sea salt is very fine)
1/2 teaspoon coarsely chopped fresh chilli of your choice (or more)
1 to 2 starfruits
1 mango (you can use either ripe or unripened)
2 sprigs fresh mint, leaves torn or very thinly sliced

1 In a mortar, add the salt and the chopped chilli. Pound, grind and smash away until the chilli pepper has released its oils. Your salt should be a pretty shade, now that it's been in contact with the chilli. Taste, and add more chopped chilli, if needed.

2 Slice the starfruit into 1/4-inch (6-mm)-thick slices. Peel the mango and slice it into 1/4-inch (6-mm)-thick slices. Toss with just a teaspoon of the fresh chilli salt (less if you are using very fine sea salt).

3 Arrange the fruit on 4 plates and sprinkle the rest of the chilli salt directly on the plates, so that each person can dip his or her fruit into more salt if desired. Top with the sliced fresh mint.

More Option
■ Try the chilli salt on watermelon, cantaloupe, Asian pear . . . really any type of fruit!

Grilled Bananas with Chocolate and Toasted Coconut Flakes

My friend, Andreea Gulacsi, of Glorious Food and Wine blog, recently took a trip to Champagne, France, and had the most awesome dessert ever. Chocolate grilled bananas. I've added my favorite flavors to the technique—chocolate and toasted coconut. It's deceptively simple, yet a showstopper on the table!

1 Lay the bananas sideways. Carefully slice the bananas open (cut through the skin and through the banana itself) without cutting through the bottoms or through the ends. You're creating a pocket for the chocolate.

2 Tuck the chocolate inside the banana.

3 Set them on a grill preheated to low heat and grill for 5 to 7 minutes, until the bottoms start to turn black and the chocolate has melted.

4 While bananas are grilling, heat a frying pan over medium-low heat. Add the coconut flakes and stir continuously until golden brown at the edges. Immediately pour onto a plate to stop the cooking.

5 When the bananas are done, top them with some toasted coconut or other topping of your choice.

SERVES 4

4 bananas (leave peel on)

3 oz (85 g) dark or milk chocolate bar, broken into pieces

½ cup (40 g) sweetened coconut flakes (or other toppings of your choice like chopped nuts or chopped fruit)

Coconut Frozen Yogurt

I'd never have known how good homemade frozen yogurt could be if it weren't for the king of ice cream, David Lebovitz (www.davidlebovitz.com). You can find Greek-style yogurt at most health food stores or large markets. If you can't find Greek style yogurt, I provide you with a easy method for making it yourself.

MAKES $^1/_2$ PINTS (430 G)
3$^1/_2$ cups (875 kg) Greek-style plain yogurt, store-bought or homemade (see below)
$^3/_4$ cup (150 g) sugar
1 teaspoon coconut extract
$^1/_2$ cup (75 g) sweetened coconut flakes

$^1/_2$ cup (110 g) diced papaya
$^1/_2$ cup (110 g) diced mango
$^1/_4$ cup (80 g) diced kiwi

SPECIAL EQUIPMENT
Ice cream maker (remember to freeze your insert if you have one)

1 Mix the yogurt with the sugar and coconut extract. Let the mixture chill in the refrigerator for at least 1 hour to let the sugar dissolve. Churn the mixture in your ice cream maker, following the manufacturer's instructions.
2 Set a dry frying pan over medium heat. When the frying pan is just getting hot, add the coconut flakes. Stir constantly until the flakes toast to a golden brown. Dish out onto a plate immediately to stop the coconut flakes from toasting further.
3 In a small bowl, combine the papaya, mango and kiwi.
4 To serve, divide the frozen yogurt into dessert bowls. Spoon the fruit on top and sprinkle with the toasted coconut flakes.

> **TIP: To make homemade Greek-style yogurt, take 5 cups (1.25 kg) of whole milk plain yogurt and strain in a cheese-cloth-lined fine-meshed sieve (set over a bowl!) for 4 hours or overnight in the refrigerator. Discard the whey (the water). You should end up with about 3 to 4 cups (750 g to 1 kg) of strained yogurt (depends on brand of yogurt) with a rich and creamy consistency similar to Greek-style yogurt.**

Coconut Frozen Yogurt

Thai Coffee Ice Cream

Thai Coffee Ice Cream

This is the type of ice cream that I eat straight out of the tub. Under the table, in a dark closet or hiding under the bed covers. So I don't have to share. Need I say more?

MAKES 1$^1/_2$ PINTS (430 G)
5 tablespoons plus $^1/_2$ teaspoon finely ground French or espresso roast coffee
2 teaspoons plus $^1/_4$ teaspoon ground cardamom
1 cup (250 ml) water (for brewing coffee)
1$^1/_2$ cups (375 ml) sweetened condensed milk
$^1/_2$ cup (125 ml) heavy cream

SPECIAL EQUIPMENT
Ice cream maker (remember to freeze your insert if you have one)

Brew the coffee with just 5 tablespoons of the French or espresso roast coffee grounds and just 2 teaspoons of the ground cardamom with the water. Transfer the brewed coffee to a heatproof bowl. Whisk in the sweetened condensed milk, heavy cream, the remaining $^1/_2$ teaspoon of finely ground coffee and the remaining $^1/_4$ teaspoon of ground cardamom. Chill in the refrigerator for at least 2 hours. Churn the mixture in your ice cream maker, following manufacturer's instructions.

Chocolate Wontons

This is a type of dessert that will make little girls giggle and squeal with delight and little boys get down with a little disco dance. My kids will pout if I don't save a few wrappers after I make wontons (see recipe on pages 60/61) so that they can make a batch of these warm, gooey Chocolate Wontons for dessert. It's so easy, too. Just add a chunk of your favorite chocolate to the middle, seal and fry.

Don't be too greedy, though. A small piece of chocolate for each wonton is fine. If the chocolate nugget is too big, the wonton won't seal properly and the chocolate oozes out when frying. No chocolate = no happy kids.

MAKES 12 CHOCOLATE WONTONS
1 egg
1 tablespoon water
12 wonton wrappers, defrosted (keep wrappers covered with damp towel)
12 pieces or nuggets of chocolate
High-heat oil for frying
Confectioners' sugar, for sprinkling

1 In a small bowl, whisk together the egg and water to make an egg wash.
2 On a clean, dry surface, lay 1 wrapper down with a point toward you, like a diamond. Place 1 piece of chocolate near the top end of the wrapper. Brush a very thin layer of the egg wash on the edges of the wrapper. Fold the bottom corner of the wrapper up to create a triangle and gently press to remove all air from the middle. Press the edges to adhere the sides. Make sure the wrapper is sealed completely. Repeat with the remaining wrappers and chocolate pieces. Keep the folded chocolate wontons covered under plastic wrap or a damp paper towel to prevent them from drying.
3 In a wok or medium pot, pour in 2 inches (5 cm) of high-heat oil. Heat the oil to 350°F (180°C) and gently slide a few of the chocolate wontons into the hot oil. Make sure you don't crowd the chocolate wontons too much. Fry 1½ minutes, then flip and fry another minute until both sides are golden brown and crisp.

Matcha Crepes with Cherry Chocolate Ice Cream

I can eat crepes any time of the day—breakfast, lunch, dinner or dessert. I love how the edges can crisp up and curl. Of course I justify to myself that crepes have less sugar than a big slice of cake, so therefore I can have two of them. And top each off with a full scoop of ice cream too. Sigh….I love my world!

Matcha or maccha is Japanese green tea powder made from the highest quality of green tea leaves. The powder is a stunning mossy color and it's incredibly healthy. Now make sure you get "matcha"—you can't just substitute with green tea leaves! If you can't get the matcha powder, you can leave it out and make coconut crepes instead—just add ½ teaspoon of coconut extract to the batter mix.

You can make the batter and the ice cream in advance, which makes it a great dinner party dessert.

MAKES 8 TO 10 CREPES
1 tablespoon butter, melted (for sautéing the crepes)

MATCHA CREPES
1 cup (120 g) all-purpose flour
1 cup (250 ml) milk
¼ cup (65 ml) cold water
2 eggs
1 teaspoon matcha green tea powder
Generous pinch of salt
3 tablespoons butter, melted

CHERRY CHOCOLATE ICE CREAM
2 cups (500 ml) heavy cream
1 cup (250 ml) whole milk
½ cup (100 g) sugar
½ lb (250 g) pitted fresh cherries, chopped
8 oz (250 g) chopped dark chocolate

SPECIAL EQUIPMENT
Ice cream maker (remember to freeze your insert if you have one)

1 Blend the Matcha Crepes ingredients in a blender on medium speed for 20 seconds until the batter is smooth. Refrigerate for at least 1 hour or overnight.
2 Make the Cherry Chocolate Ice Cream by heating the cream, milk and sugar in a medium saucepan over medium-low heat. When the mixture is hot, but not boiling, remove from the heat and add the cherries. Let steep for 10 minutes. Cool the mixture in the refrigerator.
3 When the ice cream mixture is fully chilled, stir in the dark chocolate. Churn the mixture in your ice cream maker, following the manufacturer's instructions.
4 Before sautéing the crepes, stir the batter. Set an 8-inch (20-cm) nonstick frying pan over medium heat. When it's hot, brush with a little of the melted butter. When the butter is bubbling, pour in ¼ cup (65 ml) of the batter and swirl the pan so the batter covers the bottom evenly.
5 Cook 30 for seconds. Use a rubber spatula to loosen the edges, flip the crepe and cook another 30 seconds. Slide onto a plate and cover with a towel to prevent drying. Continue making more crepes with the rest of the batter.
6 To serve, fold a crepe into quarters and place a scoop of ice cream on top.

Bubble "Boba" Tea

Bubble Tea is one of Taiwan's most famous food imports. There are Bubble Tea shops popping up everywhere there is a large population of young Chinese students. The large, chewy, translucent tapioca, or "boba", look like bubbles through the glass—thus the name for the drink. One note of caution: don't try to suck up the boba too fast through the straw. You might shoot it down the wrong way—ahem—warning based on experience.

MAKES ONE 8-OZ (250-ML) SERVING
4 tablespoons boba (tapioca)
6 oz (175 ml) very strong-brewed black tea
1 tablespoon honey (or more to taste)
2 tablespoons milk
2 handfuls of ice cubes

1 Cook and drain the boba. To cook the boba, follow the instructions on your package, as the boiling times really depend on the size of the tapioca. Spoon the cooked boba into a 8-oz (250-ml) glass.
2 In a cocktail shaker, add the tea, honey, milk and ice cubes. Shake vigorously until chilled. Strain into the glass with the boba.

Mango Julius

Remember the Orange Julius stores that were so popular in the '80s? Here's my version, only with mango instead of orange. This drink is rich, creamy and cold, and a scoop of vanilla ice cream makes it perfect for dessert (okay, I'm lying, I have it for breakfast too).

SERVES 1
8 oz (250 ml) mango juice
2 oz (60 ml) milk
2 tablespoons sugar
1 scoop vanilla ice cream or mango sorbet

Combine all the ingredients except for the ice cream in a blender. Blend until smooth. Pour into a tall glass and top with the ice cream or sorbet.

Avocado Milkshake

Mango Julius

Avocado Milkshake

One of my dearest friends, Irene, taught me this Indonesian drink. One morning I was feeling ugly and sluggish and so she zipped to the kitchen and blended a couple shots of espresso, candy-sweet condensed milk and a ripe avocado. I would have never guessed that this combination of ingredients would transform into something so luscious, velvety and sweet. I added the rum to the recipe, of course!

SERVES 1
¹/₂ ripe avocado
4 oz (125 ml) sweetened condensed milk
2 oz (60 ml) brewed espresso (or strong coffee)
3 to 4 ice cubes
1 tablespoon rum (optional)
Ground espresso beans, for garnish

In a blender, add all the ingredients. Blend until smooth. Garnish with a sprinkle of the ground espresso beans.

Passionfruit Chilli Martini

On a recent trip to Club Med Ixtapa, Mexico, with my friend Diane and my brother Jay, I fell in love with a martini. It was my first love for a martini ever. I'm not a big martini fan, even when *Sex and the City* made the drink hip. While all my friends were ordering "chocolate martinis" I would stick to my boring but affordable house wine. Until, I met Basti, the super-star bartender at Club Med. He created a chilli martini that tickled my tongue and had me madly, crazily lusting after his shaker. Basti made his martini with peach juice, but I love my version with passion fruit juice.

SERVES 1
1 fresh chilli, cut in half lengthwise, seeds
   removed
1/2 oz (15 ml) Simple Syrup (see below)
1 1/2 oz (45 ml) vodka
2 oz (60 ml) passion fruit juice

SIMPLE SYRUP
1 cup (250 ml) water
1 cup (250 g) sugar

1 To make the Simple Syrup, combine the water and sugar in a small saucepan and bring to a boil. Turn the heat to low and simmer for 3 minutes, stirring to dissolve the sugar. Remove from the heat and let cool. Store the syrup in the refrigerator for up to 1 month.
2 In a mixing glass or cocktail shaker, crush one of the chilli halves with just 1 tablespoon of the Simple Syrup—you can use a spoon or a muddler. The more you crush, the hotter the drink will be. Fill with ice and add the rest of the Simple Syrup, vodka and juice. Shake 30 seconds until chilled then strain into a chilled martini glass. Garnish with the remaining chilli half.

Passionfruit Chilli Martini

Apple Ginger Mint Iced Tea

Here in tropical Florida, everyone drinks iced tea! The sweetened stuff that's typical in the South is just uugggghhhhh....gag....much too sweet for my taste. So, I've created an ice tea infused with fresh apples, fresh ginger and fresh mint. Instead of sugar, how about syrupy honey?

**MAKE FOUR 8-OZ (250-ML) SERVINGS (WITH
   ICE)**
2 to 3 bags of green tea
One 2-in (5-cm) piece fresh ginger,
   peeled
1/4 apple, cut into matchsticks

1 to 2 sprigs fresh mint
2 cups (500 ml) boiling hot water
An ice-filled pitcher
1/2 cup (125 ml) apple cider
Honey, as desired

Combine the tea bags, ginger, apple matchsticks and mint in a tea-pot. Fill with boiling hot water and steep for 5 minutes. Pour and strain into the ice-filled pitcher. Add the apple cider and honey, as desired. Fill individual glasses with ice and serve.

Pomegranate and Soda

When we were little, my brother and I would love to eat pomegranate seeds! Mom would open a pomegranate in her biggest bowl and break apart the jeweled sections for us. Of course, the juices stain everything it touches, so our shirts, lips, teeth and tongues were painted ruby red.

This is one of the prettiest drinks, pomegranate juice or liqueur mixed with club soda and ice. Add a spoonful of ruby red pomegranate seeds to each glass. My favorite pomegranate liqueur is Pama—it's a perfect balance of sweet and tart.

SERVES 1
Spoonful of pomegranate seeds
Ice
2 oz (65 ml) pomegranate juice or liqueur
4 oz (125 ml) club soda
1 sprig of fresh mint for garnish

Spoon the pomegranate seeds in a tall glass and fill with ice. Pour in the pomegranate juice or liqueur and club soda. Stir briefly. Garnish with the sprig of fresh mint.

Vietnamese Iced Coffee

Stop! If you're scanning or browsing for recipes in this book, stop right here. If you haven't had Vietnamese Iced Coffee before, you gotta just go to the store, buy some French roast coffee and condensed milk. Yes, baby, it's *that* good! It's rich, strong and luscious. Just how I like my men.

The Vietnamese coffee is usually made with a metal coffee press found at most Asian markets (less than $4.00) but you don't even need that. Use your regular coffee maker and brew a triple-strength French roast coffee or espresso. If you don't have a coffee maker, go to your local store and get a $2 plastic single-brew coffee maker (Melitta makes a good one) that drip brews directly in a cup.

SERVES 1

2 tablespoons sweetened condensed milk
1 small heat-proof glass
1 Vietnamese metal coffee maker
2 tablespoons strong French roast coffee, coarsely ground
$\frac{1}{3}$ cup (80 ml) boiling hot water
1 tall 8-oz (250-ml) glass filled to brim with ice

Pour the sweetened condensed milk in the small heat-proof glass (it's best that you use glass so you can watch the coffee drip down). Take the metal coffee maker and unscrew the metal filter from the base. Spoon the ground coffee into the base, screw the filter back on tightly, packing in the coffee. Place the coffee maker on top of the small glass and pour hot, boiling water into the coffee maker, filling it to the top. You can use the tip of a spoon to tighten the screw of the filter more (if coffee is dripping too quickly) or loosen it (if coffee is not dripping at all). The slower the drip, the stronger the coffee. You should see 3 to 4 drips at a time. Be patient! The entire process should take about 3 minutes and the result should look like espresso. You can add more water if you want. When the coffee is done, remove the coffee maker and stir the coffee and condensed milk together. Pour this over a tall glass filled with ice. Enjoy!

Hong Kong Yinyeung Tea-Coffee

This is the perfect drink for those who are indecisive . . . coffee? tea? Well, how about both!

As a kid, we'd use to go back to Hong Kong every summer to visit our family. Back then, I didn't care too much for tea and I wasn't old enough to have a cup of coffee. But Mom let me order Yinyeung, a delicious harmony of coffee, tea, evaporated milk (Black & White brand of evaporated milk is preferred) and sugar.

It's not as simple as sticking a tea bag in your coffee, though on lazy afternoons I've been known to do just that. This drink is silky, smooth and hits that sweet spot just perfectly. You can use any type of good quality black teas, like English Breakfast. But I prefer my Assam tea from Upton Tea Imports or the Lychee Black Tea (also used in Smoked Tea Salmon, page 80).

If you don't have canned evaporated milk, you can use sweetened condensed milk (just omit the sugar in the recipe) or whatever you normally use to dress your coffee with—milk or unflavored half and half.

SERVES YOU + 3 OF YOUR FRIENDS FOR AFTERNOON TEA

4 tablespoons evaporated milk, plus more for the table

4 teaspoons sugar, plus more for the table

TEA FIXINGS

4 cups (1 liter) boiling hot water

4 teaspoons black loose-leaf tea

COFFEE FIXINGS

4 cups (1 liter) water

5 tablespoons coffee grounds

1 To make the tea, let the boiling water cool for 1 minute. Steep the tea leaves in the hot water for 3 to 5 minutes, depending on how strong you like your tea. I like mine strong! But don't let it sit for longer than 5 minutes or it might become bitter. Strain the tea and discard the leaves.
2 To make the coffee, follow the instructions for your coffee maker to brew a good strong cup of coffee.
3 Pour each cup halfway with tea, halfway with coffee. Add 1 tablespoon of evaporated milk and 1 teaspoon of sugar. Of course, you can add more or less of milk and sugar depending on your tastes.

acknowledgments

This book really is a dream come true. I wouldn't have been able to create this blossoming career without the love and support of my husband and best friend, Scott. To my squeezeable bugaboos, Andrew and Nathan, who are always there to help me in the kitchen, cook with me on TV and to be so patient and not eat the yummy food until Mommy takes a photo.

Thank you to my publisher Tuttle Publishing for giving me the opportunity to pitch a beautiful book and for having the faith in me to finish it: Eric Oey, Holly Jennings, Colin, Christopher, Ann, Donna, Samantha and Rowan. Oh yes, a shout-out to Holly's sister, Heather, who read my column in the paper two years ago and urged Holly to contact me as a possible author.

My sisters-in-blogs (yes, I know that sounded dorkish) Bee Yin Low, Diane Cu, Elise Bauer—thank you for answering late night phone calls, Skypes, IMs, emails, tweets and even last-minute flights to see you. To the gals whose beautiful writing inspired me to start a blog of my own, Tea Austen, Lucy Varnel, Sara Gim, Jennifer Jeffrey, Nicole Controneo, Deb Perelman (remember that email I wrote to you guys?! Who knew??); and to the talented food photographers who wow'd me with their luscious food styling & photos, Matt Armendariz, Bea Peltre, Lara Ferroni, Adam Pearson. And how could I not mention my foodie friends David Lebovitz, Kate Moeller, Morgan Painvan & Club Med, Andrea Nguyen, Dave Liske, Lisa Fain, Kalyn Denny, Greg & Michelle Baker, Chuck Lai, Veronica Perez, Anu Karwa, Mark Tafoya, David Leite, Michael Ruhlman, Diana Kuan, Dr. BBQ, Jeni & Dylan, Carrie Oliver, Slashfood, FoodGawker, SeriousEats, Tastespotting, BlogHer, Sean Timberlake, Eating Out Loud Alan, Lydia Walshin, Cookthink, FoodBuzz, Kim O'Donnel, Martha's Circle Pim Te, Morgan Hartman, Traca Savadogo, Lynne Halleran, Carolyn Jung, Martin Yan . . . YOU ARE ALL RESPONSIBLE FOR ME GAINING 10 POUNDS THESE PAST TWO YEARS.

Thank you to the *East County Observer*, the little newspaper that gave me my very first food column in print and to *Creative Loafing* for giving me my first paid writing gig! A big dose of gratitude to the *Tampa Tribune* staff and readers who allow me the luxury of sharing my sometimes wacky thoughts with you every single week. To Sarasota ABC7, Tampa Bay CBS 10 and of course my friends at the Daytime show, thank you for shining the spotlight on my cooking! My first experience in front of a TV camera was with the Emmy Award Winning Jack Perkins Show—thank you Jack and Jen Noble for telling my story. Of course, a warm thank you to The Chef's Table (where I taught my first cooking class), Rolling Pin in Brandon and The Epicurean School of Culinary Arts in Los Angeles who have all graciously hosted me in their teaching kitchens.

I have a very special place in my heart for Jeff Houck for being a wonderful friend and spying that talent in me. You gave me an opportunity of a lifetime that sparked my career.

To my girlfriends in my 'hood: Jules Price, Jessica Rivelli, Jan Small, Kelly Hutchins, Lisa Holler, Julie Freed, Wendy Crane, Jeanette Casey, who I hope will forgive me for being so busy that I don't have time to hang as much! And girlfriends in my old 'hood, Irene Lim and Maria Villaruel, who taught me the art of eating well and eating often. To the Digital Doctors team, thanks for taking care of things and keeping the business humming along smoothly.

See the gorgeous photos of me in the book? That's the work of Carrie Hasson and Diane Cu. And the picture perfect shots of ingredients? My good friend Matt Wright.

Thank you to the experts who took time to read my book and offer your stamp of approval, including Guy Kawasaki, Andrea Nguyen, Kim O'Donnel, Michael Ruhlman, Ming Tsai, and Martin Yan.

What would a food blogger book be without a blogroll? Come see my full list of friends at **www.steamykitchen.com/link-love.** And a hurray to all my blog readers and Twitter followers, I wouldn't be here living my dream if you hadn't thought I was entertaining enough to keep coming back time and time again.

Of course, my family, Jay, Mom, Dad, Uncle Billy, Uncle Patrick, Auntie Virginia, Auntie Rumy, Ivan, Sylvia, George, Maridel and Rob. I love you.

A big hug to my fabulous group of testers who responded to my call for recipe testing. Thank you for testing and re-testing each and every recipe in this book:

Lynne Halleran	Sarah Carter
Dickie Adams	Linda Chen
Emily Adkins	Jennifer Chess
Patricia Allen	Elizabeth Chou
Patti Anastasia	Silvia Cocco
Christine Anderson	Patti Cockerham
Zoe Baker	Angelo Comsti
Carmen Bao	Robin Cosby
Regina Benko	Kerrie Cougle
Kindra Birss	Ashley Covelli
Johanna Blanco	Alexander Cowan
Kitt Bo	Ric Crabbe
Laura Bomar	Lynn Craig
Graham Bowman	Melissa DiStefano
Bonni Lee Brown	Marion Dumas
Phil Burch	Chris Duval
Jude Cabal	Jennifer Eiler
Dani Cantor	Barry Enderwick
Maria Carrillo	Lori Falcon
Elizabeth Carroll	Brenda Falk

resource guide

Online Retailers for Asian Groceries
Amazon
www.amazon.com

Asian Food Grocer
www.asianfoodgrocer.com

Import Food
www.importfood.com

Koamart
www.koamart.com

Temple of Thai
www.templeofthai.com

List of Asian Markets by State
New Asian Cuisine
**www.newasiancuisine.com/new_asian/
map_grocery_stores.asp**

Specialty Products
Earthy Delights (mushrooms, real soy sauce, yuzu)
www.earthy.com

Vine Connections (sake)
www.vineconnections.com

Sur La Table
www.surlatable.com

The Wok Shop (woks, cleavers, steamers, teapots)
www.wokshop.com

Wok Star (pre-seasoned woks)
www.wokstar.com

Upton Tea Imports (tea)
www.uptontea.com

Zojirushi (rice cookers)
www.zojirushi.com

Asian Recipe Blogs
Appetite For China
www.appetiteforchina.com

Burnt Lumpia
www.burntlumpia.typepad.com

Chez Pim
www.chezpim.com

Asian Grandmother's Cookbook
**www.theasiangrandmotherscookbook.
wordpress.com/**

Eating Asia
www.eatingasia.typepad.com

Japanese Food Report
www.japanesefoodreport.com

Just Hungry
www.justhungry.com

Lily's Wai Sek Hong
www.lilyng2000.blogspot.com

Lunch in a Box
www.lunchinabox.net

Maangchi's Korean Cooking
www.maangchi.com

No Recipes
www.norecipes.com

Rambling Spoon
www.ramblingspoon.com/blog

Rasa Malaysia
www.rasamalaysia.com

Real Thai Recipes
www.realthairecipes.com

Tigers & Strawberries (great resource for Chinese recipes)
www.tigersandstrawberries.com

Use Real Butter
www.userealbutter.com

Vietworld Kitchen
www.vietworldkitchen.com

Wandering Chopsticks
www.wanderingchopsticks.blogspot.com

White on Rice Couple
www.whiteonricecouple.com

Zen Kimchi
www.zenkimchi.com

index

THE TUTTLE STORY

"Books to Span the East and West"

Most people are surprised to learn that the world's largest publisher of books on Asia had its humble beginnings in the tiny American state of Vermont. The company's founder, Charles E. Tuttle, belonged to a New England family steeped in publishing. And his first love was naturally books—especially old and rare editions.

Immediately after WW II, serving in Tokyo under General Douglas MacArthur, Tuttle was tasked with reviving the Japanese publishing industry. He later founded the Charles E. Tuttle Publishing Company, which thrives today as one of the world's leading independent publishers.

Though a westerner, Tuttle was hugely instrumental in bringing a knowledge of Japan and Asia to a world hungry for information about the East. By the time of his death in 1993, Tuttle had published over 6,000 books on Asian culture, history and art—a legacy honored by the Japanese emperor with the "Order of the Sacred Treasure," the highest tribute Japan can bestow upon a non-Japanese.

With a backlist of 1,500 titles, Tuttle Publishing is more active today than at any time in its past—inspired by Charles Tuttle's core mission to publish fine books to span the East and West and provide a greater understanding of each.

ABOUT THE PHOTOGRAPHY IN THIS BOOK

All of the final dish photography in this book were shot by me in my home, usually about 15 minutes before my family or dinner guests pounce and devour the dish. The cardinal rule at my home, and at many homes of food bloggers is, "don't you dare touch the food until I've taken my photos".

Violate this and you run the risk of having your chopsticks confiscated and being assigned dishwashing duty.

When I first started the Steamy Kitchen blog in early 2007, I posted a few recipes with no photos. YAWN. I'm a type of gal that needs visual stimulation. Almost every single cookbook that I own is filled with photos of the dishes. I want to see the food that you want me to cook! At the bookstore, I can pick up a cookbook and in two seconds determine if the photos to text ratio is worth reading. One quick flip. And just like a cartoon flip book, the cookbook should tell a tale of an amazing 100-course meal, starting with little nibbles and ending with a soothing treat.

Even though back in the early days of the blog I only had three readers, myself, my husband Scott and my mother-in-law (and I'm sure she only read it to make sure that I was feeding her grandkids a healthy, nutritious diet!), I had to teach myself how to use my digital SLR, a Canon Rebel XT.

The dang thing was a birthday present from months before, but it had so many buttons, settings and options that I really secretly hated it. Ok, maybe the ill feelings weren't so secret, as my kids thought that the camera's name was "Ah...Turd-Dropper!" that I would yell when it just wouldn't operate the way I commanded it to.

For a while, I found a happy place with the "P" setting on the camera's dial, which stands for "PISS away $800 for a camera to use just the automatic settings". Then when I started writing this cookbook, I got serious and upgraded to the "Av" setting, playing with the wheely-dialy thingamabobber. The pics started looking really hot, off I went. About half of the photos in this book were taken with very little knowledge of how to use a camera. It wasn't until my good friend, Diane, sat down with me and said, "Honey. The manual setting "M" isn't that hard to learn," and showed me in 10 minutes how to adjust the wheely-dialy thingamabobber with the button pushy doohickey. So, now I'm an "M" girl and a proud owner of a Canon 40D. Though, pssst . . . I still don't know all those fancy photography terms!

My fancy photography set is a cheap, wooden TV tray, a $3 foam board and another white board for reflecting light. I don't have a food photographer, food stylist, kitchen assistant or even a dishwasher. It's quite crazy how I've managed to come up with all these luscious photos, at times I feel like a one-woman orchestra! All but two photos were taken in natural light right next to my big sliding glass door. The food is real, no fancy photography tricks like schlack or glue. In fact, the food is still hot by the time I'm finished with the photo shoot and we eat it for our family meal! Sometimes, you'll even find a gorgeous photo of a dish . . . and off to the side, five tiny hungry fingers reaching for a piece of the action. It smells sooo good that the kids cannot resist!